*The Land of Naked People*

# The Land of
# Naked People

........................................................................................

*ENCOUNTERS*

*WITH STONE AGE ISLANDERS*

## Madhusree Mukerjee

HOUGHTON MIFFLIN COMPANY

BOSTON  NEW YORK  2003

For information about permission to
reproduce selections from this book, write to
Permissions, Houghton Mifflin Company,
215 Park Avenue South, New York, New York 10003.

Visit our Web site: www.houghtonmifflinbooks.com.

*Library of Congress Cataloging-in-Publication Data*
Mukerjee, Madhusree, date.
The land of naked people : encounters with Stone Age
islanders / Madhusree Mukerjee.
p.   cm.
Includes bibliographical references (p.   ) and index.
ISBN 0-618-19736-2
1. Andamanese (Indic people) 2. Andaman and
Nicobar Islands (India)  I. Title.
DS432.A54 M85 2003
954'.880049911—dc21   2002032714

Printed in the United States of America

Book design by Robert Overholtzer
Map by Patricia S. Wynne

QUM 10 9 8 7 6 5 4 3 2 1

The author is grateful for permission to quote from
*Above the Forest* by Visvajit Panya. Reproduced by
permission of Oxford University Press India, New Delhi.

*To natives unknown*
*on whose bones we stand*

# Contents

## *Jarawa*

## *Sentinelese*

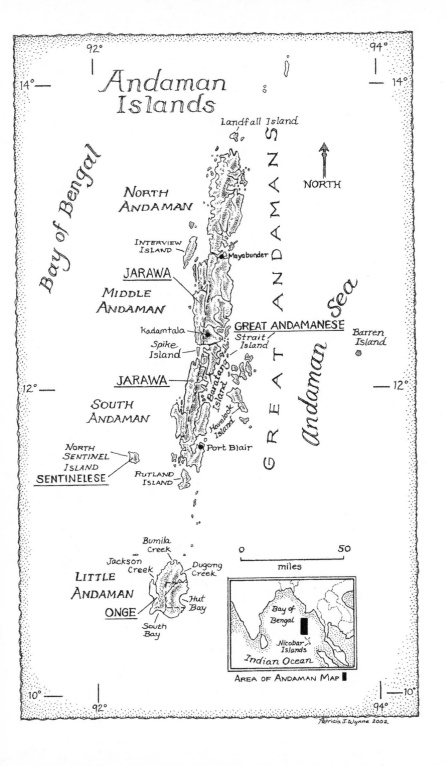

# Preface

Angamanain is a very long island. The people are without a king, and are Idolaters, and are no better than wild beasts. And I assure you all the men of this Island of Angamanain have heads like dogs, and teeth and eyes likewise; in fact, in the face they are all just like big mastiff dogs! They have a quantity of spices; but they are a most cruel generation, and eat everybody that they can catch, if not of their own race.

So said Marco Polo after coasting by the Andaman and Nicobar Islands in 1290. On his way home to Italy and immortality, he was dropping off a Chinese princess in distant India to wed a king she'd never met. After his ship left Sumatra, sailing past a spattering of small green hills in the ocean, Marco Polo did not land. Had he done so, he might have learned more about the dog-people; but by then, he'd learned something about self-preservation.

To end up on the Andamans, one had to be singularly unlucky — to be swept off course by contrary winds, or wrecked by a monsoon storm. A long, delicate chain strung off the southern tip of Burma, and aligned north to south as though on a longitude, the islands had long sheltered a race of terrible reputation. "The people on this coast eat human flesh quite raw; their complexion is black, their hair frizzled, their countenance and eyes frightful, their feet are very large, and almost a cubit in length, and they go quite naked," related two Arabs in 850. "They have no sort of barks or other vessels; if they had, they would seize and devour all the passengers they could lay hands on." Stories abounded of the savages dismembering and roasting hapless sailors. "No one to this day has landed on the Andaman where people are cannibals," recorded the eleventh-century text *Ajaib-al-Hind.* One wonders who lived to tell the tales.

Southward the archipelago gave way to the Nicobars, where lived a far more peaceable people who offered coconuts to seafarers. Almost two millennia ago, the Ten-Degree Channel separating the Andamans from the Nicobars had become a popular route for ships laden with silk, grain, elephants, slaves, and other merchandise to cross from India to Sumatra and then on to China. Even so, many early scholars seem to have confused the two island groups. Ptolemy wrote of the Andamans as Bazakata, derived from the Sanskrit *vivasakrata,* meaning "stripped of clothes." The name Andaman conceivably came from *nagna-manaba,* Sanskrit for "naked man"; the name Nicobar derived from *nakkavaram,* Tamil for "naked." So both island clusters were called the Land of Naked People, a Chinese variant, Ch'u-uan-wu, being no more helpfully translated as Testicle Display Country.

The Andamanese intrigued all who sailed by, and not just by their nudity and alleged ferocity: with their small, dark bodies and frizzy hair they resembled Africans rather than Asians. "Some have supposed that a Portuguese ship, early in the 16th century, laden with slaves from Mozambique, had been cast on these shores, and that the present Andamanese are the descendants of such as escaped drowning," wrote Michael Symes of His Majesty's 76th Regiment of Great Britain upon visiting the archipelago in 1795. Given the antiquity of legends about the inhabitants, however, he guessed that Arab slave ships of earlier centuries might have been the culprit.

Today, scientists believe that the Andamanese directly descend from early humans who colonized mainland and southeastern Asia perhaps fifty thousand years ago. These forebears, likely the first *Homo sapiens* in Asia, were elsewhere overwhelmed by later arrivals.

Some encounters surely contributed to the islanders' abiding distrust of foreigners. In 1694, Alexander Hamilton, a ship's captain, met a forty-year-old Andamanese in Sumatra who'd been sold into slavery as a boy but was freed by his dying master. The first outsider to leave a detailed account of the archipelago, surveyor John Ritchie, noted in 1771 that the islanders knew of guns and feared them; twenty years later a French merchant vessel was reported to be offering Andamanese slaves for sale. In the early nineteenth century such slaves were a regular part of the tribute paid by the raja of Keddah (in present-day Malaysia) to the king of Siam.

The wary natives took from the outside world only the fragments of shipwrecks: the nuts and bolts that washed up on their shores and which they hammered into arrowheads. Although the islands lay on a busy trade route connecting two great civilizations, India and China — and so were at the center of the world, one might say — they remained almost entirely untouched until modern times.

To this day, a hundred-odd individuals survive on tiny North Sentinel Island, repelling with bows and six-foot-long arrows all boats that approach. They may be the most isolated humans on earth.

On my first visit to the Andamans in 1995, I was entranced. It's the light I remember best of all, a clear golden glow filling the sky and touching the leaves with glitter. My father (for I went with him, my mother, and my niece) walked over hills and swam over reefs, miraculously cured of his asthma. "There is an air of peace and restfulness," I wrote in a letter to a friend. One beach in particular — strewn with soft white sand, shaded by towering green trees, and lapped by water as clear and blue as the innards of a gemstone — I recall as though from a dream, so ethereal that I felt the gods must steal down to play there.

I did not know then how deep my involvement with the islands would become or how much the Andamanese would teach me. I had grown up in Calcutta, some seven hundred fifty miles to the north of the Andamans; I knew where they lay on a map but little else. (Calcutta is now spelled Kolkata, but throughout this book I use the old spelling.) In the early 1900s, Calcutta had been home to some fiery young men who sought to rid India of British colonizers by violent means. Most of these freedom fighters (terrorists, to the British) were captured before they could hurt anyone and sentenced to life on the Andamans. I read of their hardships and of their being killed by savages in the islands' forests when they escaped from jail. Indians knew the Andamans as Kalapani, across the waters of death.

As a teenager, I met a dashing adventurer who'd traveled from Calcutta to the Andamans in a rowboat. His accounts thrilled me, as did other stories that drifted by, of beautiful corals, wild jungles, and unexplored islands. Many years later, after I'd come to the United States to study physics and metamorphosed into a science writer in New York City, I decided to visit the islands as a tourist. At the time a journalist friend in India mentioned that some of those "savages" still survived alone on an island, threatening anyone who sought to land.

Disbelieving, I read whatever I could about the Andamanese. Those still isolated as Stone Age hunter-gatherers used bone, wood, or iron acquired from shipwrecks — not stone — to tip their arrows. They had their own languages, which seemed unlike any other. They shot fish and pigs with bows and arrows, believed that birds talk to the spirits, couldn't make fire but kept it forever burning in their huts, didn't have words for numbers greater than two, adored children, and laughed a lot. In short, they lived in a time capsule that preserved the ways of our prehistoric ancestors.

I made use of that trip to interview scientists and officials, learning enough about the Andamans to write a short piece in *Scientific American,* where I worked. In 1858 British colonists had established a penal settlement on South Andaman at Port Blair, now a sizable town where my family and I spent most of our visit. "No doubt was felt as to our right to occupy [the islands]," stated colonial administrator Maurice Vidal Portman in his two-volume 1899 tract, *A History of Our Relations with the Andamanese.* Their inhabitants were so dreaded, he went on to explain, that no other nation had bothered to claim the Andamans. The islanders, who had other ideas about sovereignty, led raids into the settlement. But Port Blair spread fast, consuming the jungle around it.

At its center rose the imposing red-brick Cellular Jail, so called because of its rows of solitary cells, radiating outward from a central tower like the arms of an octopus. The cells had small windows that overlooked the sea but were too high to see out of. We met a freedom fighter in his nineties who remembered the *bulbuli* birds that would fly in and out of those slits, for days his only view of the world outside. This prison in paradise is now a museum, displaying among the sackcloth and fetters a roster of famous political prisoners, mostly Bengalis like myself. I found myself oddly moved by the list. "They gave their lives so we could make a mess of our country," I mused in the letter to my friend.

The British overlords lived on tiny, nearby Ross Island, now covered with picturesque ruins of brick buildings, ripped apart and then held aloft by the intricately twining roots of huge fig trees. Arched doorways that led to nowhere framed the stunning ocean. "This must have been a charming little town at one point," I noted. "Bakery, market, oceanside houses, church, even a hospital, and the inevitable cemetery." I couldn't make out the tennis courts or the nine-hole golf course where the expatriates had whiled away their postings; the ballroom, I later learned, was demolished during the Japanese reign in World War II. From beneath the coconut tree where I sat writing my letter, I could see the tower of the Cellular Jail across the water. Doubtless the overseers signaled to Ross Island in times of trouble.

Ross was abandoned in 1942, just before the Japanese arrived. It was a short but memorable occupation. The invaders murdered many inhabitants, most of them the descendants of ex-convicts who'd settled on the Andamans. The Japanese constructed feverishly, building an airstrip and thousands of bunkers along the periphery of the Great Andamans — the South, Middle, and North Andaman Islands — to repel the Allies who were on the seas. They also allowed Netaji Subhas Chandra Bose, a Bengali firebrand who'd recruited a ragtag army to fight the British, to plant an Indian flag.

At the end of World War II the British returned, but two years later, in 1947, left for good, handing the Andamans over to newly free India. The ex-colony then had a colony of its own, which it promptly used for dumping refugees from various mainland conflicts. Since independence the population had grown nine times, a zoologist told me. The crowding was threatening to exterminate the Andamanese.

Early administrators of the settlement had grouped the aboriginals into four categories. Some ten tribes, altogether between five and eight thousand souls, occupied most of the Great Andamans and their adjacent small islands; they had borne the brunt of the British occupation. These so-called Great Andamanese were at war with the elusive Jarawa, guessed to number about six hundred, who sheltered in the dense western forests of South Andaman. Seven hundred or so Onge tribal members lived on Little Andaman, a not-so-little island farther south, and perhaps a hundred Sentinelese — no one knew what else to call them — roamed the eighteen square miles that compose North Sentinel, off by itself to the west.

The Andaman islanders were the "most carefully tended and petted" of the "races of savages," British administrator Portman had commented. But by the end of the nineteenth century, syphilis, measles, influenza, and other ailments introduced by outsiders had driven the Great Andamanese to the brink of extinction. Having been isolated for thousands of years, the islanders had no resistance to the killer diseases that thrive in the relatively dense populations of agricultural societies. In the late 1960s the survivors were collected on tiny Strait Island to the east of Middle Andaman. A local paper recently noted their population rising to thirty-seven, "with Smt. Surmai, wife of tribal Chief Jaraki, delivering a male child on Jan. 16, 1995." They were the most assimilated of the aboriginals, eating boiled rice, wearing Indian clothes, speaking Hindi, and living in wooden cottages. The government's policy was to give them the "fruits of modern civilization" without destroying their culture, said the director of tribal welfare, whom I met in his little wooden office perched on the side of a hill.

Next to fall were the Onge. In the 1960s and 1970s, Indian authorities resettled thousands of families of expatriates from what is now Bangladesh on Little Andaman, leveling vast tracts of forest to make room for fields. A hundred or so of the Onge were still alive. The government had constructed huts in the hope of making the tribe stationary, so that it would be easier to deliver the dole they needed now that the jungle no longer sustained them. They insisted on nomadic ways, however, and spent much of their time hunting and fishing. "On the files their income level has increased," commented the director, who was new to his job, "but they have no zest for life." He envisaged teaching the children soccer and volleyball to dissipate their obvious "sadness and depression."

Because of their enmity with the Great Andamanese — and everyone else — the Jarawa had been spared the devastating epidemics of the nineteenth century. Squeezed into shrinking forests on the western coasts of South and Middle Andaman, they still defended their remaining territory with vehemence. In January 1995, just two months before my visit, they'd shot a pregnant settler with an arrow and killed a calf. At the same time, anthropologists and officials had for decades been landing on some Jarawa beaches to offer food, iron pieces, and red cloth. (The Jarawa wore no clothes, but drew thread with which they made ornaments.) "When you go there, the Jarawa don't carry weapons," said the director. "They light a fire to signal it is safe to land." The "contact mission" would last for a few hours. The naked Jarawa — who were physically exuberant — danced with joy over their presents, sat on the laps of the visitors, pinched their paunches, or claimed piggyback rides. The whole time a boatload of plainclothes policemen with hidden guns hovered near the shore.

Mercifully, neither the British nor the Indians found a reason to colonize North Sentinel. Its inhabitants saw ships and boats in the sea, and helicopters and planes in the sky, but otherwise lived free of outside influence.

In 1995 I spent all of an afternoon and evening pleading with one official after another, seeking permission to join a Jarawa contact mission leaving that night. I explained my credentials to skeptical anthropologists and seemingly sympathetic administrators, who sent me on to someone else. The Andamanese were so vulnerable to germs and harmful influences, I was told, that all visitors had to be minutely scrutinized. Around nine P.M. I ran uphill, sweat-drenched, to the gorgeous bungalow of the lieutenant governor, the islands' chief administrator and the final arbiter of who would get on the boat. The guard turned me away.

The next morning someone called with an offer to take me to the Jarawa forest. The trip was illegal and probably dangerous as well, so I declined. Now I wonder if I shouldn't have taken the chance. "This is a gold mine for anyone with curiosity," I wrote to my friend. So many questions seemed to have no answers. How did a people who looked like Pygmies happen to be in Asia? How did they get here, given that their boats are not adequate for long ocean journeys? How did someone living in the Stone Age view our world, with its ships and helicopters?

What intrigued me the most, perhaps, was the last question — allowing that many of us accustomed to the information age also find technology amazing. In my view the four groups of Andamanese, having encountered outsiders at different times, provided a clear-cut experiment displaying the stages by which a dominant culture subsumes a marginal one — stages played out in virtually every corner of the globe. But over the years the islanders came to reveal themselves as individuals, personable and poignantly clear-eyed as to the trap in which fate had flung them. My initially dispassionate, scientific interest was transformed by a vivid personal sympathy. I began to feel that in their experience lay shades of my own past.

Starting around four thousand years ago, waves of horse-borne invaders and pastoral migrants, speaking an Indo-Aryan language and wielding iron implements, pushed into India from the northwest. Their civilization came to bloom along the fertile riverbanks of the Indus and the Ganges, beating back the aboriginals. Many of the latter retreated to mountaintops, deserts, and inaccessible forests, there to hide forgotten — until modern India found a use for their remote homes, for mines, dams, and timber, and banished them once again, this time to the slums and shantytowns of cities. Others were inducted into a caste system, which reserved the most menial and distasteful jobs for the defeated — rendering them useful while ensuring they could never rise to threaten the rulers.

I couldn't help wondering if the aboriginals of eastern India — my ancestors — might be connected with the Andaman islanders. The Great Andamanese believed that before a spirit enters a woman's womb to become a child, it lives in a fig tree; curiously, fig trees are worshipped throughout India as givers of fertility. If you sneezed, an islander might have asked, "Who is thinking of you?" — just as a Bengali asks if something goes down the wrong way and you cough. Shaving the head was a common funeral rite in their culture and in mine; animals, to them, were intriguing and powerful, just as they still remain to most Indians. Such links will forever remain unexplored, for they're too flimsy to tease apart; another hurdle is the number and variety of Indian tribes, whose home ranges once formed an intricately patterned patchwork laid over much of the map.

In this ancient hierarchy, the British fit in easily: their skin, whiter than that of the purest Brahmins, attested to their right to the top of the heap. When they left, many of their policies, especially toward the tribes, made sense to the new rulers. Indian administrators and academics, trained by imperialists, were insulated from winds of change blowing abroad: the infant nation's poverty, the sheer cost of Western books and journals, and distrust of most things foreign saw to that. As a result, policies toward the Andamanese remained substantially the same for most of the century and have shown progress only now that it's almost too late.

Just five hundred or so islanders still survive, and their lives are changing fast. Their tale is one of conflict with outsiders such as me.

# First Brush

I N THE LATE eighteenth century, as the colonial race to the Far East gained in ardor, the British administration in Calcutta concluded that the Andamans would make a convenient stop for ships to replenish supplies and make repairs. Accordingly, John Ritchie, hydrographer of the East India Company, was dispatched on the *Diligent* to conduct a preliminary survey of the islands.

Soon after anchoring in an Andaman strait on January 16, 1771, the ship was hit by a squall. For the three days it lasted, the crew could see nothing except at night, when "the shore was lighted up with hundreds of Torches, which made an appearance as if we were in the middle of a great lake, surrounded by houses lighted up." But the morning of the twentieth dawned fair, and at eight A.M. the crew spied a native canoe paddling toward the ship. Ritchie ordered a boat into the water, directing his sailors not to beat the natives but to tie them up and bring them on board. The men and boys in the canoe pulled backward in panic. Just before they were overtaken, the men dived into the water and swam ashore. The two boys flailed at the attackers with their paddles, which were soon twisted from their hands.

One of the *Diligent*'s crew, a man from Burma, next stepped into the canoe to try out his linguistic skills. With many gestures he earnestly addressed one of the youths; but while he was so engaged, the other boy pulled out a torch made of dry grass and resin, blew it up into a flame, and held it to the Burmese's bare buttocks. To the merriment of his companions, "the poor old fellow roared out in a horrible manner, and leaped into the sea, to cool his posteriors."

The sailors tied up the captives and brought them to the *Diligent*. "[S]urely never were people more terrified," Ritchie wrote. "[D]espair was strongly painted in their faces, and neither of them could support their weight, but fell upon the deck, as if they had lost the use of their limbs." So far as the boys could tell, they'd been abducted by ghosts. One and a half centuries later, anthropologist Alfred Reginald Radcliffe-Brown would report that the Andamanese had believed the spirits of the sea to be light-skinned, bearded, and grotesquely long-limbed — and to have a taste for human flesh.

The captives were revived with offers of food. Having eaten some coconuts, and realizing they weren't in immediate danger, they recovered their spirits and wandered about the deck, staring at everything. They seemed especially curious about the differences in color among the European, Indian, and Burmese sailors.

Another canoe, with an old aboriginal man and a boy, soon arrived alongside the *Diligent*. The boy came on board willingly, but as the sailors struggled with the old man, he clamped his arms around two of their necks and jumped into the sea. The sailors came back up after a minute or so, declaring he was the devil himself and stronger than ten men. Later the old man climbed onto the ship of his own accord and wandered about, pulling on the ring bolts and roaring and whooping "like the American wariours."

At eleven A.M. two canoes, each with five men, approached the ship, their S-shaped paddles, which doubled as bows, betraying their intent of rescuing the captives. The two boys called out to them, and a discussion took place; eventually the youths were allowed to set off in the captured canoe with nails and cloth they'd been given. But when they drew close, their fellow tribesmen pulled them onto their canoe and made them leave their presents in the other one, which they abandoned.

They rowed toward the shore "in the utmost haste and confusion," and the old man, who remained on board, laughed uproariously to see them in such a fright. Later he too left with his son, in a canoe laden with gifts of nails to hammer into arrowheads, singing all the way.

In 1789, roughly two decades after Ritchie's survey, Archibald Blair of the Royal Indian Navy founded a naval base on a small island adjoining South Andaman merely by clearing forests, setting up cottages, and planting kitchen gardens and orchards. Even so, the base marked the arrival of civilization, of human control over the vegetative wild.

"The island is inhabited by Coffrees which were so timorous, that I could bring about no further communication with them, than their acceptance of a few presents, which they would not take from our hands, but made signs for them to be laid down on the Beach, when they gladly accepted them," Blair wrote. Not all were shy: one old woman threw stones at his boat, and, frustrated that they did not reach, "expressed her fury by carrying indecency to the highest possible pitch." She too was mollified by his offerings.

The natives to the south of the harbor came to be friendly, sometimes visiting to ask for food or bits of iron for arrowheads. "Their colour is of the darkest hue, their stature in general small, and their aspect uncouth. Their limbs are ill-formed and slender, their bellies prominent, and, like the Africans, they have woolly heads, thick lips, and flat noses," wrote Lieutenant Robert Hyde Colebrooke of the Bengal Engineers in 1794. "They go quite naked, the women wearing only at times a kind of tassel, or fringe, round the middle; which is intended merely for ornament, as they do not betray any signs of bashfulness when seen without it." Judging by his descriptions, these were Jarawa.

North of the settlement roamed the Bea, who intensely resented the intrusion. The men of this and other Great Andamanese tribes shot at the newcomers with arrows five and a half feet long but retired in the face of gunfire. Ritchie had noted that the islanders knew about firearms "and had, no doubt, been taught it in a manner that does no great honor to those, who were their preceptors." The occasional fatality from musket fire was now reminder enough.

At one time two native men in a canoe approached the *Ranger*. The sailing ship bore toward them but could get no closer than two hundred yards. Keeping their distance, the aboriginals talked to the foreigners "in a loud and angry tone." From the shore could be heard voices, including those of women, who called out to their men "as if apprehensive of their getting into danger and wishing them to return."

The sailors threw overboard two empty bottles (with such treasures are new lands purchased), which the canoeists picked up from the water. But when four soldiers chased them in a boat, they paddled off too fast to be caught. Eventually one native put down his oars, coolly baled out the water, and taking his bow and arrows from the bottom of the canoe, laid them beside him. The other man too occasionally stopped paddling to look back, gesturing to his pursuers to come on and catch him, and at length, wrote Colebrooke, "clapped his hand to his posteriors as a mark of contempt."

Later that day the natives signaled to two officers to approach. It was an ambush: some men hiding under the mangroves let fly a shower of arrows headed by fishbones. Musket fire soon dispersed them. If the natives were thus unaccountably hostile or "mischievous," they were swiftly taught that such behavior would not be tolerated. To the trespassers, their own intentions were invariably "friendly": they just intended to stay.

My seat number was 21A. But I could find no 21A — the space was taken up by a row of food carts. The stewardess glanced at my boarding pass, winked, and motioned me into 21D across the aisle. I sank in gratefully. I owed this unorthodox seat to my younger sister-in-law, an actress beloved of Calcutta's airport officials. (The return flight I would owe to my other sister-in-law — no movie star but someone with stellar connections as well, daughter of a prince turned politician. Ordinary people didn't fly to Port Blair, on South Andaman, for most of the plane was reserved for government officials. You needed to be one, to plan a year ahead, or to have the right sisters-in-law.)

Two hours after leaving Calcutta, I peered out of the window hole to see dark green tree-covered islands swelling like fungus out of a flat ocean. The plane swung in and landed, braking with a frightening rush and shudder. The Japanese-built runway was designed for World War II fighters and bombers, not for passenger carriers.

Outside, the sun was blazing. On the tarmac sat a squat aircraft painted with a doll and the slogan VISIT MYANMAR YEAR. It was 1997. A long line of men in identical green lungis — sarongs — and striped shirts walked toward the airplane, their faces looking pleased even from a distance. They were Burmese fishermen captured by the Indian coast guard, going home after months or years in jail.

My elder sister-in-law had told me to seek out a co-passenger named Tapan, described as short and fair, dragging a foot, and in a suit; but the plane was full of sour-faced men in suits. When someone finally pointed him out, he turned out to be of medium height, medium color, and limpless, albeit in a suit. "Where were you?" he scowled. His glance fastened on my wrist. "You're supposed to have a white handkerchief tied on your right hand."

Oops, I'd completely forgotten. I apologized. He was to convey me to my host, Sen, my sister-in-law's cousin's husband and a prominent lawyer. (Some names have been changed for privacy.) I was on the Andamans for only a brief look around, but nothing gets done without connections, my family had insisted.

A jeep was waiting outside. We wound our way over sunny

streets lined with small shops. Whenever the road passed over a hill the sea came into view, fringed by coconut palms. The sunlight flashed off the dustless leaves of roadside trees, just as it had two years before. I felt the beauty of the place seeping in, raising my spirits.

The jeep came to a stop under the portico of Megapode lodge, one of the tourist homes named after endangered birds. A man in a white cotton khurta and pyjamas greeted my companion. "What are you doing here?" he asked in Bengali. "This is a weekend, and Monday is a holiday, how do you expect to do any cases?"

"I didn't know Monday is a holiday," Tapan protested. "How was I to know that?"

The scolding continued while I walked in and asked the receptionist for my room. She looked me over, unimpressed, and glanced at her register. No booking, she announced, and no free rooms.

"I am Sen," a voice interjected; it issued from the man in white. A shock of hair swept back from a broad dark forehead, a hoarse voice, a rough, imperious manner and flowing clothes. A politician, surely, not a lawyer. Indian garb marks the men whose power comes from the people; it is their servants who wear suits.

"Give her one-nineteen," he told the receptionist, and she broke into sudden sweet smiles and produced a key.

"Go and rest," he ordered. "I have to go out for some work, I'll see you later." His voice contained a careful distance, as it should toward an unfamiliar woman; yet there was a familiarity, I decided, that came from being a host in a distant land.

I showered, then waited in the sunny garden on top of a cliff, enjoying the breeze through my wet hair and gazing at the sea and distant islands below. I needed to get some things done quickly, for Sen would leave the next day. I had to find another hotel, for Megapode was expensive and didn't take credit cards; book a seat on the plane back to Calcutta; and, most important, figure out how to get into tribal areas.

When Sen returned, I explained what I needed. He ordered me into his van, and for good measure Tapan too. We drove downtown and stopped outside a hotel, where Sen strode in, told effusive managers to give me the VIP suite permanently reserved for him, and swept out. I followed, amazed and embarrassed. Then to Indian Airlines, where the waiting list for Thursday had fifty-odd names. Sen's presence got me on the flight.

The van next stopped at the public works department — why, I didn't venture to ask. We walked up the stairs, Sen snapping at Tapan, "Why do you smoke all the time?" Tapan, who was soon to become a high-court judge (so Sen informed me, in a tone that took credit for it), pulled a last puff and tossed his cigarette out of a window.

We entered an enormous, dark air-conditioned office, paneled in garish red-stained wood. At one end, behind a giant glass-topped desk, sat a bulbous engineer. Sen's imperious tone vanished. Instead, in fluent Hindi, he introduced the man as his bosom friend. "Remember the time I had an omen, of you being in trouble? I thought, my friend is in trouble, I have to get to him, now, I have to save him. It was raining, so hard, trees were falling over on the road, but I went straight to the airport. They said no seats, I said, I will go, my friend needs me. I came, literally standing in the plane. Remember?"

A wary smile curved the engineer's chubby cheeks.

"I came, I got here, I took care of the problem. Remember?"

He nodded, still smiling.

"This is my relative, Mrs. Madhusree Mukerjee. She wants to write about the islands, she would like to see some tribal areas. Also Tapan here, you know him, he would like to go too. Can you arrange for a trip? Maybe a boat?"

My eyes widened. Next to me, Tapan mouthed noiseless protests. A round of soft drinks and civilities, the engineer assured us he would do what he could, and we left. From the back seat, I protested that I wasn't a Mrs. "If you are not married, you should be," Sen retorted. "I will think of you as I like."

Although the first settlement flourished, in a few years the whim of Commodore William Cornwallis, brother of the governor general of India, shifted it to the eastern side of North Andaman: the new harbor was spacious enough to accommodate warships. The view was romantic, pronounced Michael Symes, a diplomat who stopped by on his way to Burma: "[N]othing is to be seen but an extensive sheet of water, resembling a vast lake, interspersed with small islands, and environed by lofty mountains clothed with impenetrable forests."

An impediment to romance was the scarcity of females. Once two Andamanese women were captured and brought to a ship in the harbor. They were fed and dressed and soon lost their fears, "except what might be offered to their chastity, which they guarded with unremitting vigilance." Although they had their own cabin, one always watched while the other slept.

They also threw away the clothes. But they "were inexpressibly diverted," wrote Symes, by their images in a mirror; they sang, "sometimes in melancholy recitative, at others in a lively key," and danced about the deck, "slapping their posteriors with the back of their heel." One night, though, they stole through the captain's cabin, jumped into the sea, and swam to an island half a mile away. They were not pursued.

Another woman did not get away, nor did her captors. "A party of fishers belonging to the settlement induced a woman, by the allurement of food, to come so close that she was made prisoner; instead of relieving her hunger, they proceeded to offer violence; the cries of the poor creature brought a numerous troop of savage friends to her assistance, who, rushing out of the thickets, attacked and killed two of the yet more savage aggressors," reported Symes. The bodies were found pierced with sharp weapons and "pounded by stones until every bone was broken." No flesh was missing, which Symes took to be a sign that the natives were not cannibals.

Nor did the natives eat a shipwrecked European they encountered in the forest; they just took away his clothes.

Once, in the late 1700s, an Andamanese man and boy were found on a beach, "apparently in the last stages of famine." But since starvation is improbable — the shores abounded with food — they must have been emaciated by some disease imported by the newcomers. The man died, but a Major Kyd, an administrator, returned to Calcutta with the boy as a servant. Help was not in short supply in the city, so one surmises the boy's main value was "the striking singularity of his appearance," as Symes put it.

The new naval base was unhealthy for the settlers as well. Following a spate of deaths from fevers, its more than eight hundred men, women, and children were evacuated in 1796. Malaria thus bought the Andamanese a half-century's respite from colonizers — if not from adventurers.

*Great Andamanese*

# Savage

JOHANN WILHELM HELFER, amateur naturalist, practicing doctor, and newly married man, hated life in Prague. In his mind he roamed the alluring depths of the Orient, brooding about its pull. "Who knows," he wrote in his diary, "when I yield to the delight of dreaming of traveling in India as a naturalist, whether I might not start back in alarm if the future were unveiled to me?"

Watching him grow distant and depressed, his wife, Pauline, realized there was no help for it. He would have to leave home, and she with him. In 1835 the Helfers embarked from Trieste, Italy. After traveling through Arabia and Afghanistan (she was often disguised as a man for safety), they finally landed in Calcutta. There Helfer earned the job of his dreams as a naturalist with the British government, charged with surveying seeds, plants, hardwoods, minerals, and especially coal for the ever-multiplying number of steamships. The couple moved on to Burma, where they decided to settle.

While Pauline busied herself planting orchards of coconut, betelnut, and coffee, Johann planned another trip — to the Andamans. At the time, the islands weren't a British possession, and so the trip was not, strictly speaking, professional. But to his wife's dismay, the fantastic stories he'd heard drew him inexorably.

In January 1840 Helfer went to sea in a small schooner, *Catharina*, and right away got caught in a squall. Struggling against the violent winds and currents, the vessel finally reached scattered islands on the edge of the Andamans.

"The first object that met my eyes was a black, naked, Andaman negro, then came another, and then several." (Though an Austrian, Helfer wrote his journal in English for the benefit of his employers.) "They did not seem to trouble themselves much about us, and were gathering shellfish on the shore."

The sea was so rough that he could not land. After three more days the *Catharina* traveled into the Andaman Straits, which separate North and Middle Andaman, and was sucked into a whirlpool. "The vessel whirled round and round like a feather in the wind, the current rushed past like a mill-stream; and our situation was most critical." After extricating themselves, the explorers entered a wide bay where they came upon some boats. These turned out to contain Malays who were looking for swiftlets' nests, an Eastern delicacy.

Helfer spied some Andamanese, armed with bows, arrows, and spears, peeping from behind rocks. "Some came down to the beach to stare at us, and one called out to us at the top of his voice. It was a good voice; we listened, but could not understand what he said." The ship's Malay captain went ashore and returned to report that he'd tried to talk to three men with painted faces, with no success.

The next day three canoes cut across the bay. The *Catharina* drew near, but the islanders were evidently frightened, for they pulled two of the canoes into the jungle while the third vanished up a creek. Still, after the ship dropped anchor they reappeared and called out to it. Armed with coconuts, Helfer and his men approached them, rowing to a promontory of rock.

Only one of the natives had the courage to come up. "He was a young man, well-built, of middle size, quite naked, and nearly as black as coal, but with a tinge of brown. His hair, shorn on both sides of his head, formed a curly woolly crest. His body was neither tattooed nor painted. He chattered a great deal, grinning with his white teeth, and laughed aloud. I laughed too, when he broke out into roars of laughter."

He brought water to the visitors, whereupon the Malay captain of Helfer's boat took the natives a bowl of rice. The young man accepted it, returning the bowl filled with water. But one of the boatmen bumped against him, and it broke. "After that the savages would not come near the boats any more, but only peeped at us from behind the rocks."

It being terribly hot, Helfer wanted to land and get water for the ship but found his men to be afraid. At length he persuaded a good number of them, who carried guns. The natives ran away, vanishing behind a rock, and the casks were duly filled: "My people drank water till sunset." From time to time they could still see the Andamanese.

"I wished to attempt communication with them again, and landed at a spot from which, not long before, I had seen smoke rising." He found the glowing embers of a fire, with skulls of turtles hanging from poles and little bows and arrows for children lying about. Helfer wandered along the beach and into the woods, botanizing. That night he wrote in his diary: "These, then, are the dreaded savages! They are timid children of Nature, happy when no harm is done to *them*. With a little patience it would be easy to make friends with them."

The next morning Helfer, the captain, and eight sailors rowed to a sandy bank where a number of islanders were gathered. The visitors displayed their coconuts and rice, but the natives backed off into the woods. Helfer was about to follow them in when suddenly a group of natives jumped out of the bushes shouting, spears and bows raised high.

So as not to give offense, Helfer and his men had landed unarmed. They ran. The boat capsized in the rush, and they began to swim to the *Catharina*. The islanders sent a shower of arrows after them; one hit Helfer in the head and killed him.

He was five days short of thirty.

In the afternoon of that day in Port Blair, in 1997, I strolled down the road from the lodge. Although billed as a tourist hotel, Megapode was reserved for VIPs with chauffeured cars and sat in grand isolation on a hill far from town. The sun was blazing, and I soon sought shelter in a small green-painted anthropological museum. Inside it was cool and dark, with fans beating noisily. A man at a corner desk raised his head and rubbed his eyes.

Long glass-topped cases in the center of the room displayed baskets, nautilus shells used as drinking cups, and other artifacts. One section was labeled SENTINELESE, from 1967. How did we get these? I wondered. Stole them from the huts while the owners were out hunting? I stared in astonishment at a large flat wooden board etched with a square cut into smaller squares, eight by eight. Alternate squares were stippled. Surely the Sentinelese didn't play chess!

On the walls were six-foot-long arrows and some photographs. A fine black-and-white print showed two Onge sitting on each other's laps, as they did when meeting after a long time — just sat silently with their arms draped around each other, with perhaps a tear trickling down. Another showed an Onge woman with a crab-claw pipe jauntily stuck between her teeth.

A blown-up color photo of a Jarawa woman hit the eye. She had a bold, insouciant pose, long pointed breasts, and a rounded stomach, and she looked at the camera with the assurance of being admired.

In the evening, pacing in the dark driveway of Megapode, Sen pontificated. "A man and woman are walking along. Someone paints them. That is an aboriginal painting. Someone makes a copy, that is an original. Do you understand?"

"No."

"Picasso's paintings, they are all originals?"

"Yes," I conceded.

"But the true original is Leonardo, Mona Lisa's sweet smile. That is the aboriginal. Now do you understand?"

"Yes," I said, though I didn't.

"The Andaman tribes are one of the few aboriginals, *ab* meaning 'first.' They came here first, before anyone else. We are just originals."

Speak for yourself, I thought as some men approached. Soon I too had a visitor, a professor of sociology whom Sen had summoned for me. The boat for Strait Island, where most of the Great Andamanese lived, would depart early on Monday, he told me; but I would need a tribal pass. With no time to traverse official channels, I went to Sen's room to ask him if he could get me a pass.

Sitting on the sofa was a mustachioed man in an olive uniform with brass trimmings, a deputy superintendent of police. "Give her a pass," Sen said to him.

"I can't," the DSP protested. "Only the DC can. Just ring up the DC."

The district commissioner was a new arrival to the islands, and Sen didn't know him. He was plainly reluctant to ask a favor that might not be granted. "Why don't you take her without a pass, it's your police who check!"

"Call him," said the DSP.

Eventually Sen picked up the receiver and dialed, listened for a few minutes, and put it down, relieved. "Not home." He turned to me. "Is it okay if you just talk to the local Andamanese? The DSP knows one, in his force. Plus you'll be going through the Jarawa forest tomorrow." Courtesy of the public works department. "It's exciting, scary. You'll get goosebumps." Only a week ago a Jarawa had shot at the passengers of a bus.

*       *       *

At four A.M. on September 1, 1849, a monsoon storm smashed the merchant ship *Emily* onto a reef on the western coast of the Andamans. "The night was dark and rainy, with heavy passing squalls, and had been so for three days previous, so that no observation could be obtained by either sun, moon, or stars, during that time," began Captain F. Anderson's report to the owners.

When morning came, the crew built a raft and lowered it into the water, but the first man on it was washed off and the raft itself swept out to sea. The next day a few men on a pinnace, or small sailboat, somehow made it to shore, carrying a little bread and some clothes. But a longboat with muskets, gunpowder, nautical charts, ship's papers, salted meat, and other essentials overturned in the waves, drowning four men; the boat sent afterward followed the raft out to sea. Anderson, who didn't know how to swim, was saved by having on "one of the safety swimming belts." Finally an unnamed European made it to shore with a line, and everyone else followed it in — except for one man who drowned and the second officer, who preferred to stay on board rather than risk the waves.

Then they had to walk three-quarters of a mile in bare feet over the corals. "It was awful, like walking over so much broken glass; we got cut and mangled about the feet and legs dreadfully, and I have not been able to walk since," Anderson related. Not long after a new hazard appeared: the natives.

One arrow passed within three inches of a boy apprentice, Moffat. "We had nothing to defend ourselves with, but we all got large sticks and held them up like arms, which I suppose the savages took them for, as they returned to the bush shortly after." There were some thirty sailors on the beach, and the Andamanese must have been afraid to attack until they'd gathered in force.

Anderson and his men got to work repairing the longboat and the pinnace with odd pieces that had washed ashore, and by nightfall they were ready to leave. It took much persuasion to get ten men and the boy Moffat into the leaking pinnace. "Our eatables and drinkables consisted of one piece of beef and pork, and an oil tin containing four gallons of water," he noted. At daylight they finally found a passage through the reefs and parted from the longboat. But another storm hit that night, "so that we knew not which way we were steering, with a boat so leaky that we could scarcely keep her free, and having only three oars and a lascar's blanket as a substitute for a sail, our situation was anything but pleasant, having no clothing or covering but what we stood in." Morning dawned among small islands, probably at the north end of the Andamans, and after four days the unfortunates managed to land on one. They unloaded the boat and had just prepared a place to rest when, extraordinarily, a brig sailed into view.

"This cheered us up considerably, the boat was immediately launched, everything put into her with the exception of our remaining piece of beef which in the hurry was forgotten." Pulling and sailing for over an hour, the pinnace got in sight of the ship, which "saw us and hove to, which was a joyful sight to us all." But after about ten minutes the brig put up its sails and left. "No doubt they were afraid we were pirates coming from one of the cannibal islands," wrote Anderson impassively. "I steered after her until darkness hid her from our view."

Desperate, the men had no choice but to try for the Burmese coast. Anderson himself steered all night, in case a quick break in the clouds revealed a star that might guide him. In about ten days they hit land, a tribute to his sheer guts.

A rescue vessel, the HMS *Proserpine,* quickly proceeded to the scene of the wreck, with Anderson on board. At eight A.M., October 25, Captain Brooking rounded Interview Island and saw "[n]atives coming to the beach, armed as on the other Island, observed some with clothes on, supposed the same to have been stolen from the wreck, as these were the first seen with any one article of clothing on." An hour later, the journal continues, the wreck was sighted. "Natives very numerous on the beach, all armed." On seeing the *Proserpine,* however, they all ran into the jungle.

The rescue party boarded the *Emily,* "when to our horror we found, lying on the deck, the mangled remains of the late 2nd Officer." The wreck had been stripped. Curiously, the Andamanese had taken all the biscuits and liquor — beer, champagne, and sherry — on board. But they hadn't eaten the salted meat, nor the unfortunate Simpkin; he had, however, been scalped.

Shortly the lookout reported natives approaching the wreck. They'd lit fires on hillocks, "which no doubt were beacons, as in an incredibly short space of time more than 200 natives had collected on the beach, all armed with spears, bows, etc." Others were joining the group, which was coming toward the wreck. The rescue party, fearing that it would be cut off, directed the *Proserpine* to fire. "To show their daring not a man among them would move on the first round, but on the second round coming quickly and the shot falling fairly among them, a general yell was raised, and dropping their arms, they one and all took flight." At sunset, having retrieved what they could, and "having warned in writing, on several places on the wreck, any parties calling there to beware of the natives," the rescuers left.

The story has an odd epilogue. The wreck of the *Emily* was sold to a salvage company, whose vessel, the *Sea Serpent,* proceeded in a few months to the scene. Amazingly, the Andamanese turned out to be very cooperative: "[T]hey came down to the wreck and mixed with the crew of the Schooner, even assisting them in their work, and voluntarily returning articles they had plundered from the wreck."

The next year an unknown sailor from the *Sea Serpent* returned to the wreck and left a journal entry quoted by officer Maurice V. Portman in his 1899 *History.* A native man he'd befriended on the earlier trip did not turn up, "but a youngster has come in his stead. We gave him some coconuts, and invited him to sit in the boat." The youth was tattooed in horizontal stripes and daubed with red ochre; from a string around his waist hung a shell with a sharp edge all around, with which he easily sliced a coconut. When someone threw away this knife, he amicably retrieved it from the water, indicating that it was very useful to him.

Asking for a cigar, he lit it himself, "and no Turk could enjoy his hookah with greater contentment." He was acquainted with fire-arms and not in the least alarmed at having a musket discharged near him but was curious about how the fire was produced. "It was explained to him, and he laughed at the explanation," wrote the sailor. The conversation must have been in sign language. Ultimately the stripped *Emily* was abandoned, and the natives set fire to its hull "for the purpose," surmised Portman, "of getting at the iron bolts and screws."

In 1857 the Sepoy Mutiny — or the First War of Independence, depending on your point of view — threw British India into turmoil as Hindus and Muslims fought side by side against rulers who were racist and exploitative. Having dispatched the uprising with the same indiscriminate brutality it accused the rebels of, the government sought an abode for those perpetrators whose crimes were not deemed to merit death. Accordingly, in November of that year, Surgeon-Major Frederic John Mouat was dispatched in the war steamer *Pluto* to scout the Andamans.

According to Mouat, *Pluto*'s crew boasted "self dependent Anglo-Saxons, active and fiery Celts, fair Norsemen, stout Finlanders, swarthy Italians, and Maltese," a couple of Americans, and diverse other Caucasians. The darker ones were African stokers and pokers, Chinese carpenters, Indian and Malayan sailors, Burmese cooks, and Bengali valets. In motley dialects, everyone speculated about the savages they were to encounter.

The Indians supplied the "wildest imaginings," endowing the Andamanese with horses' heads, lions' tails, and immunity against bullets, lead or silver. The fanciful stories affected even the Europeans — always "ready to meet either man or devil in fair and open fight" — whose brave hearts became fearful of a hideous people who would slaughter them with poisoned arrows "and, finally, in their banquets, feast on their dead bodies."

Steaming southward from Burma, the adventurers first reached North Andaman, where they came upon bricks from the abandoned colony and a festering salt marsh, which Mouat guessed was the source of the deadly malarial fevers that had plagued it. Farther down the coast lay a small picturesque island. Scouting around it, they spied from a distance a group of natives on the edge of a large rock, gazing into the water below. Engrossed in fishing, the islanders didn't see the *Pluto* until it had crept quite close.

"As we drew towards the reef already mentioned, the native party stationed on it were observed all at once to make a sudden start, and to stand transfixed with unspeakable astonishment and awe. It is not too much to say that they seemed to be completely paralysed by our sudden appearance on their coast. If we had dropped from the clouds, or risen from the sea, their wonder and admiration could not have been more excessive," wrote Mouat. "They would start, and gaze, and look in amazement at each other, as the loud rattling noise made by the fat unrolling anchor chain, and the more unaccountable sound caused by the escaping steam, as in clouds of dense white vapour it issued shrieking from the steam-pipe, at once appalled their hearts, and excited their curiosity."

The senior officers resolved to send two boats to land near the natives and offer them "such trifling presents as they most value," to demonstrate friendship. Accordingly, two cutters were equipped with hidden, loaded guns and manned. At first the natives observed the goings-on with curiosity. But when the boats approached at a fast clip, their oars rising and falling in military unison, the islanders let out "a sharp, instantaneous shout, or rather yell," of defiance. They gesticulated and brandished their bows, until one bold man rushed into the water and "in a paroxysm of well-acted fury" shot an arrow at the steamer.

The man had judged the *Pluto*, the source of the approaching boats, to be the true threat. But the futility of his move struck the visitors as funny — so much so that "[t]he very echoes in the surrounding hills were awakened by the rollicking hilarity." The crewmen's superstitious fears had not blinded them to their advantages, especially those manifest in the guns at their feet.

If laughter was not insult enough, the boatloads of men — hirsute, weather-beaten, armed — were heading for a spit of beach on which stood a "timid knot of frightened females." The terror they expressed, by running to and fro, wringing their hands, throwing themselves onto the sand, covering their faces, or looking toward the boats with "gestures of supplication and pleas for mercy," did not induce the chivalrous visitors to turn away. Rather, the naked women presented to Mouat "as ludicrous a spectacle" as he could imagine.

"[T]hey were not merely plain and unattractive, but absolutely hideous — and far from pleasant objects to look upon. Their complexions were as black as soot could make those of our Ethiopian minstrels at home. Their small dwarfish figures were hard and angular, and their general contour the very reverse of graceful." What seems to have annoyed him most was the lack of "that natural ornament," hair: most Andamanese women cropped their curls very close.

As the boats landed, the terrified creatures raced into the jungle fifty yards away, leaving a scramble of small footprints in the sand. Despite their ugliness, sentries were posted to prevent the men from following "the less repulsive" of the females into the forest.

After leaving some trinkets, the visitors tried to approach the enraged men on the rock. "[We] waved white handkerchiefs, exhibited numerous dazzling strings of beads, unfolded pieces of cotton cloth," but all this effort was met by ungrateful showers of arrows. Eventually the boats returned to the *Pluto*.

To the Victorian imagination, the Andaman islander became the stuff of nightmare. In the Sherlock Holmes story "The Sign of Four," such a native killed out of the sheer malevolence of his nature. Cornered after a boat chase down the Thames, he stood revealed to Dr. Watson as "a little black man — the smallest I have ever seen — with a great, misshapen head and a shock of tangled, dishevelled hair." Watson continued, "Never have I seen features so deeply marked with all bestiality and cruelty. His small eyes glowed and burned with a sombre light, and his thick lips were writhed back from his teeth, which grinned and chattered at us with half animal fury."

Compare this character, and the Andamanese women depicted above, with Dr. Watson's ladylove in the same story: "She was seated by the open window, dressed in some sort of white diaphanous material, with a little touch of scarlet at the neck and waist. The soft light of a shaded lamp fell upon her as she leaned back in the basket chair, playing over her sweet grave face, and tinting with a dull, metallic sparkle the rich coils of her luxuriant [blond] hair. One white arm and hand drooped over the side of the chair, and her whole pose and figure spoke of an absorbing melancholy."

What greater contrast could be drawn between ugliness and beauty, viciousness and gentleness, savagery and civilization?

In the nineteenth century, some Andamanese taken to Calcutta were displayed at the zoo, where Bengali visitors often took them to be descendants of the monkey god Hanuman. "Their nervous organization being less developed, they are happy in not feeling pain with the same excessive poignancy that white people of the twentieth century experience when wounded or injured," opined an Englishwoman writing in 1911. As late as 1925, a paper published in *Man,* a journal of the Royal Anthropological Institute, defined the Andaman native as a new species of human, *Homo mincopoeus* (after Mincopie, a word that Colebrooke, the eighteenth-century explorer, mistakenly used for the Andamanese). Henceforth, wrote W. P. Pycraft, the term *Homo sapiens* should be restricted to the Nordic races.

## Uprooted

"THE ANDAMAN BOY: A TRUE STORY," a poem published in 1819, described how a ship passing the archipelago picked up a native child floundering in the sea. By sign language, he explained that at dawn he'd seen the vessel pass, and, out of curiosity, had plunged into the water to follow it. But the ship went on and on, and by the time he was spied and rescued, the sun was setting and the outlines of his homeland could barely be discerned. The ship was headed to Sri Lanka:

> Oh! then to see that anxious boy,
> Gaze tow'rds his native land;
> And hear his sighs, as he at length
> Trod on a foreign strand.

All day he would sit and stare at the ocean, perhaps hoping that the islands would miraculously appear in the distance. It was in vain:

> For day by day he pin'd away,
> And soon sunk to the grave.

After scrubbing off the grime of my weekend trip, I chose a flowing chiffon sari in pale yellow and pink. I had to look as Indian and unthreatening as possible, for it was a Monday of official visits, and questions about the Andamanese, I already knew, made bureaucrats suspicious. Sen was gone, but I was to meet his friend, the DSP.

The office was small, with a no-nonsense desk and basic wooden chairs. The DSP sent for tea and asked a deputy to bring in Joe.

Joe, a Great Andamanese, was in the home guard. He marched in and stood at attention, staring over everyone's heads. He was pimply and red-eyed. The DSP asked his name in Hindi.

"Joe, sir."

"Surname?"

A shake of the head.

"How old are you?"

"Twenty." Sixteen, I would have guessed.

"Look at his hair." The DSP turned to me. "You can see he is a negro." Joe was expressionless, stiff as a board. "But lighter skin. He is a mixture."

I squirmed.

"Would you like to be a constable?" the DSP asked Joe. A barely perceptible mark of pleasure flitted across Joe's determinedly pursed lips. "Yes, sir."

The DSP turned to his deputy. "We have to enroll him in some classes." Heads nodded.

I couldn't convince myself the DSP's interest was anything but momentary. I asked if I could talk to Joe alone, perhaps in the afternoon. It was decided he'd come to my hotel at two P.M.

Back in my room after the morning's interviews, I paced, tired and strangely nervous. Joe was due any minute now. What did he think of himself, his people, us? Could there be anything but resignation?

A knock on the door and there he was, hands clasped behind him, impassive as before. I let him in but decided my room was too odd a setting. We moved to the rooftop restaurant, where I asked a few basics. Every time, he looked at me and answered yes or no. Some questions required other words: his father's name was Dulu and his mother's name was Diu. He liked the home guard but wouldn't say what his work entailed. Anything requiring more than two syllables evoked only silence and sometimes a shy twist of the lips.

He'd studied till grade three on Strait Island. "Then they brought me to Port Blair. I studied again till three. Then they took me back to Strait. Again from the beginning till three."

The outburst was so fast and unexpected that I made him repeat what he'd said. Something had changed between us; he was enjoying my incredulity. Out of frustration, he'd refused to go to school anymore. I asked what he'd learned there, but he stared in silence at the tablecloth. So I tried provocation. "Do you know your people have been on these islands for thousands of years?"

"Yes." The ends of his mouth turned up more definitely, his eyes meeting mine.

"How do you feel that we have taken them from you?"

"At first . . ." He looked at his hands while I waited. "At first it was bad, not now." Earlier, his parents had no homes. But now they were better off, he explained, because the government had made them cottages.

I asked if he'd met the Jarawa boy who was in Port Blair some months ago. The youth had broken his leg while raiding a settler village and, having been caught, was kept at a hospital in Port Blair while the leg healed. He was grandly entertained with everything anyone could think of for impressing a visitor from the Stone Age — glass bangles, a harmonica, air conditioning, TV — and even a few of his estranged brethren.

"Yes. They took me."

"You could talk to him?"

"Tried. He would talk, but I couldn't understand. First when they brought him he was crying. Later he was playing. I saw him once, then later went to see if he is okay." After three of probably the most surreal months in his life, the Jarawa boy had been returned to the beach where he lived.

Nearing the end of their exploration of the Andamans in the 1850s, Mouat and other officers of the *Pluto* realized that they had failed to collect enough curios, "as indispensable as letters of introduction" in the elite circles of Calcutta. Lady Canning, the wife of the governor-general — Mouat's boss — had her personal collection of Indian antiquities to which she strongly encouraged contributions. Accordingly, when the *Pluto* circled Interview Island to the northwest, bringing into view hundreds of natives on a nearby shore, the visitors prepared two cutters for landing.

Mouat claimed he was merely executing the order to gather information. He stood in the prow of his boat, waving a white handkerchief and strings of beads that "flashed brilliantly in the sun." But some natives in canoes responded with a volley of arrows, one of which, emanating from a "fierce-looking savage" who seemed to be a chief, hit the thigh of an officer.

The soldiers, being "ready for any unexpected attack," instantly felled the offender. "Covering his face — not with his robe, for he had none, but with his hands, to shut out the blinding flash of the fire-arms which we were now discharging rapidly — he sank in his canoe with a grace and dignity in which there was something really touching and melancholy."

In the skirmish that followed, several in the British party were injured, mostly from friendly fire: one of the boats had misjudged distances. At least three Andamanese died. The rest abandoned their canoes to swim ashore, "diving every two hundred yards like ducks baited by water-spaniels." The hunters chased down several of them and managed to catch one.

They also picked up two of the bodies: "Their features, distorted as they appeared by the most violent passions, were too horrible for anything of human mould, and I could regard them only as the types of the most ferocious and relentless fiends," exclaimed Mouat. After a minute scientific examination by the ship's doctor, who wanted to keep the heads — Mouat drew the line at that — these "repulsive" creatures were lowered into a canoe and pushed toward shore.

Meanwhile the captured savage, having been dressed in "trowsers and a jacket," was affording amusement to the sailors, who made earnest efforts to teach him to smoke, nearly choking him. "He appeared to submit to all his trials very patiently, as if he considered them necessarily involved in his captive lot," Mouat wrote. The prisoner was named Jack Andaman. Shortly afterward, the ship's dog, Neptune, plodded up to observe the newcomer. Jack must never have seen a dog before, for his first reaction was utter amazement. But acting from some deep-seated instinct — or perhaps the conviction that any being was preferable to his captors — he threw his arms around Neptune and lay down with him on the deck. From then on the two were inseparable.

At night Jack was placed in irons to preempt escape attempts: "[F]or we were anxious to convey him with us to Calcutta, as the only specimen of a native Andaman who had, at least in recent times, been seen in a civilized city."

With Jack on deck, the *Pluto* turned away from the islands. "Savage as he was, he evidently regarded the gradual disappearance of his native shores with feelings of a melancholy nature, remembering, no doubt, as we should do, the friends he left behind, and the scenes of infancy and boyhood he might never see again." If Mouat had second thoughts, he instantly banished them, noting that the widening sphere of civilization was improving some savages and necessarily annihilating others, for "man must constantly advance or perish." Darwin had his adherents.

The souvenir was a hit in Calcutta: "Our friend Jack was regarded by all who had an opportunity of seeing him as an object of great interest, such as the contrast between the extreme barba-

*Jack Andaman in a sailor suit*

rism of savage life and the highest state of civilized existence must ever excite." He was given quarters in Mouat's residence, and, decked in fancy clothes, displayed to the Lord and Lady Canning. Jack spent most of the visit admiring himself in the full-length mirrors of the governor-general's home and bursting into fits of laughter.

When news spread of the arrival of a genuine savage, huge crowds of Bengalis gathered daily outside Mouat's house. They were dispersed by means of a cannibal caricature: a scarecrow made of black silk, with woolly hair, huge staring eyes, formidable teeth, and a ferocious howl, displayed at a window. The onlookers fled in fear but, soon realizing the trick played upon them, had a hearty laugh and left for good.

Jack was liked by all except, for some reason, Mouat's female

Indian servants. He adored babies, of whom there were two in the household, and he would have fondled them thoroughly if he was so allowed. As it was, he had to be content with just looking, with "curiosity and affection." Sometimes he would hold up several fingers and gesture toward his distant home with an "indescribably sad expression of countenance," probably trying to say that he too had children.

Touring Calcutta in a carriage, Jack met Africans on ships that docked at the harbor, but understood nothing of their dialects. He was curiously calm at all the wonders presented to him, until he saw a man on a horse. Evidently he thought of it as a monster with six legs, for his astonishment knew no bounds when the man got off: Jack leaped out of the carriage and examined the horse's back, looking for tears.

That very night he came down with cholera. Though the intense phase of the disease passed with treatment, he remained weak. Mouat, himself a physician, realized that Jack's only hope for survival might be returning to his native land.

Mouat redeemed himself by coming to love Jack enough to send him back. He was left at South Reef Island, near where he'd been caught, on the presumption that his people would find him. In a strange reversal of the events following his capture, the crew persuaded him to strip naked so that his friends might more readily recognize him. The condition embarrassed him now that he'd imbibed the moral stigma civilization attaches to nudity.

"He took an affectionate leave of all who had accompanied him, appearing very dejected and low," and remained standing "silent and melancholy" until he disappeared from view. He was never seen or heard from again.

Hailing from a long line of displaced Andamanese, Joe's mother, Diu, was living in Port Blair. I asked if I could meet her, and Joe smiled slightly, nodding. We walked along the streets under a scorching sun: there was no shade left, for the public works department had diligently cut down the trees. Only three majestic survivors reigned on the hill near the government offices, several hundred years old to judge by their trunks. Up a road winding from Aberdeen, the main bazaar, Joe led me to a small house guarded by a large sign: ADIBASERA.

ADIBASERA IS A TRIBAL RESERVE.
ENTRY INTO ADIBASERA WITHOUT TRIBAL PASS
IS AN OFFENCE UNDER ANDAMAN AND
NICOBAR ISLANDS PROTECTION OF
ABORIGINAL TRIBES REGULATION 1956.
BY ORDER.

A small, dark, pretty woman in red clothes, standing by the door, welcomed me in. Inside, lying on a bed, was an older woman, light-skinned. Diu turned out to be the one in red, with the lively smile, sweetly sloping cheeks, painted eyebrows, and *bindi* — the dot Indian women wear on the forehead. "You look so young," I exclaimed, "you could be Joe's sister." That pleased her, and Joe too. Glad to relinquish me, he lay down behind the other woman, hidden but listening. Thankfully, Diu was loquacious.

I offered her a pair of silver earrings I'd brought along. "No holes," she said, pointing to her ears. I was taken aback; she looked so Indian, and every Indian woman had holes in her ears. It was only her smooth lobes, the frizzy hair pulled back in a ponytail, and, perhaps, the delicacy of her bones that betrayed her difference. But her daughters had pierced ears, and she kept the earrings for them.

Diu was thirty-five. Having spent some early years in Port Blair, she was accustomed to Indian ways. I asked about life on Strait Island and got an earful.

The authorities made the tribals work for a daily wage, clearing undergrowth. "The ladies" — she used the English word — "have trouble, have to leave small kids and go to work." A government-run body, the AAJVS (Society for Upliftment of Andaman Aboriginals) took care of Andamanese affairs on behalf of the Department of Tribal Welfare. It provided rations and medicine but kept most of the money the tribals earned, giving them only a little in hand. Diu wanted permanent work and a salary she could keep. "I taught small kids for fifteen years," she pointed out indignantly.

"My mother says old times were better. Five kilograms of rice would last a long time, there were fish, shellfish you could gather. Now there are so many people. There used to be forests here."

The Jarawa youth had intrigued her as well. "I liked seeing him," she said with a smile. "But they think we are enemies, they think we show outsiders the road to them."

"They did that, in British times," I replied, and instantly regretted it. Diu looked down at her fingers and nodded. The old men and women, she offered, still told many stories: "They say British killed half of us, and then these people came." My people, Indians.

One evening I found myself seated by a lone Englishman in a restaurant. "You're alone?" he asked in surprise, and I joined him. He was young and thin, with matted hair and unfocused hangdog eyes. He'd been traveling in Asia for the last six or seven years. He spent about two weeks a year in England, selling things he bought in other countries.

He didn't get lonely, he said, for he ran into the same individuals year after year, in places as diverse as Pushtu and Port Blair — all wandering, like himself. In October or November he would go to the Himalayan foothills for "the best *charas* [marijuana] in the world."

I asked if he was happy, and he considered. "Not always, sometimes. I feel I want to do something. It's not right, somehow, to hang out in this country. I'm not helping anyone. I want to help." He grew agitated. "My parents don't like what I do. But parents, they have to offer an alternative, right? What do I do? I have no qualifications."

I watched as he counted ten spoons of sugar into his tea and stirred. I offered to pay for his meal, but he had enough money for now. I left, feeling unaccountably saddened.

# *Pacification*

I N   T H E   S P R I N G  of 1858 the British government in India started a penal settlement on South Andaman, at the same harbor where the first colony had stood almost a century earlier. It was named Port Blair. Three months later, on June 16, Superintendent James Pattison Walker recorded the following tally of convicts:

> Total received 773
> Died in hospital 64
> Escaped and not recaptured (probably died of
>     starvation, or killed by the savages) 140
> Suicide 1
> Hanged for attempting to escape 87

Of the surviving 481 prisoners, 60 were hospitalized.

Before being executed, the recaptured convicts told of their companions having been massacred by the natives. But their fearsome tales did not deter other escapes. The conditions of imprisonment were horrific. The men were permanently handcuffed in pairs, with the less cooperative of them being pinned to the ground while they worked.

As the prisoners cleared the jungle, the natives began to hit back. On April 14, 1859, about 1,500 of them attacked a group of workers, killing three and carrying off six who had fetters on. The remaining prisoners waded into the sea under the covering fire of a military vessel.

Curiously, the islanders had targeted the overseers, being disinclined to injure those with marks of imprisonment. "They called upon the convicts to stand aside and let them go into the water and attack the Naval Guard in the boat," wrote Maurice Portman. But the prisoners had more in common with their jailors than with the *junglees* (a Hindi or Bengali term meaning jungle-dwellers or savages), or history might have taken a different course. Eventually the overseers begged to have their signs of authority taken off, so that the Andamanese would not single them out.

One of the prisoners who'd escaped in the first months was Dudhnath Tewari, an Indian who was convicted of mutiny and desertion. His group of about 130 fugitives had made their way through the jungle near Port Blair, slowly starving. On the fourteenth day they were surrounded by about one hundred natives, who shot at them with arrows. Tewari, though wounded on his temple, shoulder, and elbow, managed to flee the carnage with two other men.

The next morning the natives again spotted the three fugitives and pursued them, killing Tewari's companions. Tewari feigned death but was dragged out of his hiding place. His captors withdrew to a short distance and shot at him again, and once more he did not die, though he was injured.

The islanders now helped him onto their boat and treated his wounds with colored earths. For many months Tewari wandered with them, naked and shaven, eating the fish, boar, and fruits he was offered. After four months he married a twenty-year-old named Leepa.

About a year later, Tewari learned of a plan by the natives to attack the main encampment at Port Blair and escaped again. On May 14, when the islanders arrived in force, the British were ready. The Battle of Aberdeen, named after the jetty where most of the action took place (the *Charlotte*, moored offshore, fired into the ranks of the "savages") was a decisive conflict. How many of the islanders died is unclear — one estimate is four hundred — but they never again attacked in force. For his services, the crown pardoned Tewari, who returned triumphant to the mainland.

In the forest, Leepa was left pregnant.

I woke up in high spirits: it was my day on the beach. I had to get to Wandoor jetty, and from there take a boat to Jolly Buoy, a coral-rimmed island southwest of Port Blair. I ended up sharing a taxi with two tourists.

Olina, a German, had seen a documentary on the island's history. "I don't like the way they talk about the tribals, they look down on them," she complained, her hands pushing an invisible something away. "You enter the anthropological museum, the first thing you see is a naked woman. She isn't even doing anything, just posing for the camera. I don't like this arrogant attitude."

I agreed she was on to something. At Megapode lodge I'd viewed an official documentary on the islanders. The lens focused repeatedly on the bare torsos of Jarawa women, but hardly ever found a man. When it came to the Onge women — who were dressed — it noted only the faces. It had no interest at all in the assimilated Great Andamanese.

We finally arrived at Jolly Buoy, a toy of an island: a good swimmer could probably circle it in half an hour. From its mangroves abutted a soft white sand beach, sloping into transparent water. From the shore, one could tell where the corals were by a change in color, turquoise to deep sapphire.

After borrowing a snorkel from boat hands, I swam to the reefs and hung above, watching damselfish hiding in the anemones, one fish trying to clean another's gills, and large green-patterned parrotfishes busily chasing invaders away. At one point I found myself suspended in a shoal of glittering yellow and blue creatures, close enough to touch.

Farther on, the sea floor suddenly fell away into midnight-blue depths, out of which I imagined giant white tentacles reaching. I returned to the beach.

"When I'm out there," a tourist said, "I feel completely at peace."

My sister, who'd called me at the hotel, had insisted that her friend in Port Blair, Souren, was a very decent young man. His family was in the timber business, but he himself had branched out into condiments.

I met Souren at the hotel's rooftop restaurant. A lovely breeze was sweeping off the bay, threatening to blow out the candle on the table. There was a power cut, an evening feature. I settled down to enjoy my food; tonight, I wasn't taking notes. I told him about random things I'd learned in the last days, and mused, "I meet people I like, in official posts, but everything is still such a mess."

"The Andamans are very corrupt," he volunteered. "One of the most corrupt places in India. There is lots of money coming from the center. Some people here have made crores of rupees" — hundreds of thousands of dollars.

The engineer I met had been charged with corruption. "He's due to retire, so he's amassing as much as he can." The police officer who'd introduced me to Joe was under investigation for corruption and wrongful arrest. I ventured a guess. "Sen defends these men?"

"Of course. That's the source of his influence." A gust blew out the candle. "He's also close to the member of parliament, campaigns for elections."

So my first instinct had been right, Sen was a politician. One of a new breed of rulers on the islands.

In 1861 three captured Great Andamanese men, dubbed Crusoe, Jumbo, and Friday, were sent to Burma. They boarded the ship in high spirits and scrounged cigars from the officers on board, evidently believing they were being returned to their own islands after being held in Port Blair. When unloaded at Moulmein, a colonial port in Burma, they were miserable.

One rainy night, they ran. Their footprints were traced to the Moulmein River, where they'd made a raft from a few planks of wood and set off. Their sole provision was one yam. The next day they were spotted on an island twelve miles downstream and that very night must have reached the sea. But the rough waters shattered their makeshift raft, and to their chagrin they were obliged to swim to shore. Returned to captivity, Jumbo, who was described as cheerful and gentle, died a month later of pneumonia. His skeleton was duly preserved for science.

Over the next months Crusoe and Friday became familiar with life in Moulmein. At first they danced for a Burmese audience, but, hearing the howls of laughter, refused to perform anymore. They would wander around the bazaar, using cash to buy pork, or sit for hours watching blacksmiths at work on iron tools, which they coveted. If they came upon a pony, they would hug it, and Friday had once to be restrained from fondling a tusked elephant. They were "uniformly tractable and good humoured," according to a British official in Moulmein, and especially fond of children. But they were deeply homesick. Told they would finally be returning to "Blair," as they'd learned to call their own country, they lay awake singing for two nights prior to their departure. Once in the jungles, they vanished.

Nonetheless, they'd been sufficiently impressed with their "insignificance and weakness," as Portman put it, in comparison with the enemy. Now they knew — as some escaped prisoners from the Andamans discovered on landing in Burma — that much of the earth belonged to their captors. The story of their adventure was to persuade many of the Great Andamanese that resistance was futile.

Soon the islanders were killing fewer of the escaped prisoners. Instead, they often captured them and treated them well, offering them pork and other delicacies. "The Andamanese may have had some idea of getting the convicts to make common cause with them against the Government," wrote Portman.

The Government was similarly taking aboriginal prisoners, keeping them awhile and releasing them with presents. The object was to impress the savages with the technical advantages and friendly intentions of their conquerors, and to create "artificial wants" such as for tobacco and alcohol that would become "the nucleus of increasing intercourse with a superior race," noted one Colonel Tickell (who'd hosted the three captives in Burma).

Although the islanders were becoming more compliant, acts of violence did occur. In January 1863, a boatload of guardsmen paid a social visit to a Great Andamanese village. Though the islanders seemed friendly at first, they suddenly attacked, killing a navy man named James Pratt. In retaliation his companions fired into the crowd and fled.

Colonel Robert Christopher Tytler, the settlement's commander, succeeded in capturing two natives named as the murderers, Snowball and Jumbo. (The Andamanese were given the same ridiculous names over and over again.) They were held in fetters at Port Blair. Near the end of March, two canoes full of natives tentatively approached the settlement and were interrogated by a navy brigadesman, who reported: "The Andamanese hailed us from the shore. Two or three swam off and wanted us to go on shore with them. We would not, and anchored the boat. I told them to bring bows and arrows, and we would give them presents. I asked for women. They said they were in camp and asked us to go there."

The negotiations were largely by means of signs. Eventually the naval brigadesman returned with two Great Andamanese men who'd voluntarily boarded his boat to come to Port Blair. There they met Jumbo and Snowball, were pleased to find them alive, and returned to their beach the following morning. Next to visit was Jumbo's wife, Hira, who came to be called Topsy, and a boy, brother of one of the prisoners. So began a tradition in which the islanders routinely came to Ross Island to live with relatives held hostage at the "Andaman Home."

Topsy, clever and personable, stayed for a long time and made herself useful as a guide to Reverend Henry Corbyn, the keeper of the Home. She adored Jumbo and was distressed whenever parted from him; she seems to have served Corbyn in order to ensure her husband's well-being. Along with Jumbo, another man named Jacko, and five children, she was taken on a tour of Calcutta — distinguished by both men attacking, on separate occasions, sightseers who spat on their trousers. But sometime after their return, all the inmates of the Home escaped. Topsy was ill and evidently drowned while trying to swim a channel.

The Andaman Homes — soon several were built, in diverse locations — became outposts at which the islanders would deposit recaptured convicts, bring news of shipwrecks, or receive medical care, returning to the forest laden with gifts and germs. The Homes became invaluable tools for establishing "friendly relations" with the natives: that is, for eliminating their opposition to the colony. "Though not immediately apparent," wrote Tytler, "we are in reality laying the foundation stone for civilising a people hitherto living in a perfectly barbarous state, replete with treachery, murder, and every other savageness; besides which it is very desirable, even in a political point of view, keeping these people in our custody as hostages, for it undoubtedly secures the better behaviour of these inhospitable people towards our Settlement."

Given the devastation the Homes came to wreak, it's curious that their initiation was an accident. In a few months Tytler was obliged to release Snowball, for he had had nothing to do with Pratt's killing. Jumbo remained in prison for some years until the true murderer was identified: Jacko. Pratt had tried to rape his wife.

Near the end of the nineteenth century, John Hagenbeck, a German adventurer, animal dealer, and filmmaker, joined a punitive expedition against an Andamanese village deep in the jungle. Some of its inhabitants had killed a couple of their "half-civilized" brethren who frequented Port Blair. The colonial authorities saw the act as a challenge, for it fell to them to implement British law in every corner of the empire.

The party consisted of four officers, twenty soldiers, and 250 prisoners, the latter equipped with axes and knives for cutting through the jungle. Hagenbeck went along as a "battle tourist." After steaming a couple of hours up the coast, the party landed on a beach near a native camp. With the help of two Great Andamanese from Port Blair, the officers interrogated the locals as to where the offending village was. Hagenbeck, who held the natives to be "capable of every falsehood and treason," sniffily noted his reservations on the methodology of the British officers and smugly added that he was to be proved right.

That evening, by the light of the moon, he witnessed the funeral of a native chief. Men and women, their bodies covered with lime, danced around the painted corpse, which was tied to a tree; a horrific howling rent the air: "It was a bizarre and spooky scene, this crowd of white forms shining in the bright moonlight, as with writhing limbs and wild expressions they danced around the stiff, white corpse in whose honor the awful lamentation was performed." At dawn the expedition set off in the direction the natives had pointed to. The village was supposedly only five kilometers away, but the rain forest was so impenetrable that it began to look like a two-day march. Hagenbeck, seeing no tracks to follow, opined that they should turn back, take hostage some natives from the coastal camp, and force them to show the way. The officers demurred, believing they would soon come to their goal.

That evening they set up tents and shot a couple of hundred wood pigeons for the pot. In bed, Hagenbeck tossed and turned, tormented by leech bites and haunted by the awareness that at any time the convicts could rise as one to murder the whites; they could then march back to the coast and commandeer the waiting steamer. "But luckily for us those people around the tent were Indians, this means people without will power and initiative, without audacity and drive, in addition crippled from long imprisonment." Soothed by this thought, he fell asleep.

He was woken by screaming. The fires had gone out, leaving embers that glowed on pandemonium. People rushed about, shots sounded, a convict swayed, wailed, and fell to the ground, an arrow in his shoulder. The Andamanese were in the trees, shooting down. The officers had so underestimated the enemy that no one had thought to post a guard.

The soldiers now fired hundreds of shots up into the trees and continued to fire long after the arrows had stopped. Magnesium flares revealed that the party had sustained only a single injury, but two of the attackers had died and a wounded native had been caught. One of the dead men Hagenbeck recognized as belonging to the coastal camp, and under interrogation the captive revealed that the coastal and jungle villages had colluded in the attack.

When the punitive force arrived at the jungle village, it was deserted. Everyone, including Hagenbeck, gathered weapons, pots, and other trophies before the huts were set on fire. When they returned to the coast, the village there was also discovered to be empty and was burned to the ground. Pacification required leaving no doubt as to the consequences of resistance.

As the ship steamed back, the captured native jumped through a porthole and swam away — one who escaped, if only for the moment.

My last evening in Port Blair I spent on the Marina, a brand-new complex featuring a toy train, a large swimming pool, a velodrome for bicycle racing, and a paved walkway by the sea. Everything was brilliantly and garishly lit. I stopped by an electric "tree," a decorative structure hung with fifteen light bulbs, calculating that it alone cost a few dollars a night in fuel burned. All the electricity on the islands came from imported diesel, at great cost for a poor nation.

This ugly expanse was hardly in aid of tourists, who came here for the sand and moonlit surf. The true reason for its existence was grotesquely obvious: the more projects there were, the more ways bureaucrats could divert money. Air-conditioned government offices were going up everywhere, complete with fountains and fancy lighting, and so were tourist lodges, to be packed with civil servants whose bills were borne by taxpayers.

The islands also paid. Sand for all the building came from the beaches. When these were dug up and trucked away, the sea turtles had nowhere to nest and the trees fell into the water. They rotted and poisoned the surrounding corals, while seawater moved inland and polluted the freshwater table.

In addition, much forest on the Great Andamans had been felled for timber and for settlements. As a result, the monsoon rains would run right off the naked hillsides, carrying large loads of silt. The mud settled on the nearshore corals and suffocated them; those farther from shore died too, because the opaque water blocked life-giving sunlight. In the old days, the islands were almost entirely encircled by vivid coral reefs. But now only marine reserves such as around Jolly Buoy, and the territory defended, with their lives, by the Jarawa, preserved pieces of the paradise that was.

In one corner of the Marina I came upon a red-and-black-tile obelisk with a plaque:

MEMORIAL FOR
THE BATTLE OF ABERDEEN

THIS MONUMENT IS BUILT IN THE MEMORY
OF THOSE ANDAMANESE ABORIGINES,
WHO BRAVELY FOUGHT THE
"BATTLE OF ABERDEEN" IN MAY 1859,
AGAINST THE OPPRESSIVE AND RETALIATORY
POLICY OF THE BRITISH REGIME.

A nice thought, to remember the resistance.

## Native Morals

BACK IN PORT BLAIR a year later, it took me a month or more of genuflection to the authorities to get a tribal pass. One early morning, armed with the precious document, I boarded the launch from Port Blair to Strait Island. It stopped at two islands on the way, unloading settlers and loading up with coconuts, bananas, and vegetables, so the trip took seven hot, cramped hours. To my surprise, I wasn't the only one to get off at Strait Island: several men jumped off as well. But I was the only one who needed papers.

A path led from the jetty to a coconut grove nearby, under which were dispersed wooden cottages, the homes of the Great Andamanese. The social worker was away, so I got to stay in his room. His deputy, Paul Patrick, a pleasant young man with a squint, broke the lock to let me in and chased away the goats whose droppings littered the front porch. The room was new, made of concrete but bare and smelly from the expanse of trash that the staff had tossed into the backyard. At least there was a mosquito net.

Curious kids peeked through the window, looking shyly away when I beckoned them in. They seemed habituated to outsiders and looked quite healthy. A woman with a mass of curly hair entered with an adorable little boy and seated herself. It was Etal, one of the two women whose lifestyles were the topic of much gossip in Port Blair. I asked after Joe and Diu.

Joe had left his police job and was now on Strait Island, she said; Diu too was here. Buli, Etal's son, stole shy glances at me while he bounced a rubber ball. He had the straight hair of an outsider. "Who is his father?" I asked after a while.

"Golat," she replied. Her husband was part Andamanese and part Karen Burmese. According to anthropologist Sita Venkateswar, however, Etal had abandoned Golat to live with an Indian man. Just a few years earlier, Venkateswar had found Etal to be "articulate and humorous, a streetwise and irreverent urchin." But the lover had since left, and Etal's youthful good looks were now overcast by layers of sadness. She doted on Buli, always keeping him by her side; nor did I see her dressed up and made up, as Diu was.

Diu seemed to have a flame, a handsome young Indian. I found the two busy repairing the wooden rails bordering her porch while her three youngest children played nearby. They all looked happy and absorbed.

In 1872 George Edward Dobson, a British army surgeon, made an excursion to an Andaman Home in the interior. The journey was by boat, seven miles up a creek, its banks "clothed with probably the densest and loftiest forest in the world." The azure kingfisher flitted about "like a flash of many-coloured light"; slatey herons sat motionless among the mangrove roots, while paradise crows and other brilliant birds could be glimpsed in the jungle.

A dugout with two natives announced the Home. Dobson and his men were welcomed by a local chief's wife, who quickly put on a government-supplied frock; but "very soon afterwards, perceiving that no ladies were in our boat, she got rid of that unnecessary encumbrance, and presented herself in nature's garb, adorned by a single leaf, a garter tied below one knee, and a necklace composed of the finger- and toe-bones of her ancestors," Dobson wrote in an anthropological journal. The Home, which consisted of two long sheds, contained 110 Andamanese of all ages, cooking fish, mending bows, or otherwise engaged, and remarkably incurious about their visitors. The chief, who wasn't feeling well, dozed off. Even when Dobson set up his photographic tent, none of the natives seemed surprised.

Dobson recognized one young woman, who'd been brought up from infancy at an "orphanage" on Ross Island, designed to train native children in the crafts of civilization. "This girl I had seen almost every day, sitting in front of the school-house, and on Sunday at church, neatly dressed in white, and her head covered with a fair quantity of black, woolly hair," he wrote. Four days earlier she'd gotten permission to rejoin her people, and "she was now destitute of clothes, shaved and greased with a mixture of olive-coloured mud and fat, and married, wanting but the finger- and toe-bone decorations to complete her toilet." A year later she was to recognize another white visitor, and, pointing to her swollen stomach, say with much pride and no shame, "buchcha hai!" — Hindi for baby here!

To many Victorian observers, such frankness about bodily matters was proof of the "ineradicable savage element" in their subjects.

On reaching puberty, a Great Andamanese girl would receive the name of a flower blooming in that season. It preceded the name given while in the womb — which was irrespective of sex — and yielded to a more dignified title when she became a mother.

Adults tolerated teen flirtation until they thought it was serious. Then the pair might be subjected to a trick. "[O]n a given day it is arranged by the friends of the suspected couple that they shall (without the knowledge of either) be painted respectively with the red oxide of iron unguent, *koiob*, and the white clay *talaog*, for, as they would not meet till night-fall, the risk of their discovering the trap laid for them is reduced to a minimum, while a glance on the following morning would suffice to betray them if guilty," wrote Edward Horace Man, Officer in Charge of the Andamanese during the late 1870s. The couple would thus be embarrassed into breaking up, unless they were ready to get married. A girl's being found pregnant would be sure to result in a wedding. (Peculiarly, though, the Andamanese did not know that intercourse leads to the condition, believing that it came from swallowing spirits who were living in certain foods.)

In brief, the ceremony consisted of the coyly reluctant groom being dragged to the bride's presence, and, despite her feigned weeping and protests, being forced to sit on her outstretched legs. Torches were lit to allow everyone to witness their embarrassment, and the chief pronounced the couple wed. Others showered the couple with presents: the nets, bows, arrows, and other objects required for setting up a household. For a few days the couple remained too bashful even to look at each other.

The marriage was complete only when a baby arrived. If a childless man returned after an absence, he would first greet his parents and only then his wife. But if he were a father, he would go straight to his own hut. "[T]he wife hangs round her husband's neck sobbing as if her heart would break with joy at their reunion; when she is exhausted with weeping, he leaves her, and, going to one of his relations, gives vent to his pent-up feelings of happiness by bursting into tears." Adultery was uncommon and could result in violent retribution.

Parents thoroughly indulged their children and almost universally gave them away. "It is said to be of rare occurrence to find any child above six or seven years of age residing with its parents, and this because it is considered a compliment and also a mark of friendship for a married man, after paying a visit, to ask his hosts to allow him to adopt one of their children," Man recorded. The parents would in turn adopt the children of others. Still, they paid frequent visits to their own, sometimes taking them away for a few days with permission of the new parents.

*    *    *

The Great Andamanese had a number of taboos against taking the lives of creatures, many of which were under the protection of Biliku or Puluga, the northeastern monsoon wind. In North Andaman, Biliku was supposed to be angered by the killing of a spider (also known as biliku), an insect that hummed like a cicada, a type of beetle, and a particular bird. Anthropologist Alfred R. Radcliffe-Brown, who visited the Andamans from 1906 to 1908, also noted prohibitions against harming two kinds of fish, a certain mollusk, another bird, and two types of trees.

The cicada was a child of Biliku, who would be infuriated if anyone interrupted its singing — in the early morning and late evening — by making a noise, especially that of chopping or banging wood. At these times an islander would be silent as a mouse, even ceasing to hum a tune. Biliku expressed her displeasure by means of storms, which everyone was anxious to avoid.

Nonetheless, the Andamanese loved to eat the cicada's grub, and they indulged this taste between October and November. At the end of the season they would perform a rite known as the killing of the cicada. Everyone would be careful to be in camp by day's end. "As soon as the sun sets and the cicadae begin their shrill cry, all the men, women and children present begin to make as much noise as they possibly can, by banging on the sounding-board, striking the ground with bamboos, beating pieces of wood together or hammering on the sides of canoes, while at the same time shouting," recorded Radcliffe-Brown. "They continue the noise, which entirely drowns that of the cicada, until after darkness has fallen."

After this ceremony the cicada would vanish, and four months of clear, beautiful days would follow.

To the colonists, the islanders' religion made little sense, for it had nothing to do with their idea of morals. When Edward Man translated the Christian Lord's Prayer into a South Andaman language, Puluga served as God. Although Puluga was male, most of the tribes seem to have thought of the spirit as the female Biliku. But that was the least of the translation's problems. Unlike the Christian God, neither Puluga nor Biliku was omniscient and could easily be deceived. Worse, he or she did not care about matters of great import. "Although I made very careful and repeated enquiries, I was unable to meet with a single native who believed that such actions as the murder of one man by another, or adultery, aroused the anger of *Puluga*," wrote Radcliffe-Brown.

Andamanese religion — that is, their world of spirits inhabiting the sea, earth, and sky — seems akin to our science, in that it was an attempt to understand nature. The color of the moon, the shape of a rainbow, a spark of lightning, or an earthquake were all explained in terms of spirits or animate celestial bodies. The moon became red with anger if he spotted a rival light, such as from a fire or torch, when he rose; a rainbow was a cane bridge that the spirits used to visit the earth; lightning was the streak of a pearl shell flung by Biliku; an earthquake happened when spirits under the earth danced. So on the stories went, each phenomenon evoking several explanations, depending on whom you asked.

In the evening I strolled with a Great Andamanese teenage girl, Boro, on the beach, while a band of small kids skipped and shouted around us. The western sky was streaked with pink, and from the shimmering blue and pink waters rose dark green islands nearby. Boro stooped to pick up a shell from under the surf and handed it to me; she seemed very shy and sweet. She was engaged to Joe. What either of them thought of the match I had no way of knowing.

We stopped to watch a rowboat come in from the sea with several Andamanese men and boys. Joe jumped out to pull it onto the beach and dumped two smallish sea turtles upside down on the sand. He gave me a passing nod. He looked older and more confident, far more in his element than when I'd seen him the year before.

Two young boys were fishing from the jetty, Indian style, throwing in their lines and jerking them out. Farther along the beach an old woman, Boro the elder, was also fishing, breaking up snails to use as bait. From time to time she scanned the sea anxiously. Another boatload of men had gone turtle-hunting early in the morning and hadn't yet returned. We too squinted at the waters until it got dark, and then strolled back to the cottages.

"Sometimes the Jarawa come out, that's why we worry," said Boro the younger. "In the hot season, they are looking for water and they end up on this side. We've seen them a few times near here, on that island in front." She pointed. The Jarawa would swim across Middle Strait, which separated Middle and South Andaman, and make the rest of their way through the jungles.

A German traveler, Fedor Jagor, had noted two Jarawas' fortnight-long social visit with the Great Andamanese in May 1873. (The guests took to matches, but not tobacco, which their hosts were by then using.) Such cordial encounters were rare, and the colonial policy of exploiting the tribes' differences soon ended all possibility of friendship; after subduing the Great Andamanese, the British used them as trackers to find Jarawa huts for burning. The memory still troubled some of the Great Andamanese with a vague guilt, as well as a fear that the Jarawa harbored resentments from the past and could attack even their fellow aboriginals. They were saddled with the responsibility of moral choices that others had bestowed on them.

Radcliffe-Brown was the first university-trained anthropologist to do fieldwork — anywhere. He did not live with the natives; instead, he interviewed residents at the Andaman Homes by means of interpreters. He later developed his findings into a grand new framework for understanding primitive societies.

According to Radcliffe-Brown, two Great Andaman tribes (not including the Jarawa) would sometimes meet for nights of dancing and feasting. Everyone would get decked up in clay patterns or with ornaments of shell or leaf. The hosts would make a special effort to supply ample delicacies such as pork, turtle, or honey, and some of the men would compose new songs and train the choir. Only the composer was allowed to sing the lead, and a few individuals were in great demand for their creations.

The visitors and guests would exchange presents. It wasn't, strictly speaking, barter; but if someone was disappointed with what he got in return, the dispute could lead to blows and escalate to a fatal feud between the tribes. If a man happened to kill some-one — even from another tribe — he would have to reside alone in the forest for weeks or months, undergoing a kind of penance. He could not touch a bow or arrow or even food; instead, he would have to be fed by his wife or a friend. For a full year he would wear the shredded plumes of a particular wood.

When one group decided that enough blood had been spilled, it would dispatch female emissaries to discuss matters with the women of the enemy tribe. It wasn't that women were more peaceable; rather, they were the ones who had to be pacified, for it was their anger at the deaths of loved ones that kept the feuds alive. The men, who had to do the killing, preferred to let bygones be bygones.

One English visitor, writing in 1911, described murder as "a sport and a pastime" for the natives. But in reality, killing was a serious matter — and rare enough that the aboriginals had no weapons specific to warfare; instead, they made do with hunting implements. In fact, the only homicides the Great Andamanese routinely committed were on behalf of the authorities. The na-tives were encouraged not only to catch escaped prisoners but also to murder them, "the returning of the head being the easiest and quickest way of earning the reward." Elsewhere in British In-dia, the government conducted punitive expeditions to wipe out headhunting; in the Andamans, it introduced the practice. In the 1920s, one Captain West returned from a campaign against the Jarawa with severed heads hanging from a pole, alongside a Jolly

Roger, a pirate flag complete with skull and crossbones. Around 1939, reported anthropologist Triloki Nath Pandit, policemen transported to civilization the decapitated heads of Jarawa men in the same dinghy as their captured women and children.

Nor did the islanders eat people: they were horrified by the suggestion that they did. An apocryphal story described some English soldiers on a boat watching with horror as their compatriots, who'd been captured by the Onge, were dismembered and thrown live onto a fire. Such practices, if indeed observed, could have been what led to charges of cannibalism.

Apart from celestial beings, the aboriginals' universe contained spirits of the land and sea. The Great Andamanese called the sea spirits *lau*. These were tall, pale, whiskered, and grotesque, while the land spirits might be dark. At night, both kinds of spirits carried lights. The beings were associated with death and disease and were also believed to have a taste for human flesh. Ironically, the legendary Andamanese ferocity toward mariners — whether would-be slavers or shipwrecked sailors — may have arisen from their fear that the *lau* were themselves cannibals.

By our standards, the Andamanese were gentle to one another. Edward Man recorded the following words of abuse in an unspecified Great Andamanese language:

> *ngab-tedinga tapaya!* (You liar!)
> *ngun-lamaya!* (You duffer!)
> *ngun-jabagya!* (You fool!)
> *ngi-chona!* (You long-head!)
> *ngig-choronga-lanta!* (You long nose!)
> *ngig-panamaya!* (You sunken-eyed one!)
> *ngid-kinabya!* (You skin and bone!)

The insults were tame — compared with the slurs on birth and family that we often trade when angry. True, an Andamanese man might further have expressed his rage by destroying objects, his own or others'; sometimes weeks of work to replace them would be entailed. Women would similarly tear one another's baskets or nets, or bang a burning log on the ground, shouting, *"Ngig mugu jabagike!"* meaning "May your face become hideous!"

But the Andamanese shared food, nursed one another when sick, were loyal to spouses, indulged children, and treated most everyone with consideration. This moral code is familiar because human behavior likely evolved in such small bands, where everyone was answerable for his or her actions.

Their distrust of strangers, which allowed the Andamanese to survive as long as they have, also has its counterpart in the modern moral landscape, being manifested as our racism. "We have to teach them some morals," the secretary of tribal welfare told me in Port Blair, speaking of the Great Andamanese.

"They have morals," I pointed out indignantly.

"They do?" he asked in surprise.

## Civilized Vices

O NLY TOTAL IMMERSION in civilization gave hope of "reforming" the natives, many colonial officials believed. Around 1840 an Andamanese family — a man, woman, girl, and boy — was taken to Penang, Burma. In a few years the man and the boy died of cholera and the woman of smallpox, but the daughter, who was named Mary Andaman, survived. She remained in school until she reached fourteen, when she was removed to become a maid in charge of small children.

She was an accomplished pianist and regular churchgoer and was later heard to have moved to Singapore, where she opened a school for native girls. At one point, rumor had it she was engaged to a European schoolmaster, but whether the wedding took place is not known. Mary was often pointed to as proof that savages could be civilized.

In another case, Topsy (at least the fourth Andamanese to bear this name) was "clothed, Christianized, civilized" but nonetheless committed a sexual offense — apparently cohabiting with a man. She was punished and married off, then "turned into a nurse for white babies." Topsy traveled to England, from where she wrote to a former mistress. Part of this missive, dated October 28, 1907, was published by Violet Talbot, an officer's wife in Port Blair. Since these are the only words from the pen of an Andamanese that I have chanced upon, I quote from the letter at some length.

Predictably, Topsy hated the climate. "[S]o far I'm thankful to say I'm keeping well. I used to get fever every day. I feel the cold dreadful, although I wear nothing but warm things, and most of the time spend by the kitchen fire to keep myself warm. The weather here is so changeable, sunshine one, pouring rain, the next, and the nights are simply awful."

Topsy was independent enough to visit London, a few miles away. There she called upon Edward Man, who "did seem pleased to see me, just as much as I was to see him." She also met Sir Richard Carnac Temple, a prolific scholar who was Chief Commissioner on the Andamans for some years. The Lord and Lady Temple took Topsy out for tea in a salon and showed her Hyde Park and other sights. They also gave her a copy of *The Arabian Nights*, hoping that she would enjoy it, but Topsy "felt inclined to send it flying [to] the other end of the street."

Along with another maid, Topsy made an extensive tour of London. "Went underground tube Railway, felt a bit frightened at first when the lift was going down and everything so wonderful. Got out near Westminster Abbey, went round saw where all the Royalties are buried, and the chair on which King Edward was crowned and all the kings of England, it is such a beautiful old abbey. From there to Whitechapel where King Charles was imprisoned, then to the British Museum, went and had tea at the shops. Oh! London is a grand place." They went on by train to Windsor Castle: "When I got there wonder of wonders, I never saw any place so beautiful."

"So you see," she summed up, "I am enjoying England, in spite of fog and cold." The next month she planned to travel to Calcutta in the service of another woman, but I don't know if she ever made it back home. Observers would say she'd been completely amended.

*          *          *

Joseph's was a different story altogether. He belonged to the orphanage, where native children, not necessarily orphans, were
trained so that they'd grow up to become ambassadors of civilization and help bring their brethren into the fold. The eight-year-
old's name caught the fancy of a visitor, Deputy Surgeon-General
Joseph, who adopted him in 1880 and took him away to Rangoon
and Bangalore. The boy learned to read and write English and
Burmese and acquired a fair knowledge of literature; he could also
calculate with decimals and trained as a pharmacist.

After his mentor died, Joseph wandered around southern India,
picking up the languages Tamil and Telegu, of which he spoke remarkably pure versions. Amiable, intriguing in appearance, and
multitalented, he drifted into — and out of — a variety of jobs. He
was a flutist in the band of the raja of Vizianagram, a cabin servant and understeward on British liners, and even a pharmacist at
Rangoon General Hospital.

But he ultimately landed in prison for theft and was sent home
to the Andamans. At the time Joseph was just twenty or so but
had frequented "the lowest quarters of various native cities and
had acquired the habit of drunkenness, and (to a phenomenal extent) of lying," according to the head of the orphanage, Reverend
Chard. Soon he'd forged Chard's name to get liquor and been
locked up for inebriation.

Portman, who was then the Officer in Charge of the Andamanese, prided himself on his ability to deal with such "incorrigi-
ble[s]"; he sent Joseph to the jungle, where he married an aboriginal woman. "He is healthy and strong, gets on very well in the
jungle, has become entirely an Andamanese, and will I hope, in
time, forget the vices which civilization and the outside world
have taught him," Portman wrote in his report for 1890.

A year later Otto E. Ehlers, a German explorer, sought Joseph
out in the jungle, finding him "clothed just with bow and arrow
and covered with paint from top to bottom." Although reticent
at first, Joseph thawed enough to have a "vivid conversation" in
English and to introduce his "ridiculously fat and small wife" as

well as a bevy of female friends. He was informative about his people and behaved "like a perfect gentleman," Ehlers wrote. Joseph could readily adopt Western clothes and manners — along with his Christian name — when the occasion demanded, and he served as an interpreter not only for Ehlers but also for the Frenchman Lapicque, who visited the year after.

Ehlers found it astonishing that "this strange youth," who was more erudite than millions of Europeans, and who'd earned a comfortable salary in his earlier life, could give up the amenities to which he'd become accustomed and instead live in the jungle and "play the wild savage."

The vices of civilization are not easy to evade, especially if the very soil that nourished one's roots has been replaced by rubble. Joseph, extraordinary though he was, had an intact culture to return to.

In 1998, anyone in Port Blair would tell you that the Great Andamanese men were addicts. One of these was Diu's husband, Dulu. A tall skinny man who might at one time have been handsome, he strode by the next morning on Strait Island, muttering angrily to himself. Dulu was one of only three men around who knew how to perform a traditional dance. Elaborately painted in white clay and adorned with clinking shell ornaments, dancers like him would provide a spectacular display of male beauty and vigor. These days, though, the youngsters preferred Michael Jackson's moves.

Worse, anthropologist Venkateswar had learned that Dulu suffered from an "extreme addiction to a 'cocktail' of sedatives, with a shot of methylated spirit for good measure," given to him by a pharmacist. Dulu would procure birds' nests and ambergris (whale ejecta that floats up on beaches and is an expensive ingredient in perfumes) for this man in order to satisfy his cravings. He'd once stolen into the clinic on Strait Island to look for narcotics, I was told; another time he'd broken into a bank on Long Island, east of Middle Andaman, presumably for cash.

The alcohol problem dated from the occupation, for the aboriginals had no brew of their own. In the early days naval guardsmen would visit their camps, offering alcohol and demanding women, and until around 1875 rum was part of the rations distributed at the Andaman Homes. In later years, Portman noted, "Several cases have occurred of persons having connexion with the Andamanese women, and it has been such a common amusement for a few people on Ross Island to make the Andamanese boys drunk, that I have had to prohibit the Andamanese from visiting that Island." It's one of the rare allusions to Englishmen preying on natives.

While Reverend Corbyn toured Calcutta with the captive Jumbo, his wife, Topsy, and others, the Andamanese left behind at the Home seemed "to have been assaulted, suffered the unwanted advances of a naval rating in charge," he confided to his journal. The incident did not show up in his official reports; but syphilis did, in epidemic form, a few years later.

Sometime in the 1880s, a visiting sailor named Stanley Coxon witnessed the Annual Regatta and Sports at Ross Island. The entire population of Port Blair had gathered for the event, its highlight being the Andamanese women's race at four-thirty P.M.

Whenever the natives came to Ross Island, an official was charged with making sure they were clothed. This time — Coxon wrote decades later — they were all wrapped in pieces of sacking tied around the waist.

"The parade being over, some sixteen dusky damsels formed up abreast of the starter. The course was cleared and all eyes were on the starting-point. 'Are you ready?' said the starter. 'Off!' and off went every wrap they had on them! 'Not theirs to reason why, Theirs but to do and die,' and no stupid piece of English sackcloth was to be allowed to interfere with the chances of any of our black beauties winning the much-coveted money prizes. We were all simply in convulsions, and the laughter of the Tommies could be heard reverberating in the hills." Evidently the women had undone the knots of their coverings while on the way to the starting line. "What a priceless snapshot this race would have made! But alas! we had no Kodaks in those days."

At a photo store in Port Blair, forty prints of the Jarawa were displayed for sale. Out of these, twenty-two were of women alone, with bare breasts; the rest were groups of men, women, and children. Only three shots showed just men.

The islands seemed crazed with sex. Broken families were common, and the many orphanages were stuffed with abandoned boys and girls. According to gossip in the bazaar, fully four-fifths of the bureaucrats had mistresses. A few of the senior officials — including one who offered help with the tribal pass if I spent time with him — had harems, office staff who got attendance when they didn't come to work, and other perks. A former district commissioner invariably employed women to type letters on his office computers. One of these women had four or five abortions, after which her father killed himself, out of shame.

In a penal colony, men inevitably outnumber women; as a result, any female around becomes fair game. A women's jail was started in 1860 to ameliorate the problem: prisoners who'd lived out their sentences could choose a spouse and settle down. But family life continued to be a matter of scandal.

One historian, Ramesh Chandra Majumdar, has noted a few instances that entered the records because of violent crime. In 1895 a convict was murdered because he was about to be released: his wife, who had a lover, did not wish to return to him. The next year an ex-convict attempted to kill a neighbor's wife, for she'd had a liaison with him but proved unfaithful. "In nearly every administration report of the penal settlement unnatural crimes of this kind were referred to as regular or normal incidents," Majumdar concluded.

Men still outnumbered women on the islands, about five to

four. That was because the islands continued to be run like a colony: men visited for a few years to make money while their wives stayed on the mainland and minded the children.

None of the vocabularies compiled for Andaman languages includes a word for rape — and in all of Andamanese history, not a single settler has so much as accused an aboriginal of rape (though the Jarawa have slain several village women). But one of the Great Andamanese women was reportedly gang-raped in the 1980s, and the girls on Strait Island, Sita Venkateswar observed around 1990, were being routinely seduced upon reaching puberty, usually by welfare staff. Gone were the days when a Great Andamanese woman would wear no more than "the smallest piece of green leaf between the thighs" — of a species chosen for its quality of staying green longer. I found every teenage girl in the settlement to be enveloped from neck to ankle in a maxi, a shapeless garment that hid breasts, waist, and legs. I was lucky to be female, the social worker's assistant told me, for strange men wandering around the tribals' cottages were liable to be beaten up by the Great Andamanese men.

Such measures provide only an illusion of security and can never shield an adolescent from a predator. A few months before my visit, a fourteen-year-old Great Andamanese girl had a baby. Upon being grilled she named a social worker as the father. Jirake, the raja, submitted a petition, signed by all adults of the community, which caused the lieutenant governor, the islands' chief administrator, to suspend the social worker. But Jirake later retracted the petition, leading some of the Great Andamanese to believe that he had been induced, by means of bribes or threats, to change his mind.

In Calcutta, I got into a heated argument at the office of the Anthropological Survey of India. Jayanta Nath Sarkar, an authority on the Jarawa, protested that I wasn't giving credit where it was due. "Do you know how many Great Andamanese were there when we settled them in the 1960s? Nineteen. Now they are forty-two. We saved them from dying out."

Most of the men, I pointed out, were alcoholics and many of the children were fathered by the welfare staff. A social worker had even been accused of having a baby with a fourteen-year-old.

Missionaries in India also had children with tribal women, said Ranjit Kumar Bhattacharya, the director of the Survey. Andamanese females had a history of sexually serving outsiders, Sarkar added, his tone suggesting to me that the women's morals deserved scrutiny.

But the welfare staff had immense power, for they controlled food, money, medicines, travel privileges, and many other details of importance to the aboriginals. "If they want something, how can you say no?" I argued. That a teenager should have a baby by an adult — worse, one who was entrusted with her care — seemed to these experts to be an unremarkable law of nature. "He was caught in her snare," the pharmacist on Strait Island had told me, excusing an affair his male colleague had with a fifteen-year-old Great Andamanese.

To these men, an adolescent girl was devious enough to entrap a man far her senior in age, power, and sexual knowledge. But where they saw a precocious promiscuity, I saw a helpless and terrorized child.

# Death

As the throbbing tones of the [sounding board] grew louder, heads, hands, and feet began to gyrate and whirl. Faster and faster they went round and round; then came wild leaps into the air, with arms and legs swinging wildly . . . They would leap and fall and rise and sway and whirl until nothing was clear but a vision of black bodies and arms and legs and feet in a cloud of dust.

— Frederick Taylor, *Century Magazine*, 1911

T HE OLDEST Great Andamanese couple were lounging on the porch outside their Strait Island home. Having no children, they were Chachi and Chacha — Aunt and Uncle — to everybody. "The Jarawa are coming to the settler areas to look for food," said Chachi, a plumpish old lady who sat on the floorboards, fanning herself desultorily. "The things that are happening to them, they can't accept," she continued in a slow, tired drawl. "That's why they kill people."

"They didn't use to kill anyone before," agreed Jirake, the raja, joining us.

Chacha, an imposing old man with an aura of confidence and integrity, reposed on a deerskin deckchair he'd made himself. The others say he'd refused to be raja. The post was created by the British to designate someone who would communicate orders to his tribesmen; he garnered favors and influence but not respect.

Chacha couldn't see much, for one of his eyes was a milky gray. Nor could he hear much. So he carried on his own conversation, in a mixture of Andamanese and Hindi, of which I understood only snatches. He talked of spying on the Japanese: of hiding in the jungles to watch a blaze, of running in the darkness to report to his British masters, of warning his people to flee.

The South Andaman tribes, being nearest to Port Blair, were the first to die out. As a result, most of the surviving Great Andamanese descend from a northern tribe known as Jeru, whose elders speak an amalgam of the Jeru language and other dialects. But even this remnant was destined to vanish. "The kids don't know the language. They know no songs. What is left?" asked Chachi of no one in particular. "Let the cinema show, let the radio play, that's all they care for."

The interiors of most cottages on Strait Island were decorated with posters of Bombay movie stars, and in the evening the entire younger generation gathered in the schoolhouse to watch TV. *Baywatch* — with its synthetic seminudes of global utopia — was a favorite, I was told, with these now prissily dressed people. What the children aspired to was clear: integration with the mainstream.

In truth, they could scarcely learn their traditional songs and dances even if they wanted to. The characteristic Great Andamanese musical instrument was a huge, hollow board carved out of fragrant hardwood; in the nineteenth century, Frederic John Mouat mistook one for a shield until he heard Jack Andaman accompanying himself on it while singing a sad tune. Normally the performers would beat time by dancing on the board. But in the 1950s, anthropologist Lidio Cipriani relieved the natives of their sounding board, "the last specimen of its kind"; it now reposed, silent as death, in a Calcutta museum.

"I speak to them in Andamanese but they reply in Hindi," complained Jirake, who had several children. Two small boys were playing around as we chatted. "The Onge keep their language," Jirake continued wistfully. "They said to us, you have given up everything of your own, but we haven't. They say, you let your kids run around, go to Port Blair. I say, what can I do? The previous raja would let them run free, now if I tried to tighten things up they wouldn't listen to me."

He became quiet. "I lost three kids." Blood dysentery, the pharmacist had told me, from bad water in the well. Something that might not have been fatal had a doctor been around. "One day, took a dead body over on the ship. Came back, heard another had died. Had to go right back."

"The children went away, of illness," Chachi added sadly. "They said, tummy hurts."

In the old days, when an infant died, the parents would weep over the little corpse, shave their heads, smear themselves with olive-colored clay, and place a lump of it over their foreheads, where it would harden. The mother would decorate her child with white and red clay, shave its hair, and fold the limbs into a fetal position. Meanwhile the father would dig a grave in the center of his hut, where a fire normally burned.

The parents would then blow on the infant's face a few times in farewell, seat the body, wrapped in large leaves, in the grave, and bury it. They would tie wreaths to the trees around the hut. After rekindling the fire, the mother would place a shell full of her own milk beside the grave so that the baby's spirit might not go hungry. Then everyone would abandon camp and set up another one several miles distant. (This last ritual belonged to a northern tribe; in some others, the parents would continue to live in the hut.)

After three months, the mourners would return and destroy the wreaths and exhume the body. The father would take the remains to the nearest creek or seashore, clean the bones, and bring them home. The mother would paint the delicate skull with red clay, decorate it with strings of small shells, and wear this precious memento about her neck. Out of the bones she would craft necklaces for giving to friends.

Finally the mourners would remove the clay lumps from their foreheads and the mother would paint her husband in a ritual pattern. Friends would gather, "whereupon the bereaved father sings some old song of his, which he last sang, perchance, with his little one alive and well in his arms," wrote Edward Man. Everyone would start to cry and the women would chant while the father and mother performed a dance known as *titolatnga*, the shedding of tears. Long after the parents had retired, wearied by grief, their friends would continue the melancholy song and dance.

"[T]here were several births (the average being two monthly,) at the Home," noted a report in 1867. "But the infants all died, some of them living only a week, while others existed only for a couple of months." From 1864 to 1870, one hundred fifty children were born in the Andaman Homes, but not one lived beyond two years.

The Andamanese adored their children, and every woman who could would suckle an infant; Man surmised that the babies were imbibing syphilis with the breast milk. Since such transmission is unknown, it's likely that the infants were instead infected in the womb. The disease was blamed on the ex-convicts who staffed the Homes, and who were armed with sticks and even loaded muskets. They intimidated their charges and had their way with them. But a navy man who'd raped some women might instead have been the source.

The Andaman Homes and the orphanage became the origin of several other epidemics: measles, influenza, and ophthalmia, which can cause blindness. The diseases spread unchecked to remote islands and deep forests of the Great Andamans, extinguishing tribes who might never have encountered outsiders. Portman reported: "On the 29th [of July 1890] ten men and six women came in from Long Island and reported that, with the exception of a few people at Mount Kunu, Juruchang, and the Archipelago Islands, they were the only survivors of the tribes between Port Blair and Rangat" — that is, in most of South and Middle Andaman.

Henry Corbyn once encountered a "fierce looking virago," an aged woman who cursed loudly and gnashed her teeth as though she would bite him. He considered her insane. "Such cases are often seen," commented Portman in 1899: these women seemed to hate outsiders because they'd caused the deaths of loved ones. Although he recognized the havoc the Homes were wreaking, Portman approved of their role in bringing the islanders within the fold of the empire. "Under any circumstances the Homes should certainly be maintained until the whole of the Andaman Tribes are friendly," he opined.

The fatal effect of the colonial presence came to be seen as proof of the inherent weakness of savages. "Primitive man is a puny creature as a rule, accustomed to gratify every sensation as it arises," wrote a visitor, Patrick Balfour, in 1935. "Andamanese vitality is low." Certainly the outsiders had greater resistance: epidemic diseases breed in densely populated societies, whose members acquire a large measure of immunity through constant exposure.

The Westerners were not immune to malaria, but by that time had acquired quinine — a gift from another crushed people, the so-called Indians of South America. The dosage was in part refined by experimenting on prisoners in the Cellular Jail. To erudite observers, the Andamanese march toward extinction, although regrettable, was natural selection taking its course with an expendable breed.

At the Anthropological Survey in Calcutta I viewed a collection of photographs, taken by Portman around 1893, as a record of a dying people. One frame showed a woman painting a man's forehead with the white clay of widowhood. In another, Ira of the Bea tribe was noted as being thirty-four years old. "Her husband having recently died, her head is plastered with white earth, Og, as a sign of mourning," noted the caption. "She wears a necklace of human bones 'Chaoga-ta-da.'" Her eyes glistened with tears; the anguish in them was repeated in hundreds of other faces, some staring uncomprehendingly at the lens, some looking bitterly into the distance.

The only smile in the twenty-six volumes was that of Hermes, a young man photographed many times; his resemblance to a Greek god did not escape his overlords. Another photo, entitled "Three Athletes," depicted three men with exquisite bodies, as if carved in black granite, decked only in the jewels of European ladies. The homoeroticism behind the camera was inescapable.

One of the volumes contained descriptions of fifty females, filled out in black ink on forms designed for the study of race. Everything from skin color (usually sooty black, rated 2; absolute black would get a 1, while rosy white would win a 10) to body temperature (about a degree Fahrenheit higher than average), and excruciatingly detailed dimensions of head and body were to be found, along with outlines of the small hands and feet. No free people would submit to such measurements. Tellingly, the form had no place for a person's name, which was only noted at the back of each form, along with other odds and ends.

Choaga Luka of the Bale tribe, nicknamed Telima ("Jungle Fowl"), was described as "[a] very quiet, sad woman. Intelligent, but silent. Married to No. 17 of the Male series. Has had four children, 3 male, 1 female. All dead." Flipping through the volume, I saw similar afflictions everywhere:

"Twice married. Three children 2 male, 1 Female. All dead."

"Married once. 2 Female children. Both dead."

No wonder everyone looked traumatized. The women must have married repeatedly because their husbands kept dying, along with their kids. The collection had no portraits of babies, but a few of children and many of adults held in the prongs of a measuring device. It was the fate of the Great Andamanese to be documented into their graves.

In 1858 the population of the Great Andamans was estimated at between five and eight thousand, but the census of 1901 counted only 625. The census also turned up a hitherto unknown tribe on North Andaman, the Tabo, whose members had reportedly killed off all those infected by some contagious disease — acquired from other tribes — until only 48 were left.

With their steep decline in numbers, the Great Andamanese became passé for scholars and officials alike, though their skulls and skeletons, preserved in museums, continued to elicit new theories. We catch glimpses of survivors in the journals of travelers — harvesting turtles for a Ross Island dinner party, retrieving birds' nests from sheer cliffs for the Oriental trade, scrambling for small change thrown by visitors or otherwise performing. "One of the show sights of the place was to take a party of these merry mites off in a boat to this buoy, and at a given signal they would dive down, and forming themselves into a ring, with linked arms, sit down round the anchor absolutely immovable for the space of from two to three minutes," related the sailor Stanley Coxon. Since the depth was almost twenty feet, this was no mean exploit. Coxon also witnessed the aboriginals fishing at night by the light of a resin torch: "I remember accompanying them on one occasion with a 12-bore shot-gun, hoping to astonish them by my prowess. I shot and missed by yards, when a naked little nigger five yards on my left presented me with that identical fish on the end of his arrow."

Some residents of Ross Island visited Havelock Island, on the eastern side of Middle Andaman, around 1910. They met Luke, who headed a band of up to twenty Great Andamanese, and who as a youth had been taught English, Hindi, Christian theology, photography, and the piloting of small ships. Portman had de-

scribed him as "the best behaved, most intelligent, and most refined of any of the Andamanese." But the adult Luke confessed
that he'd not liked Port Blair, for it was "[n]o fun, and always sick-
ness." (That seemed odd to one of the tourists, who recalled that
"Portman had made pets of the Andamanese, and given them bi-
cycles and champagne, relieved by occasional beatings.")

Trekking into the jungle, a later visitor chanced upon two Andamanese women, one old and carrying a small child, the other
young and wearing a skull down her back — a widow in mourning. The three were likely the last of their band; they ran.

In 1927 Egon Freiherr von Eickstedt, a German anthropologist,
found that around one hundred Great Andamanese survived, "in
dirty, half-closed huts, which primarily contain cheap European
household effects." The Andaman Homes were no more, but the
natives had settled near timber camps supplied with laborers
from India and Burma, who offered opium for the services of aboriginal women and fathered half the children.

Von Eickstedt did not fail to collect the skeleton of "the last Bea"
— from the tribe that had put up the fiercest fight of all. The Great
Andamanese had always resisted giving up the remains of kins-
men, as Reverend Henry Corbyn had noted in passing: "They
showed reluctance to part with the human skull, probably of a
chief, and tried to recover it, but being required by Colonel Tytler
to be sent to the Ethnological Society, for scientific purposes, I
persuaded them to let me retain it."

What the persuasion entailed he did not say: the Andamanese
were emotionally tied to the bones of loved ones, and their loss
must have felt like a second bereavement. Among the Onge,
someone whose bones were not retained by his relatives was
feared to have become a malevolent spirit, threatening those he
once loved; the Great Andamanese probably had a similar belief.
Edward Man would wait until a tribe had wandered far from a
burial site before he retrieved the skull from the corpse.

By the early twentieth century, the Great Andamanese were

selling relic skulls at the Andaman Homes, along with shell orna-ments and other artifacts. Violet Talbot, an officer's wife, was dis-heartened to find skulls priced at three or four pounds — but "managed finally to get one in exchange for a pair of khaki knick-erbockers." As late as 1951 a slain Jarawa's head was pickled for the Indian Museum in Calcutta, and, if another report is to be be-lieved, five years later an entire body.

Flesh and bone weren't the only items claimed by outsiders. So much Andamanese material — bows, baskets, harpoon arrows, nautilus shell cups — resides in museums around the world that it's clear why the original owners took to hiding all possessions when they had visitors. Von Eickstedt did not state whether his acquisition caused any protest, but probably the last Bea had no one around to mourn him — or her.

A living Great Andamanese whom von Eickstedt encountered in the 1920s was Loka, described as "roguish." Loka died in 1986 as a revered elder.

In his life of ninety years Loka did astonishing things, such as spying for the British during World War II. The Andamans had been abandoned to the Japanese advance, but Allied ships were blockading supplies. Fearful of food shortages, the Japanese com-mandant shot or threw into shark-infested seas many of the old, the young, and the infirm; at the same time, aware that Allied commandos had been landed by submarine on outlying islands, he tortured and killed some inhabitants who spoke English, on the conviction that they were spies. According to Ajoy Kumar Ghosh, a former chief commissioner (the post has since been replaced by that of lieutenant governor), the population of the Andamans decreased by three thousand during the occupation because of such deaths; a postwar British estimate was seven thousand.

Similarly suspecting the Great Andamanese to be British col-laborators, the Japanese confined them in Port Blair. But Loka was fearful that they might be killed. So one day, lighting a huge fire to mask their escape, they all fled into the jungle. "The women and children got into the canoes first, followed by the men. They rowed the canoes all night to reach the Archipelago at dawn. As this place was only too familiar to Loka . . . it was easy to hide their canoes in the creeks," wrote anthropologist Dilip Kumar Chakraborty in a 1990 monograph. The Archipelago referred to Havelock, Strait, and neighboring islands, where Loka had roamed as a child of the Balawa tribe.

The Great Andamanese hid in the jungle all day, emerging only after sunset to catch fish and turtles. At this time they met some British soldiers who offered tobacco, sugar, and tea to induce Loka to serve as an informer. He obliged, pretending to catch fish while he gathered information on Japanese troop movements.

Later, Loka served as a tracker in the "bush police," a force charged with hunting down Jarawa. In 1951 he and his band were spotted turtle-hunting near Middle Andaman, "with formidable harpoons in their frail canoes swirling round and round a huge turtle trying to make its escape." It was a last, grand image of a once proud people.

In the 1960s, a mere nineteen Great Andamanese still clung to life. Utterly destitute, they hung around Port Blair, trying to feed dependencies on opium and alcohol. Some lived in an abandoned Japanese bunker and fully half were suffering from tuberculosis. Indian officials asked Loka his opinion of tiny, uninhabited Strait Island, and moved the remnant Andamanese into the only real homes they'd ever known.

But Loka himself did not live there for long, preferring to wander. Sometimes he'd visit the island to leave tobacco and water by the grave of his third wife, whom he'd adored.

# Life After Death

The woman "Ruth" is still living at Haddo with her half-breed child, which she takes very good care of. As she declines to return to the Andamanese, there seems nothing for it but to permit her to marry the convict for whom she has an affection. Her children will be interesting scientifically.

— Maurice V. Portman, *Report on the Orphanage*, 1892–93

A MONTH AFTER my first tour of Strait Island, I again showed up at a Port Blair jetty at five-thirty A.M., along with a few hundred other people. I needed to find Diu, to hear her story, for I'd come to feel that she held the key to my understanding of the Great Andamanese.

Once arrived on Strait Island, I went in search of Diu. She was tending to her man, Sibu, who had a bandage around his forehead from some injury. One of her small sons was playing with a *dao* — a vicious-looking blade a foot and a half long — while his sister, just a wee bit older, tried to keep him from chopping off his arms. "I'll come later," Diu promised. I went to the schoolroom to wait. Three men — Dulu, Golat, and Joe — were watching cricket on the TV, with small boys leaning against them.

Finally Diu made an appearance, all dressed up in a *salwaar kameez* — a long, loose pants outfit popular with young Indian women — and curly hair flowing, uncommonly pretty for her age and her six children. We walked to my room. "I want to hear your life story," I told her. Diu laughed.

She spoke Hindi fluently, for she'd attended boarding school in Port Blair, then returned to Strait Island when her grandmother died. Soon after, at the age of twelve or thirteen, she'd been married to Dulu. "Now you don't live with him," I added, partly as a question.

It launched a tirade. "For the last five-six years we are not living together. He would go to Port Blair, make friends with bad people. He would take [drugs] and shout around all night, keep the whole community awake. The things we had at home, to eat, to wear, milk, rations, whatever . . . he would take and sell."

"Joe and Tong are Dulu's children?" I asked. I'd met Tong, her eldest, a poised and beautiful young woman with a halo of tiny curls.

"All. All six are from Dulu."

I stared in disbelief. "Doesn't seem like it, from the way they look, your small kids," I pointed out. "The smallest one, Pharro, Dulu is his father too?"

"Yes, it's Dulu."

The little one was just two or three, and she had just told me she hadn't been living with Dulu for five or six years. I had to press the matter, but it was awkward. "In Port Blair they say — that's why I came to ask you — they say about you that each of your children has a different father. Is this true?"

She was unfazed. "People say all kinds of things. All of them say such things about me. Just because I am a woman."

I wondered what she meant — that no one gossiped about men sleeping around? She was certainly a woman with personality. "You don't get angry that they say these things?"

"They don't say it in front of me." But she was smiling and didn't look annoyed or even flustered. Maybe she liked being talked about, liked to display her freedom from convention. I

wondered how she came to be this way, whether rape or moles-
tation had turned her away from a more commonplace life. But
though she commiserated with the fourteen-year-old mother, she
brushed off questions about her own adolescence.

I asked about Joe. "He is to marry Boro, isn't he? Does he like
her?"

"He doesn't say." After a pause, she went on. "Our men don't
take so much interest in their women. They say nothing, just be by
themselves, eat, drink, wander, sleep, come, go . . . If a man doesn't
look after his wife why should she stay with him? And then she
gets on the boat to Port Blair, she sees how nicely an Indian man
treats his wife, how he looks at her, how he wants her . . ."

"You're saying she doesn't get love?"

"No, they don't get so much love from our men." For this reason, she held, Andamanese boys attracted neither Indian nor
Andamanese girls, though they might be interested in both.

"So you sought your own way," I concluded.

Diu laughed. "After a lot of trouble. I had to do it to save my
children's lives." Dulu could be a dangerous father, she charged,
when he was under the influence. "If he goes to sleep, it's like he'll
never wake up. If he doesn't sleep he wanders about all night. He
could kill someone and he wouldn't know. He does such things at
home. One night I was sleeping with the kids, he filled a bucket of
water and poured it over us. All the clothes, all the bedding, got
wet. I woke up and thought, what happened? Why is there water
everywhere?"

Paul Patrick, the social worker's assistant, came in, and all of a
sudden I noticed Diu throwing him startlingly flirtatious glances
out of the corners of her eyes. Was she interested in him or did she
act like that with all men? I liked her, for she was lively and gutsy
and had sympathy for other women, but I hadn't begun to understand her. I could believe she was the victim she portrayed herself
to be, but not so much a victim of Dulu as of history. And, unlike
her husband, she'd found a strategy for survival.

The next morning a ship arrived at the jetty with Etal and her little boy, Buli, whom she'd taken to a doctor. Watching the tenderness with which Golat swung his wife's son off the deck, I found myself thinking that these men might be drugged and drunk, as Diu charged, but they sure seemed loving.

The fate of Andamanese women is not very different, I suspect, from that of other aboriginal women in my ancestry. In India, subjugated natives became the lower castes, destined forever after to cremate, butcher, dig, scrub, and otherwise toil at tasks the high-born defined as beneath them. The caste system also included a basic imbalance between the sexes.

In 1998, Michael J. Bamshad of the University of Utah and his collaborators scrutinized the connection between caste and DNA in regions of India. The DNA found in mitochondria, tiny bodies within a cell, is transmitted by a mother to her children: it traces the maternal line of descent. The Y chromosome, on the other hand, is DNA transmitted from a father to his sons and traces the paternal line. The study found that mitochondrial DNA had diffused through different layers of society. Hindu mores allowed an upper-caste man to take lower-caste wives, giving the women of the subjugated tribes a means of making their way up through the strata. Their children were accepted into their father's caste, so that the maternal DNA they carried made a transition upward: women's DNA is buoyant.

In contrast, Y chromosomes were stratified and caste-bound. "The men are stuck," one of the scientists stated: they had no means of changing their status. To this day, a low-caste man in Bihar can be lynched for daring to marry an upper-caste landowner's daughter. A further study published in 2001 found that upper castes were more Caucasian than lower castes — probably a relic of the prehistoric Aryan influx — and that Indian men were more Caucasian than Indian women, who more closely resembled other Asians. It's conceivable that some Y chromosomes, characterizing the DNA of defeated males, have died out entirely.

When Trucanini, a Tasmanian woman, passed away in 1876, her

*Great Andamese boys*

people were officially declared extinct. But the hundreds of aboriginal women enslaved by whites bore children whose descendants now describe themselves as Tasmanian. What did become
extinct was likely the male chromosome.

"Andamanese women seek to have children by non-Anda-
manese men," Sita Venkateswar wrote, "often plying their husbands with large quantities of alcohol before going to their current paramours." Another anthropologist had asked Diu how she
happened to have such a light-skinned child. She must have been
unprepared, for she became furious. "Do you want we should stay
*junglees* like this?" she shouted, pinching her arm. "With black
skin?"

In 2002, I found Diu at Adibasera, the tribal house in Port Blair,
looking unkempt and harassed by motherhood: she'd had a sev-
enth child. She was doing the rounds of offices to help Joe look
for a new job — a difficult chore, since he'd received hardly any

schooling. Travel restrictions on the Great Andamanese had been lifted, and several others were working and studying in Port Blair.

The teenage mother had since had another baby. She ultimately stated three names for the father of her first child, so the accused social worker was reinstated and sent to another Andamanese settlement. (A later visitor found him in what seemed to be a drunken haze.) Alcohol continued to be a problem on Strait Island, and at the women's request the authorities had confiscated the engines from boats supplied to the Great Andamanese, so that the men could no longer travel to other islands for supplies. The revered old man, Chacha, had died.

In the tribal welfare department I found a new officer, Kritish Ghosal. A female voice, speaking in English, interrupted us: "May I come in, please?" Two Great Andamanese teenagers, Ria and Renga, walked in the door; with short, pretty haircuts, plucked, painted eyebrows, and in bright *salwaar-kameez,* they looked cool and self-possessed. "Why don't you apply for a job?" suggested Ghosal in Hindi. "I want to study another year," Renga replied.

Joe entered as well, clean-shaven, trim, and confident, to complain about some payment he hadn't received. "Anyone else would shout," he said quietly. "We're the Great Andamanese, we don't shout."

*Onge*

# A Fiery Arrival

> It is impossible to imagine a more varied or richer sight than the Andamanese forests at any time of the year. The colours, and the light effects . . . the myriads of flowers of every hue and scent, every shape and size, the strange noises, all combine to produce an effect which stuns the outsider. The spectacle reaches its climax at night when the moon is full; the tops of the trees are bathed in a silver light and the great lianas seem to writhe like serpents.
>
> — Lidio Cipriani, *The Andaman Islanders*, 1966

IN LATE 1825 the vessel *Earl Kellie*, en route from Madras to Rangoon, found itself short of water just as it was passing Little Andaman. Along with the chief mate and six soldiers, James Edward Alexander of His Majesty's 13th Light Dragoons approached the shore in a boat, surprising a woman and child who ran into the forest. Scouting for freshwater streams, the visitors spied some natives lying in the bushes, "armed with spears, arrows, and long bows, which they bent at us in a threatening manner." The officers calmed the soldiers and approached the natives, making "signs of drinking" while an Indian interpreter tried out various languages and gestures. The islanders continued to crouch menacingly.

"I counted sixteen strong and able-bodied men opposite to us, many of them very lusty; and farther on six more," wrote Alexander. The Onge were the most "ferocious and wild-looking beings" he'd ever seen. Their "hideous faces" were painted with red ochre, and their bodies were smeared with mud that did not completely hide their sooty skin.

The party withdrew for reinforcements and resumed its search in another direction in the forest. The trees rose to immense height and were interwoven with rattans and other vines. "The sunbeams being unable to penetrate the entangled foliage, the atmosphere, in consequence, bore the semblance of twilight," Alexander related. "The broad boughs hung rich with heavy dewdrops, and the air was loaded with a damp and pestilential vapour, occasioned by the rotting twigs, leaves and fruit, with which the swampy ground was thickly strewed." The canopy was too dense to allow even a glimpse of the parrots that winged by noisily overhead.

They came upon a conical hut, thatched so low that it could only be entered by crawling. Inside were raised sleeping platforms with skulls of pigs hanging from above, drinking cups made of nautilus shells, bows and arrows, fishing nets, nails, bolts, and a piece of red-and-white cloth, probably from a shipwreck, as well as other artifacts. At a fire were roasting several seashells and mussels; the occupants had just run off.

The soldiers amused themselves by shooting the arrows into trees and collecting souvenirs. Shortly those waiting in the boats raised an alarm, for they could see about sixty natives waiting in ambush for the scouting party. The visitors resumed the search for water, however. "So little intention had we of molesting or injuring them," Alexander claimed, "that we had brought with us several looking-glasses, cloth, and baubles." And guns.

When the arrows came, the soldiers returned a round of musketry "which killed and wounded several of them. Fixing bayonets, we then charged them; but they, well knowing the intricacies of the jungle, and being extremely nimble, succeeded in not only effecting their escape, but also in carrying off the disabled of their party."

Farther on, the soldiers came upon a pool of sweetwater just inside the jungle, and, hoisting the Union Jack to signal the ship, began to fill the casks. But the natives repeatedly made "desperate attempts" to stop them, killing one soldier and wounding others. (Some Australian aboriginals had similarly defended their water sources from outsiders.) The skirmishing continued till sunset, with several Onge falling to bullets. Finally, the barrels brimming, the visitors departed with armloads of bows, arrows, and other trophies, as well as a "parting volley" of gunfire.

My ticket placed me in the hot, cramped "bunk class" below the *Yerewa's* deck. I got only a plastic chair; any sleep would have to be garnered on the filthy floor, or, if no one shooed me off, on deck. It was seventy-five miles — most of a day and a night — from Port Blair to Hut Bay, the biggest town on Little Andaman.

The deck, however, was breezy and pleasant. I leaned against the rails by a Nicobarese man with a weathered face; he could have been forty or fifty. Sitting on the floor, in a green sarong, was his wife. She had gone to Port Blair to have an operation so that she would have no more children, he told me in a mixture of Hindi and what must have been Nicobarese. In the 1960s and 1970s, when Indian authorities settled refugees from Bangladesh on Little Andaman, they also introduced a few migrants from the Nicobars. The couple lived in a village bordering the forest left to the Onge; he hunted pigs in their reserve, the man said.

Next to me a stream of males approached the rails to spit, each intently watching his flecks and blobs as they floated down to the sea. The wind blew one traveler's effluent into a fine spray over my face. The sea seemed to be of interest to these men primarily as a recipient of their ejecta: empty juice cartons, plastic bags, trash of all manner and form splashed onto the surface. I crouched next to the Nicobarese woman and stared through the rails at the foam-tipped waves.

When it got dark, the couple beckoned: we were moving to the upper deck. Silently we ate our packed food: they some rice and fish, of which they offered me an odorous piece, I some potato curry and roti, or flatbread. The woman lay down next to me and sang under her breath. The moon was out, the wind was blowing, and as I leaned back and stared at my feet up on the rails, against the dark sky, I felt perfectly at peace.

My companions slept soundly, but the deck was hard and I found myself turning as one side after another ached from the contact. At some point I opened my eyes and saw the stars, brilliant in an inky blue night; the moon was gone. When my neighbors woke me for the day, pointing to land, a crimson hue had spread soft over the horizon. I sat in a daze, watching the island approach and a red sun rise. It was 1998, and from a distance, Little Andaman looked forested. I was to discover that was an illusion, caused by a slender ribbon of trees left intact around the island's eastern rim.

The Onge wars began forty-two years after the *Earl Kellie*'s visit. The captain and seven crew of *Assam Valley* landed near a large rock at the southern end of Little Andaman in order to cut a spar. An hour later those left on board saw natives on the beach, dancing, but the men who'd landed did not come back. After two days of waiting in vain for their comrades to return, the remaining sailors went on to Rangoon.

It took almost a month for sea mail to bring the news to Port Blair, whereupon a surveying vessel that happened to be around was sent to scout for survivors. But the heavy surf prevented a landing, and the captain returned after seeing only a sailor's blue cap and a coil of rope lying on the beach.

The administration now dispatched a second ship, carrying navy men as well as some Great Andamanese under the supervision of Jeremiah Nelson Homfray, the guardian of the Homes. Homfray and his would-be translators approached the beach — on which stood four camps with thick smoke billowing out of the huts — but couldn't land because of the surf.

The ship then steamed north to what the British knew as Hut Bay, where a number of natives were gathered. Three boatloads of visitors, including some Great Andamanese women and children — naked, so their identity was evident — disembarked, holding up gifts. On seeing them, the Onge vanished; later two men reappeared, beckoning Homfray toward the jungle. He followed them in, but spying eight armed men creeping up behind him, retreated to the boats. The Onge discharged a shower of arrows, whereupon the party fired back and left.

The IGS *Arracan,* with twenty-odd soldiers, next arrived. One group, led by a Lieutenant Much, disembarked 150 yards from the landmark rock where the *Assam Valley's* sailors had landed. They marched toward it, coming upon a skull in the sand, an ankle boot, and beyond it the white-painted planking of a boat. The natives hid in the jungle, occasionally shooting arrows. The soldiers must have retaliated, for although Much's report omitted mention of any firing, it noted that "ammunition was running short."

At length the lieutenant signaled to the boats to come and take the soldiers off. The first one to approach overturned in the surf, drowning an officer. So the troops marched along the beach to Hut Bay, where the waters were calmer, discovering on the way bodies of four men, too decomposed to be identified.

It took several hours for the party to be brought off the island, by an effort that was to earn five Victoria crosses. The drowned officer was ultimately the only loss on the British side (apart from clothing, such as black silk handkerchiefs). In passing, Lieutenant Much estimated thirty Andamanese had died, although his Indian deputy, who'd ventured into the jungle, reported "fully 100 killed."

Six years after this affair, in 1873, the Onge slew five crewmen from a junk that had stopped for water. Accordingly, the authorities organized a punitive expedition.

Captain Wimberley reported that the expedition arrived at Hut

Bay on the morning of April 11, and searched the jungle, finding three pieces of blood-stained clothing. Wimberley then marched his troops for two miles along the beach and, not seeing the enemy, decided to burn their homes. These "consisted of four huts, each distant from the other about half a mile, and in each of which about 40 men could be accommodated, and one enormous hut about 60 feet in diameter, and which was capable of holding at the least some 150 men," Wimberley reported. These communal huts, in which were hung several canoes — and under which revered ancestors were buried — had given the bay its name.

When the second hut went up in flames the natives attacked, and "a sharp fight, lasting about ten minutes, ensued, which, however, as might have been expected, ended in favour of the Enfields and Sniders." The islanders fled, abandoning their weapons but carrying away their dead and wounded. Wimberley estimated that their casualties were at least ten or twelve dead. One Onge man was captured alive.

"We then proceeded to burn the remaining huts," Wimberley wrote. The islanders again appeared, this time on the open beach about one and a quarter miles away. They didn't risk attacking, having lost their bows and arrows, and retreated when the troops advanced. "As by this time the surf had increased to a very great extent, and as I had carried out my orders, and taught these Andamanese a lesson which they will remember for some time, I gave the order to reembark in the boats."

The captive was kept in a hilltop cell near Port Blair and shown the "greatest kindness," but he pined away. "He used often to sit and watch the North Sentinel Island which is visible from the summit of the mountain, as if he knew it, or perhaps fancied it to be Little Andaman." A Jarawa couple was captured "in the hope that they might be able to communicate with the Onge," but he died before they could meet.

"Strenuous efforts will be made next season to bring about a better understanding with them, as it is impossible to tolerate their barbarous propensities any longer," concluded General Donald Stewart, who'd ordered the punishment.

The sun blazed mercilessly onto a scorched brown expanse. The land had been rendered treeless, as though a tree were a parasite that needed to be exterminated, its stump uprooted and purged. Turning a dew-dripping jungle into a desert would seem to require ferocity, but all it took was a bureaucrat's signature.

In the 1960s, Hut Bay was again set on fire, this time to clear space for settlers. The Andaman jungles, characterized by towering dipterocarps, had been essentially unchanged since the Miocene age. It must have been a spectacular blaze, 25 million years of rain forest growth going up in smoke and flame.

Now the barrenness was uncanny; I heard no birdcalls except for the crowing of cocks in neighboring yards. Around the guest house were planted some deodars, a fast-growing foreign species that, being thin and vertical, provided no shade. After nine A.M. one needed resolution and an umbrella to venture out of doors. When the electricity went off in the afternoon, I lay listlessly on the bed, stunned into a stupor by the heat.

When the sun finally retired, leaving a salt-scented breezy evening, I walked back along the road, past a hospital, to the shops of Hut Bay, beyond which I could stroll on shore. At one time the bay offered the Onge prime fishing. But the corals had since died, drowned in silt swept off the parched land, and so had the reef fish. The sand was strewn with worn coral bits, torn shoes, and human excrement. With the protective trees and reefs gone, the beach was being washed away. I watched hermit crabs, assiduous scavengers of dirty beaches, scurry by in green-, white-, red-, or black-patterned shells; somehow they occupied all the pretty shells.

Trucks loaded with tree trunks five feet thick trundled down the Little Andaman Trunk Road, which ran along the island's edge. Near the jetty was a huge lumberyard with hundreds of logs, some even thicker, with a couple of elephants — introduced from the mainland — rearranging the piles. According to Samir Acharya, an environmental activist based in Port Blair, virgin forest was being felled, illegally from within the Onge reserve, by the Andaman and Nicobar Forest and Plantation Development Corporation, a government-owned firm. Officially, more than two-thirds of the island's 285 square miles belonged to the Onge; but the Corporation's "working plan" assumed that 234 square miles — pretty much all the remaining forest — was available for logging.

Oddly, I saw no signs of wealth. The island had a truly colonial economy, its timber exports building mansions for men who lived elsewhere.

Already Little Andaman had severe shortages of water, for any rain ran right off the naked earth. Two dams completed by the public works department at enormous cost — and by flattening a large tract of forest — were leaking, because the engineers inexplicably forgot that the limestone underground was porous. In three decades my people had ravaged the island that nurtured the Onge for millennia.

Farther on, the shore was buttressed with black basaltic rocks, and a few trees lined the sand. They stood 100 to 150 feet tall, bearing sad witness to the grandeur of eras past.

## Sugar and Starch

IN SPRINGTIME, the spirits entered the honeycombs to eat honey, their favorite food. But the Onge also loved honey and had placed marks of ownership on all the trees from which hung beehives. They performed the ritual of *gitankare* to anger the spirits, carving phalluses and selecting trees from which to make dugouts. Furious, the spirits left, taking with them the accompanying wind and rain. So the Onge's heroic defiance brought about the hot dry season of *torale* that prevailed from March through April.

When the spirits were gone, the Onge gathered all the honey they wanted by covering themselves with a paste of *tonjoghe* leaves, which they also chewed. At first the bees clustered around the hive in a protective cloud, but when an Onge climbed up and blew the leaf vapor onto them, they recoiled and flew away in a swarm without stinging. Then everyone had a great feast, including the birds, which ate the bees that had fallen dead from the honeycombs.

But sometimes a spirit might have been trapped in the honeycombs, the Onge told anthropologist Vishvajit Pandya, and when a woman ate the honey it would enter her womb and grow into a baby. When a man ate honey, on the other hand, a pig hunter would become good at hearing while a turtle hunter became good at seeing. Then the men could hunt even when the rains came.

Without honey, Mayakangne, the northeast wind, and Kwala-kangne, the southwest wind, would find nothing to eat. So they would wake up their mother, Dare. Furious, she would descend on Gaubolambe (Little Andaman) to see for herself what was going on. Her grandchildren, the winds and rain, would secretly follow her to the island, bringing sudden showers and rejuvenating the plants. Dare would see the pigs were putting on weight and would be pleased, for she liked to eat them. The rains would also cause the women, and the spirits trapped within them, to fill out.

The Onge, who were dispersed in the forests searching for honey, would then move to the creeks and mangroves to collect crabs, fish, and fruit. Day by day they would watch the pigs getting fatter, hunting one or two and hanging the skulls from a scaffolding at the shoreline, where earth, sea, and sky met. Dare would see that the Onge were killing pigs and become infuriated.

When a dark waterspout appeared, connecting the sea to the sky, the Onge would know that Dare, enraged by their defiance, was climbing up to her home. Once there, she would send down her vengeance — Kwalakangne, the monsoon fury. The coasts would thunder with crashing waves, and the Onge would move to the deep jungle. Near the end of the rains, when the forests in turn became treacherous with falling trees, the Onge would go back to the beaches to hunt turtles and feast on cicada grubs. Kwala-kangne would leave so that her sister, Mayakangne, who also loved cicadas, could return and eat some before the Onge finished them all.

Thus the coming and going of the spirits determined the seasons, the places where the Onge lived, and the foods that they ate.

After two days of waiting, I was perched on a stool that jumped on a tractor's trailer, on my way to South Bay. Bisweswar Das, the social worker for the Onge, was delivering rations to this small coastal settlement lying south of Hut Bay. A bearded man in his thirties, wiry and commanding, Das was somewhat wary of me but not hostile.

Also on the trip were two nurses who were to inoculate a baby, their two nieces, and some little boys along for the ride, as well as a couple of men whose roles I couldn't figure out. It had taken me a month of appeasing the gods to get permission to visit the Onge; all that was required, evidently, was to be friends with Das.

At our feet were a sack of rice, a sack of wheat, and large boxes of cereal, tea, and milk powder. The tractor was required because a stream had to be forded: a bridge had given way under the weight of a truck laden with sand stolen from Onge beaches.

We were traveling southward along the island's rim. Some trees showed up, too scattered to provide a canopy. The sun reached right to the ground, where it scorched the undergrowth or reflected off the road, scalding my face. We came to a patch cleared by burning, where the plants were shriveled black corpses. Concrete cottages with asbestos roofs stood in it; they must have been like ovens inside.

Soon the road gave way to a coconut plantation, in the scant shade of which were wooden cottages on stilts. It was Harmander Bay, the Nicobarese settlement created at the same time the bulk of the island was gifted to other immigrants and timber traders. The shade under each hut sheltered a cot, on which sat older men and women, husking coconuts or stripping the spines off palm leaves to make baskets. Under the cots lay phlegmatic pigs with chickens pecking around them. The sandy floor of the village was unlittered, and a sense of quiet industry prevailed even in the heat of midday.

The tide was low when we got to the stream, and we drove across without incident. We passed more trees and a lighthouse, and then arrived at the Onge settlement. Stark wooden cottages, government-made in some past time, burned in the sun. They were decorated with an occasional poster: MAKE MY WORLD POLIO FREE, and a smaller sign, REGISTER EVERY BIRTH AND DEATH IN YOUR FAMILY. Never mind that the Onge couldn't read English or anything else. They'd built their own cooler, breezier shacks close to the ground, but not a soul was visible any-

where. After washing my face by the well, I wandered off to sit under a tree by the beach, idly upturning dazzling white clam shells.

In the distance, rounding a bend in the shoreline, they suddenly
came: a man, a woman with a baby on her back, and a lanky boy.
The Onge trooped along the blazing beach, weighed down by baskets hanging on their backs from straps over their foreheads, preceded by dogs and trailed by scrawny puppies. I followed as the
family entered one of the shacks and sat exhausted on the elevated
platform within, perspiration falling in rivulets down their faces.
They'd gone to look for honey and found none; now they'd returned, trekking three hours in the sun, to collect their rations.

The man, Botaley, got up to draw water from the well; he
poured it over himself, dirty shorts and all. He walked around
picking up bits of firewood. They hadn't eaten all day; now that
there was rice, they would cook. His wife, Minare, her furrowed,
wizened face and shaven head making her look like ET, just sat
there, too exhausted to move. Once in a while she lifted a hand to
wipe sweat off her forehead. The baby watched me with large
frightened eyes.

The boy scratched a boil and then lifted the hand to scratch his
eye. The eruptions covered his arms, back, and legs, but his fingers
were long and delicate, and his smile shy and sweet. He tended the
fire while Botaley fetched a large pan and rinsed it.

The welfare staff was lounging in the shade, sipping the water out of green coconuts. The teenage nieces were complaining
about the heat; they'd expected a pleasanter place, a picnic spot.
"Why don't they stay in the cottages made for them?" one asked,
expressing the general resentment at the Onge turning their backs
on the things done for them.

"Don't they have an easy life?" nurse Shukla began conversa-
tionally. "They just take their rations and cook. Don't have to
work. We, we have to get up in the morning, hurry up to wash and
get dressed, send the children to school."

Only one of the staff, a young man newly arrived from the

mainland, was trying to do his job. Another Onge family had turned up, and I watched as he felt and prodded each man, woman, and child, looking for leprosy. The Onge didn't have it, but since they visited Hut Bay and the other Indian settlements, where it did exist, he'd been deputed to check. The boy with boils he sent to the nurses; once again, I followed.

The women were revolted by his wounds. Getting up with great reluctance, one opened the medicine cupboard and handed the boy a strip of ampicillin, one of vitamin B, and a wad of cotton wool. She threw him instructions about dosages, which I don't remember and I'm sure he didn't get, and told him to clean himself with the cotton wool.

Two Onge children with swollen bellies and snotty noses came up to watch. I asked why the stomachs were distended.

"Ringworm," Shukla replied.

"Do they get treated for it?"

She nodded unconvincingly.

Botaley walked by with a bunch of plantain bananas for the meal. It would be another two hours until the food was ready: the children and puppies stood around waiting. All the while Minare stared into emptiness. Finally she got up and fetched frocks for two girls who'd arrived with the second group. They looked at me, shy and proud to be dressed, but I could only think: Why? It was too hot for clothes, which looked full of germs.

From what I'd read, the Onge hadn't gotten the hang of clothes. They didn't wash them and so got skin diseases; they didn't change out of wet clothes, and so contracted colds and tuberculosis. They were far healthier before being forced to cover up. They also harbored all manner of parasites from having given up their nomadic lifestyle, which would routinely remove them from sullied locations.

Some odd customs of the Onge were in fact beneficial, discovered Lidio Cipriani, an Italian anthropologist who camped on Little

Andaman during the 1950s. The Onge believed, for instance, that the creepers with fleshy edible roots, which they dug out and ate, were under the protection of a spirit. So were the yams, which the Onge had to steal from the ground: "On no account must there be any signs of the theft for the spirit to see, so they quietly take off roots or tubers some way from the main stem and leave the rest, patting the earth down afterwards and covering the place with leaves." The plant continued to flourish, evidently helped by the pruning.

Curiously, plants protected by benign spirits tended to be edible, whereas those belonging to malevolent ones were poisonous. The Onge also had taboos against the killing of birds and of boars in the breeding season.

Some of these prohibitions clearly aided the Onge in using and preserving their environment's resources. Richard Dawkins, a scientist and visionary, has suggested that a few simple, elemental ideas (known as memes) win a Darwin-like competition with other ideas and catch on, because they somehow enhance the survival of their adherents. Indeed, the islanders might have suffered from hunger if they'd routinely uprooted tuberous plants or shot pregnant sows.

Cipriani found Little Andaman to be so rich in boar, lobsters, fruit, and other delicious fare that he did not have to carry rations. Indeed, the Onge would throw away any fish they deemed to be even slightly stale. "So easily is sea food procured that they do not consider any laying up for the morrow," another visitor, Suydam Cutting, wrote in 1932. "When a man is hungry he goes out and catches the food for his immediate use and that is all." The islanders lived in such plenty at least in part because of their seemingly whimsical beliefs.

But with rice and wheat having replaced their varied diet of forest and reef produce, the Onge now suffered from nutritional deficiencies such as of vitamin A and iron. One anthropologist, meeting some Onge men in 1949, had been awed by their powerful and exuberantly healthy bodies. Years later, a glimpse of them on TV shocked him: "The 44-inch chests I had seen were shrunk to 34 inches, and necks so thick that their heads would turn only with effort now looked thin enough to be encircled by my fist." The descendants of the lusty men who'd waylaid James Alexander of the *Earl Kellie* were defeated and diseased.

Botaley had been put to work by Thangarajan, one of the welfare staff, in scaling coconut trees. Thangarajan, a vermilion and sandalwood mark on his forehead proudly proclaiming his Indian caste status, ordered Botaley around as though he were a slave, shouting at him and complaining about the meagerness of the coconut supply he'd culled. The nurses were eating again, a meal of rice, vegetables, and egg curry.

When the Onge's dinner of banana and mounds of rice was finally ready, Minare laboriously ladled it out on a plate and handed it to one of her girls, who took it to the next hut. A third family had shown up. One young woman, breast escaping from a blouse held together with safety pins, carried a tiny baby, while another was pregnant.

At long last, having fed and washed up, the nurses emerged regally, needles held ahead like sabers, to inoculate the baby against polio and the triad of whooping cough, tetanus, and diphtheria. That's why they'd come: the immunization had to be reported to the authorities, to whom the Onge's declining numbers were an ungrateful slap in the face. We all watched and winced as the large needle entered. The infant cried inconsolably, and one nurse gingerly extended a hand to massage its thigh; for a few seconds brown fingers touched black baby. The mother walked off bouncing it in her arms.

It was time to leave. At Thangarajan's order one of the Onge men, Bada Raju, fetched a heavy cardboard carton, about 2 by 2 feet by 1 foot.

"What is it?" I asked, curious.

"Just some honey," Thangarajan said dismissively.

The carton contained jerry cans of at least four gallons, perhaps all the honey the Onge had gathered. Spirit food in exchange for government-supplied starch.

On the way back from South Bay, the tractor got stuck in the stream. After an hour of trying to help — one of my unwelcome suggestions was to offload the ten sacks of coconuts — I picked up my backpack and started to walk. It was a lovely evening and soon I was near the Nicobarese settlement, where the beach was blissfully white and shell strewn. Boys raced toy sailboats, exquisitely crafted, outrigger and all, from palm leaves and wood and bamboo. Farther on two women were bathing in a rough sea; they smiled so invitingly that I put my backpack down on the sand and waded in, fully clothed. The coral underfoot was worn, covered with algae and slippery; the large waves knocked me off my feet, and soon I was completely wet and cleansed.

Das was so exhausted by the trip that he decided to put off the one to Dugong Creek, the main Onge settlement, north of Hut Bay. (The dugong is a sea-dwelling mammal distantly related to the elephant.) That meant more waiting around, so I resolved to try and return to South Bay by bicycle, which I could rent. It was about twelve miles away, and the part through the forest was sandy, so I wasn't sure if I could make it. Not being certain of the legality of the venture — my pass mentioned Dugong Creek but not South Bay — I told only the two paleobotanists I'd met at the guest house at Hut Bay and whom I trusted.

Having arrived at long last, I went to the well and washed my burning face. On the sandy ground two puppies were licking at the remnants of a can of powdered milk. In one shack the infant who'd been immunized slept by his mother. He'd been painted with yellow clay on the forehead and down his back, while red clay filled the scalp between the curls on his head. He seemed none the worse for yesterday's ordeal.

The mother, pretty and quietly confident but shy, fanned him with a large leaf, putting it down occasionally to break off a piece of paratha, Indian fried bread, and chew it. She was eating just that and nothing else, pure starch and oil. The young, muscular father, Nomai, sat on a bamboo platform, arranging palm leaves in parallel rows and deftly tying them onto a bamboo slat to make a thatch. He sang under his breath as he wove, and his work was sure and beautiful.

Everyone seemed more relaxed now that the welfare staff was far away. The clothes the kids had donned yesterday had come off, and some had clay on their foreheads. One of the boys was playing with a stick, scaring a scrawny puppy. *"Tumko marega,"* he said, Hindi for "I'll hit you." I wondered why the only Hindi I heard the children speak was aggressive; it must have been what they heard.

When I left in an hour, Nomai had woven two feet of thatch. It would take him two months to complete the hut.

Returning through the forest, I found I was exhausted. I couldn't get on the bike anymore after I fell off on sandy patches, but had to wheel it to the next tree stump, on which I stood to haul my leg over the bar. Thanks to the efforts of the Corporation, a suitable stump was available every few yards. At Harmandar Bay, I fell off one more time and leaned in the shade of a hut, totally drained. A woman called to me: it was my Nicobarese swimming companion from yesterday. She offered me a green coconut, slashed diagonally, and I drank gratefully of the cool water, sugar, and salt.

## Gifts, Traps

AFTER THE BATTLES in the mid-1800s near Hut Bay, which must have killed a large fraction of Little Andaman's men, no Westerner visited for years — until Maurice Portman became Officer in Charge of the Andamanese. An ambitious and scholarly aristocrat, he had theories on how to pacify the Onge.

Portman began in March 1880 by leaving presents in a few canoes found moored at a creek. The next day all the goods were taken, and thirty Onge stood at the water's edge, beckoning to him. At length a canoe approached, barely concealing several men lying in the bottom with bows and arrows; when the British boat turned to meet them, they panicked and left, shooting. This time the visitors did not shoot back.

For a few years the trips followed a similar pattern, with the Onge accepting offerings but remaining suspicious. Once they embraced some Great Andamanese emissaries and seemed very friendly but later shot at them. Another time an officer rowed up and down in front of a beach with a fiddler, who played to the Onge over the roar of the surf. "[P]robably the savages thought we were mad," Portman opined.

In January 1885 he went to leave gifts in a beachside hut while Colonel Thomas Cadell, the Chief Commissioner, took a boat up a creek on the western side. But on returning to its mouth, Cadell found that the tide had gone down and many Onge had gathered on the sand spits exposed on either side. Apprehending a fight, he decided to wait in the broader part of the creek for the tide to rise. Evidently taking this as surrender, six native men in two canoes came alongside, ordering the British boat to shore and the rifles to be given up. When one canoe was pushed away, an arrow pierced the helmet of an apothecary who'd come along for the ride, wounding him slightly. (His name, Jackson, has been that of the creek ever since.)

"On this several shots were fired by our party, which appeared to take effect as the savages threw up their arms and fell into the water as if dead," Cadell wrote. They were only pretending, though, and one man who'd fallen over the bow of his canoe was found to be towing it to shore with his teeth. Being caught, he escaped in the melee but the Great Andamanese aides captured him again. His name was Taleme, and, according to Portman, he was "a fine well-built young man of about 22 years of age." He was taken to Port Blair, where he soon after died of pneumonia.

On the way back, Portman stopped at various islands, noting signs that the Onge made trips northward in search of turtles or other game. On Great Cinque — quite a small island, actually — he captured an old man, who spat in his face. While Portman returned him to shore as too intractable for his purposes, his presence on the islands gave the officer an idea. Returning to Great Cinque with a large party of Great Andamanese, convicts, and police, he had them "beat through the jungle" — walk through it in a single row, sweeping animals and aboriginals ahead into waiting arms. (This *shikar* technique was a favorite with officers of the Raj.) The Onge fought valiantly until their arrows were exhausted. The hunt bagged eight men, six women, and ten children, of whom Portman released fifteen.

Back in Port Blair, all the new arrivals fell sick, as expected, with one man dying. Portman kept the three remaining unmarried men and a boy in his house, hoping to form personal bonds.

When they were better, he took them on tours of the Andaman Homes and orphanage to demonstrate the benefits of friendship. One man, Tomiti, grew "much attached" to Portman, following him about everywhere "like a dog." The Onge boy, Eketi, became great friends with Api, a young Jarawa boy captured earlier, and Portman was amused to catch the two of them stealing sugar out of his larder.

After several months Portman took the Onge captives on a tour and landed some on a small island near their home; they left and did not return. With the remaining individuals he circumnavigated Little Andaman, learning native names for the coves and bays. Finally he put them ashore at Bumila Creek, near the northern tip of the island.

Over the next months he continued to visit, leaving gifts, and in March 1886 his policy bore fruit. Three of the former captives, Tomiti, Talai, and Kogio Kai, showed up at Bumila Creek to claim the goods, introducing some twelve others. Portman landed alone, donating two large turtles. Two days later many others appeared, whom his contacts induced to lay down their bows. Word spread fast, and group after group of men, women, and children emerged to shyly take his offerings at different points along the coast.

On a subsequent visit, a tall Onge man unexpectedly smote a ship's engineer with an adze, inflicting a bloody wound. Kogio Kai, who was serving as interpreter, called on Portman to shoot the man, and later Tomiti and Talai managed to grab him and drag him onto the boat. "None of the other Onges attempted to rescue him, or to offer any resistance," Portman noted with satisfaction. The offender was taken to the ship *Kwang Tung*, given twenty-four lashes, and transported to Port Blair, to be kept "until he has learnt to obey our orders and appreciate our power."

The Onge never again attacked representatives of government, which would have met with reprisals. But in the 1930s, they wounded the crew of a Japanese pearl-fishing vessel and in 1949 killed the sailors of a shipwrecked Chinese junk. Doubtless these weren't the only casualties.

During the Japanese occupation, a Burmese policeman escaped to Little Andaman and lived there. His interactions with the Onge seem to have paved the way for future comers. In 1948, Indian anthropologist B. S. Guha visited Dugong Creek, which then could only be approached by wading for two miles. On the northern bank he found three beached canoes, a communal hut, and several lean-tos containing thirty-nine men, women, and children and a few dogs. The village was called Tambebui. One of the men, Ukla, could speak a few words of Hindi, but everyone seemed deferential to another man painted with red and yellow ochre and armed with bows, arrows, and knives; the ship's crew described him as the raja. The Onge took the cigarettes, food, cloth, and iron pieces given to them, and allowed themselves to be measured and their blood drawn.

I was up at five A.M., pulling on clammy jeans and sneakers, which hadn't dried from my trying to wash them the night before. Finally we were leaving for Dugong Creek. When Das's truck showed up I got to sit in the cab, between him and the driver. In the back were sacks of wheat, rice, and sugar, boxes of tea, a drum of kerosene, and other provisions, as well as laborers to help with the load.

The truck rumbled along the Little Andaman Trunk Road, northward this time. After half an hour we stopped at a town, Vivekananda Puram, had breakfast, and set off along a side trail that ended in a green, shady creek with overhanging trees. Several boats were moored there; we'd be taking two. Across the creek was a gigantic sawed-off tree stump, ubiquitous signature of the Corporation. We were in the Onge reserve.

The bags having been divided between the boats, we set off on the dark green channel, navigating past overhanging branches and dripping aerial roots. The creek soon widened, and in half an hour we met the gorgeous sea. It was shallow but rough, and the vessel tossed up and down on the waves. The boat followed the coastline northward over turquoise water until, an hour later, we came to another creek bordered by casuarinas and coconut palms. The boat moored by a concrete jetty; it was Dugong Creek.

Wooden cottages on stilts were strung along a shadeless path leading inland from the jetty. The sun glared mercilessly onto the trail, and it took me a while to gather courage to explore inward. The area had been cleared in the familiar scorched-earth style to make room for the welfare staff's cottages. Farther on a small shrine featured a statue of Hanuman, the monkey god; I wondered about its significance there. (A popular theory even has the name Andaman deriving from Hanuman.) Nearby was a well, with water barely two feet deep and covered with fallen leaves and skittish water skaters. The surroundings smelled of chicken shit.

The path led past a powerhouse, a closed store with pink lilies incongruously waving in front, a field paved in concrete that turned out to be a helipad — for emergency evacuations or, more often, for VIP tourists — and arrays of solar panels. The infrastructure was elaborate.

Beyond, the homes of the Onge baked in the sun. Unlike in South Bay, many of the wooden cottages were occupied, though a few families had made their own shelters. Dogs rushed barking at me; I'd never seen the familiar Indian pye-dog so ferocious or so painfully thin. Their owners peered from behind windows and slats.

I felt like a weird alien, striding down the blazing path in my white baseball cap (with "Andaman Tourism" embroidered on it), holding a towel over my burning face. Here the Onge ruled with a vengeance expressed, if not by them, by their dogs.

Dogs were introduced to Little Andaman sometime in the 1800s, and the Onge took to them immediately. Lidio Cipriani, visiting in the 1950s, wrote that the Onge "pet them like little girls with their dolls, and the Onge women will suckle the family puppies quite naturally with their own children." The animals were kept hungry so they'd sniff out and hunt down pigs, making it easy for their owners to spear the prey (and vivisect it in a gruesome manner, according to Cipriani). They were the only domesticated animals the Onge had.

Late in the afternoon I found Das handing out batteries, candles, matches, Horlicks (a health drink), biscuits, and tea in the darkening store. The heavy stuff, the rice and wheat and sugar, they'd get tomorrow. Three Onge boys were playing on the dirt path in front, noisily pushing around plastic carts, one decorated with a pink spray of bougainvillea, brilliant in the setting sun. Another rolled a dustbin lid with a stick, running with it like Indian boys. The wheel seemed to be a hit with the kids, if not with their elders.

Tube lights were on, lit by solar power, when I walked the path to the Onge huts. The dogs raised a crescendo at my approach, snarling and making passes at my ankles, and I sought shelter by a shack. It belonged to a man known as Tanageru; he helped out with the diesel generator, currently broken. He was lighting a fire for tea.

"Won't you cook food?" I asked in Hindi.

"No. We didn't get rice or wheat tonight, will have to wait till tomorrow." He had some dried boar, in case he got hungry.

In the darkness, on a low platform, lay an ancient, decrepit woman, his wife. Fluid dripped out of one eye, and breasts hung as heavy and hopeless as her mien. She was well past sixty. Once the tea was ready, Tanageru handed her a mugful. She tried to open a pack of the biscuits and, failing, handed it to him. He tore the waxed paper and with startling tenderness passed it back. They ate, dipping biscuits into the tea.

A three-quarter moon had emerged. Farther on a man sat under his thatch on a platform, making small notches on a smoothed log. I asked in Hindi what he was doing. *"Kuchh nahi,"* he said, drawing back sharply. Nothing.

As I walked on, I saw a woman wearily trying to button her blouse, which was missing most buttons. There was nothing shy or vain about the gesture, just a resigned recognition of an outsider's presence. Radios were on in several huts, but I turned back. I was unwelcome there.

In January 1949, Indian anthropologist Asutosh Bhattacharya traveled to Little Andaman with two colleagues. When their launch, *Molly*, reached the island, a new moon had pulled a powerful tide high onto the beach, all the way up to the trees. Looking for a calm spot, the boat operator went around the coast to South Bay and dropped anchor for the night.

The vessel continued to roll from side to side while Bhattacharya, holding tightly onto the rails, gazed at the looming forest. It was past eight P.M., and, but for *Molly*'s lights falling on a small patch of sea, everything was dark. As he stared intently into the jungle, however, he spied a faint light. Indeed, a boathand confirmed, it was a fire, lit by the aboriginals.

Bhattacharya's two companions scoffed at the idea, so the boathand suggested an experiment: "I'll blow the whistle of the launch, see what they do. If they are near the fire, they might snuff it, out of fear. If there are no humans nearby — if they have lit it and gone away — or if the fire has some other origin, it will continue to burn." He went into the engine room and let off the siren. Instantly, the light vanished; there were indeed people in the depths of the jungle.

But why, wondered the anthropologist, had they put the fire out? The Onge were reputed to be friendly. If they truly were so, wouldn't they have been delighted to learn of the ship at their shore, wouldn't they have lit more fires, come forward to welcome the visitors? Instead, their instinct was to conceal their presence. "They had learned fear," he concluded, "and that was why, whether they wanted to or not, they had accepted the 'friendship' of civilized society."

Asit Kumar Banerjee, a skeletal but lively old man I met in Port Blair, was in a team that Cipriani took to Little Andaman in 1954. Nominally the wireless operator, Banerjee was also gifted with languages, being fluent in at least six, and had the task of compiling an Onge vocabulary. His group, which included many policemen and laborers, camped at Dugong Creek for six months. Although initially wary, the Onge were much intrigued by his electronic equipment. Over time they grew to like him enough, Banerjee related, to give him the tasty name Koechange, meaning "pork fat," and to bring him buckets of honey. They also made themselves comfortable in his tent, to the extent of often using the sleeping platform for romantic trysts.

Heinrich Harrer, of Tibetan fame, accompanied King Leopold of Belgium on an official tour of the Andamans in 1974. They spent some days at Dugong Creek, living in cottages specially built for the illustrious guests. One evening the king announced a distribution of food, and about forty Onge turned up on the beach with leaf, plastic, enamel, or wooden dishes and mugs.

After collecting the flour and tea, the women began silently to dance. "Men and children sat in the sand, the sea surfed, palm trees swayed in the wind and millions of fireflies glittered in the mangrove swamps," wrote Harrer. The performance was curiously restrained: "The women only turned, wound, shook and bumped their hips back and forth," keeping their upper torsos still. The flashes of cameras lit up the scene. The dancers, young and old, now formed a circle, their yellow fiber aprons swinging up and down and remnants of the day's body paint glowing in the darkness. Then the circle dissolved and a row formed, the women stamping ahead, back and to either side as they gyrated their hips. It was a fertility dance, Harrer concluded, held to honor the king "who came from a faraway country to visit the last Onge, and who handed presents to them and sat down with them in the sand."

But then the men rose, urging departure. They stroked the children and lifted them onto slings hanging down their mothers' backs. As silently as they had come, the Onge disappeared into the dark, leaving the tourists alone on the beach.

In the afternoon the Onge men came to the concrete outhouse by the jetty to take their rice and wheat flour. I hung around, hoping to stop someone, but while they talked Hindi to the caretaker, and Onge among themselves, they ignored me. I watched as one of them stripped a long even length of bark from a tree branch and used it to suspend a sawed-off jerry can full of flour from his forehead and down his back. One by one the men left with their loads. The man in front set up a lilting chant that each took up in his turn, throwing it back and forward along the track until it faded off.

The last out was Prakash, a youth in red shorts. He threw me a self-possessed and not unfriendly glance, so I decided to stroll along with him. "I'd like to talk to the Onge, but no one talks to me," I began.

"They don't talk to me either."

"Why not?" I asked in surprise, since he too was an Onge.

"I live alone." His mother was in South Bay, he explained, and he stayed at Dugong Creek for school. "I'll go back after the hunt."

What hunt? I wondered to myself. Was he one of the adolescents who had to kill a tusked male boar for his initiation?

The line of men ahead, by then walking silently with their loads, vanished into the gathering darkness. Although we spoke almost in whispers, our voices were floating down the path; we too fell quiet. By and by we came to the huts. That evening electricity flowed from the generator, and many huts had lights on inside, and fires. The dogs came up and sniffed at my ankles but didn't growl because I was with the men.

Near the far end of the colony Prakash veered off to one of the cottages and up the few wooden steps to its balcony. The entrance was barred by a high plank. He stepped over it and deposited his load on a bench. A fire flamed on the verandah, children were peeking out of an open door, and a portly man beckoned me to sit. I asked what they would eat that night; roti and dal, or lentils, Indian food, he replied. An obese woman in a long dusty dress came out of the hut and sat by me. It was she, I could swear, whose picture we once published in *Scientific American,* clad in only a shredded-cane skirt. Her eyes were red and watery; she wiped them with her left hand while with her right she drew a wheat tin closer and ran her fingers through the soft powder. She looked at me and through me; again, I wasn't wanted.

Prakash was leaving for his cottage, so I followed him. Inside, a tube light glowed onto a bare room. A short, high wooden cot stood in the center; it bore no mattress, but was carefully covered with a cloth. A mosquito net hung over it, the sides neatly folded over the top for later use. On the walls were pasted a few pages from Bombay movie magazines, and in a corner lay a metal tray with ashes. I could see nothing else.

"It's clean," I said.

"I keep it clean."

We moved onto the dark verandah; I stepped carefully over gaps where the floorboards had fallen through and leaned against the far side. The moonlight spread white on the sand below. Across the path, seeming like a world away, figures silhouetted by firelight moved in the hut we'd just left. Prakash would eat there later that night.

"How do you see your life?"

In the darkness, he made a gesture I couldn't see. "How else?"

"You should learn something, perhaps an electrician's job, like Tanageru."

"They don't teach us much," he replied, referring to the welfare staff. "They say, 'If you know this, what will we do?'"

A wave of emotion engulfed me and sat between us like a presence. The matter-of-fact tone betrayed his awareness of the forces arrayed to keep him in place. I, who'd spent much of my life fleeing traps, had a visceral, almost nauseating sense of the one that loomed high around him.

"They don't teach us much in school either. One hour, and it's over." To fill up his time, he wandered in the forest, hunting; he'd killed two small pigs yesterday.

Visible from where we stood was a thatched shack at the end of the colony, nearest the trees. Two aged men lived there. "I'd like to hear their stories," I said.

"They don't talk."

"The others isolate Prakash, because he talks to outsiders," said the wireless operator. Once Prakash, who was one of several young men named by Indians, had gotten into trouble with the Onge elders for promising to show the welfare staff a favorite fishing hole in the forest. I mentioned that he'd take me pig hunting at six A.M. the next day.

"He won't show up," said the wireless operator cheerfully. "They have no sense of tomorrow or time."

It was I who didn't show up. I spent the night doubled up with stomach cramps or throwing up onto the sand. When I finally fell asleep, to the companionable sound of a gnawing rat, it was five A.M. Around noon I roused myself and eyed the thirty feet of scorching sun that lay like a sword between my cottage and the caretaker's. It separated me from food. Eventually hunger drove me to cross it, a towel draped over my head. I could barely walk.

"We were all sick," the caretaker told me. "It's the heat."

Having chewed painfully spicy food and downed some medicines, I made a trip to the well and slowly carried back half a bucket of water for a bath.

I looked hideous. My forehead had broken out in a dense mass of tiny oily bumps, and my chin, left unshaded by my Andaman

Tourism baseball cap, was peeling. Lying on the bed, I fantasized about a facial in my sister-in-law's air-conditioned beauty parlor in Calcutta. Soft supple fingers massaging my face and neck with delicious ice cubes and cold cream, followed by steaming towels and a cleansing, drying mask.

Refrigerators, computers, satellite connections, pharmaceuticals — I had a lifestyle that drew resources from all over the world and beyond. The Onge's needs were limited to this island; mine had brought me even here. Not that I could live here. Already I felt confined, longing to escape.

A few years later, I learned that 1998 was no ordinary year but the hottest of the entire past millennium. Although I experienced Little Andaman as a cauldron, others had found it pleasant and mild in all seasons. Nor were the Andamanese tolerant of heat, as I'd assumed: they're prone to sunstroke, and at midday used to shelter in the dark depths of the jungle.

Their lives had been made intolerable not only by timber sharks, settlers, and the civil servants who put them there, but by people like me, living at the other end of the earth. Airplanes and air conditioners might be the meat of my lifestyle, but the gases they spew are poison to others. Global warming is here.

## Cultural Exchange

M ANY MOONS AGO, before the winds of many seasons had gone by, the Onge of Jackson Creek made a big canoe, related the raja Tambolai to anthropologist Vishvajit Pandya. So they all went to Aberdeen bazaar in Port Blair and returned with tea and tobacco. These had very tasty smell and smoke, so the Onge gave up smoking and drinking their forest's leaves. Women repeatedly told the men to go to Aberdeen to bring leaves of various sorts.

Then one day some young women went with the men, making the spirits very angry. The forests were full of leaves but the Onge did not take them, making the spirits even more furious. They came down with violent winds of all directions and warred with the Onge. The canoes returning from Aberdeen overturned, and the people in them turned into stones.

White men followed the new rocks in the sea, until they arrived at Bumila Creek. They wanted to take Onge men and women away to Aberdeen. Once again there was a big war, and many more Onge were turned into stones.

After that, when the young boys grew up they had to marry within their father's sister's home. That was how the Onge went from one relative to the other and avoided encounter and war.

\*     \*     \*

Onge men had arrived in force at the caretaker's cottage, chatting loudly in their musical voices. An old man with beads around his neck, who'd turned away when I tried talking to him the day before, came up unexpectedly to ask me for *zarda*, a highly potent form of tobacco chewed by Indians. The Onge hung around the caretaker until he produced boxes of the substance, which they took to Das's quarters for distribution. Apparently *zarda*, along with tobacco leaves and betel nut, yet another intoxicant, was part of their rations. I'd been advised, while in Port Blair, to bring a stash of tobacco with me to loosen Onge tongues, and I'd indignantly declined. Now I saw it wouldn't have mattered.

The Onge had a tradition of smoking local leaves, which they stuffed into pipes made of crabs' claws. The British and all subsequent visitors — possibly including foreign poachers in search of valuable decorative shells — offered the far more addictive tobacco. "Armed with gifts of mirrors, glass beads, cloth and, above all, tobacco, I was able to make friends with the reputedly ferocious people of the Andamans," boasted Cipriani.

He was much impressed by the Onge's physical attributes, such as their canines: "The teeth, which are never filed or cut, as many primitive peoples do for decorative purposes, are very white; caries is rare, and although never cleaned the teeth are retained till late in life." Commonly the incisors were as pointed as the canines, Cipriani further noted: "This, with the whiteness of the teeth and eyes against the blackness of the skin, gives the Onges a sinister appearance, which may account for the old description of the Andamanese as men with ferocious dogs' heads." The teeth were so powerful that children of ten to fifteen could "crush nails up to two millimeters thick, and dent lumps of iron."

"When we first came," a shopkeeper in Hut Bay told me, "they were laughing. They had such solid, shining bodies and white teeth, and they were laughing." Now all the Onge adults had hideously red, decayed teeth from indulging in their multiple addictives. And I saw hardly a smile, let alone a laugh.

Late in the afternoon I heard a loud calling: Who'd taken the bucket from the well? Not me — I'd returned it after my bath. The bucket finally turned up, hours later. One of the Onge boys, Rakesh, had stuck it on top of a palm tree.

The top of a palm tree was also a favorite hideout, if a risky one, for anyone in the mood for a binge. One time, when the dead leaves were trimmed, several empty bottles were discovered up there. Alcohol, introduced by the early colonists, could now be obtained from the settlers at Hut Bay. But according to anthropologist Sita Venkateswar, Onge elders had accused at least two medical officers of supplying alcohol to anyone who would bring in ambergris.

Venkateswar held that Onge males drank to assert their independence — from the women. Since their abject defeat in battle by the British, the men had been forced to become collaborators in their own demise. A raja, for instance, transmitted the wishes of the welfare staff to the other Onge and so had to be fluent in Hindi. The women expressed their contempt for such submission by refusing to speak Hindi — although they understood it perfectly. Not a single woman would answer my queries. Sometimes, Venkateswar suspected, they even used a mode of speech unintelligible to their men.

When Onge men drank, no women were on the scene. The men joked lewdly about their exploits in the manner of the welfare staff, enjoying a heady defiance of women's rules and opinions and a momentary assumption of the dubious powers of Indian men.

"In the morning they rub their skins with mud, and wallow in it like buffaloes," Robert Colebrooke, the eighteenth-century explorer, had written in disgust. But naturalist Charles Boden Kloss,

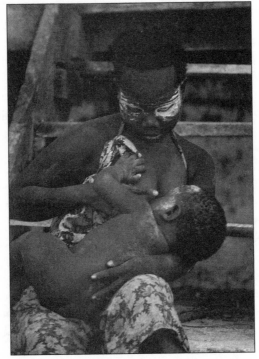

*Onge woman and child*

visiting Little Andaman in 1901, found body paint to be hilarious: "[W]henever I attempted to adjust the focus, the picture on the screen gave rise to such fits of laughter that the camera was in danger of being upset." The attitude persisted. At Dugong Creek I saw only a mother and child with patterns on their faces, and the reason soon became clear. "Why do you put clay?" the pharmacist complained to an elderly Onge man. "You should put oil." Like Indians.

In the Portman volumes at Calcutta was a portrait of five naked men, standing. One wore a plain clay wash such as Colebrooke might have seen, often a sign of mourning (and acquired without wallowing). But another sported a delicate white line of a herringbone design, like a silver chain, reaching from his shoulder down the length of his body to his toe, from his shoulder blade to his fingertips and probably down his back as well, the pattern being repeated on the other side. I could think of no ornamentation to better show off his perfect body.

George Dobson, on his visit to an Andaman Home, noted a more colorful young man strutting about. "His full dress consisted in a coat of fresh olive-coloured mud paint on one side, and bright red paint on the other. Half his face was red, the other half olive, and the red paint on his body terminated in a festooned border along the middle of the chest and abdomen; the arms and legs were similarly adorned, the festooned border running down the outer side of the legs like the gold stripe in military trousers." The Onge were exceedingly vain, commented Cipriani: men and women alike would return from the forest adorned with garlands they'd woven from fruits, flowers, and leaves, "delighted with their own beauty."

It was always women who did the painting. "[T]he more a wife loves her husband the more magnificent the designs she executes on him," Cipriani noted. "A man returning from an exceptionally successful hunting trip is met by his wife with a specially unusual and elaborate design, which she carries out with great devotion."

Painting was not just an expression of love or creativity; it was central to the identity of an islander. The Onge were divided into four clans, each claiming a quarter of Little Andaman. (A clan further contained two groups: turtle hunters, who occupied the coastal areas, and pig hunters, whose territory included more forest.) Every clan was befriended by a bird — a hornbill, an oriole, or one of two kinds of buntings — that aided it in matters relating to the spirits. This feathered ally inspired a design that, drawn on the face with red or white clay, identified an Onge's loyalties.

"Each woman has the right to use the design that belongs to her matrilineal group throughout her life," noted Vishvajit Pandya. A boy's face would be painted by his mother until he grew up, married, and moved to his wife's camp. (A man from a turtle-hunting group would marry a woman from the pig-hunting group in the opposite corner of the island, and vice versa.) Then she would adorn his face with her band's emblem.

The body patterns, on the other hand, were based on the season of a person's birth. Those born during Mayakangne, for instance, bore designs inspired by the dugong. During the season of his or her birth, an Onge would be painted every day. In so decorating with clay those she loved, a woman invoked the protection of the spirits. She was the healer, using clays and herbs to reduce fevers and cure illnesses.

Paint even made the difference between night and day. "Sun is wife of Moon," Pandya quoted. "Sun paints her husband's body with red and white clay. She applies more and more white paint on Moon and the husband becomes cold. Thereby the night becomes cold when white-painted husband comes out. In the day the sun remains hot because she is making paints for her husband."

In December 1936, some Onge men and boys, visiting Port Blair for tobacco, were spotted by officers of the HMS *Enterprise,* which was in the harbor. Deciding that the crew would enjoy viewing this "almost extinct race," the officers requested the local police commandant to bring the Onge on board. "Before they knew what had happened they were climbing up the starboard gangway like monkeys, all very surprised and very frightened," related an article in *Blackwood's Magazine.* Evidently, some of the Onge believed that the 171-meter cruiser was an island.

The crew of almost six hundred men came up to the Onge onboard in small groups, so as not to scare them further. Soon the aboriginals were relaxing with cigarettes and chocolate. The sailors felt their "wool," examined their spears, bows, arrows, and baskets, and watched them go through the motions of a dance. In return the Onge received bread, meat, milk, sugar, and other foods from the ship's stores, bead necklaces for the "girl friend," as well as mirrors, mouth organs, and other artifacts. One man, given a small clockwork tank with an imitation quick-firing gun, "carried it ashore as though it were made of solid gold."

It was also a chance to get rid of old clothes. The Onge tried these on, roaring with laughter at one another. One individual, who came to be dressed in a yellow soccer shirt that hung below his knees, a stiff evening collar, and a nautical cap, was much photographed. Another, in bell-bottom pants, a red and white soccer shirt, and a bowler hat, also "had many admirers." But the most amusing of all — to the sailors — was a man who, given a square of red cloth, used it to proudly adorn his behind rather than to cover up his front. He "was the envy" of all the other aboriginals, who were oblivious to the snickers that nudity attracts in civilized society.

To me, the Onge looked not funny but sad in their dirt-colored and torn garments.

A plant that the Onge used to reduce fever has been found to kill the exceedingly dangerous cerebral malaria virus. The plant's name remains secret, especially after a scientist tried to patent the discovery.

The Onge had cures for many other ailments, deriving from their intimacy with the environment. They were blessed with "botanical and zoological knowledge which seems almost innate, and they know of properties in plants and animals of which we are quite unaware," wrote Cipriani. "They could tell me which trees flowered and when, because they knew this affected the whereabouts and the quality of the honey, and they knew which flowers and roots had medicinal properties." (Although his informants were men, the true repositories of botanical knowledge were the healers — the women. They could not, of course, treat introduced diseases such as tuberculosis, which require the medicines of outsiders.)

But with the removal of timber, the jungle that held this phar-macopeia was vanishing. A wilderness that to the Onge was made of a myriad trees, vines, and shrubs, each with its seasonally vary-ing personality, its unique flowers and leaves and fruits, its aroma and taste and medicinal power, was to the outsider an amor-phous, impenetrable mess. In the empty spaces left after logging, the newcomer often practiced agriculture, inserting the trees he'd brought along. Curiously, it was Cipriani who initiated the project of clearing the Onge's forests to make space for coconut groves: "In order to plant coconut trees for the benefit of the islanders I had even to do the planting myself, so utterly ignorant were they of agricultural methods; we even had to do all the clearing of the undergrowth in a patch of forest, and prepare the ground. The Onges watched curiously but were quite uninterested. Why should they care for a tree for ten years to get its nuts when the is-land and seas around are teeming with food for the taking?"

Quite so; and yet he persisted. Almost a hundred years earlier, the Great Andamanese, watching convicts at work in the fields, had been similarly unimpressed. According to Edward Man, they regarded agricultural labor as "a degrading occupation and fit only for such as have forfeited their freedom." The islanders' ways of acquiring food — hunting pigs, shooting fish, digging up tu-bers, plucking fruit, or wading into the lovely cool water to find clams — allowed for plenty of leisure.

"If a man has a painful dream he will often not venture out of the camp the following day, but will stay at home until the effect has worn off," Radcliffe-Brown had noted in passing. An odd de-tail, but of significance: which of us can take the day off because of a bad dream? By all accounts, the islanders' body and psyche were far better nourished than those of the modern Indian peas-ant. Man stated that the Great Andamanese had no concept of suicide and had coined a cumbersome compound word, *oyun-temar-toliganga*, upon observing it in outsiders.

But agriculture is synonymous with civilization, with enlightenment, with emancipation from bestial ignorance. So Indian officials had followed the British (and the Italian Cipriani) in striving tirelessly to teach cultivation to these unwilling students. The Jarawa contact trips often involved the planting of coconuts, which the *junglees* promptly dug up and ate.

Unfortunately, agriculture was a double-edged sword. Its advent allowed many more mouths to be fed and encouraged humans to multiply. But, as scientist and writer Jared Diamond relates, the balance between food and population was never quite right. Time and time again people became too numerous for their fields to support, and so they migrated and conquered until they reached the ends of the earth and had nowhere left to go. Hunter-gatherers were the only peoples who knew how to live within their means.

Gaubolambe — Little Andaman — had been the Onge's universe. Their worldview and perhaps even their psyches were wrapped around its contours. Every beach, every stream, every redwood tree, every beehive they used to know and cherish.

"When outsiders settle and destroy, they resist. When they can't, they get demoralized," related Biswanath Sarkar, a young anthropologist I met in Calcutta. "While I was there a little girl died in an accident, a stone another child threw hit her. I said to some of the elders, 'I am sorry the child died.'

"'What does it matter?' they replied. 'Our god has died.'"

# Outsiders and Other Ghosts

WHEN A GROUP of us outsiders left for Hut Bay, one of the Onge men, Bada Raju, came along. I'd first met him at South Bay, from where he'd trekked alone to Dugong Creek. Now he was returning to fetch his family, so he could stay in the larger settlement and organize the cleanup of the coconut groves.

A boat took us back to the giant tree stump by the creek near Vivekananda Puram, from where we walked to the roadside to catch a bus. Bada Raju moved right to its front, claimed a seat by the driver, and stuck his nose to the windscreen. A small plastic bottle of tobacco dangled onto the back of his neck from a string hung around his forehead. He watched avidly as the bus passed miles of shorn lands. I asked if he remembered a time when this was all jungle. He glanced at me dismissively and curled his hand in a classic Indian gesture: What does it matter?

He got off near Hut Bay, where he had a friend. Hours later, while waiting at a local store at Hut Bay to use the phone, I spied Bada Raju across the street. I waved and he came up, smiling; I was flattered. He was waiting for the bus to Harmander Bay, from where he'd walk to South Bay. He rubbed together finger and thumb in a familiar gesture: Give me some money.

"Don't give him any," interjected the shop's owner. "He'll buy alcohol."

"No," protested Bada Raju, annoyed. "I need food for the children."

Indeed, he was said never to touch alcohol. He beckoned me to a nearby stall and pointed to packs of spicy fried lentils. He also got two packs of colorful balls, food of some kind, I imagined. I suggested a packet of cookies, and he turned it around suspiciously. "Good?"

"Good," the shopkeeper said.

The change was a five-rupee note, which I handed to Bada Raju. He looked confused by it. *"Panch,"* I said, holding up five fingers.

He nodded, stuffing the packages into his shoulder bag. "Go back to your store," he ordered, striding off in the opposite direction. He had no more use for me.

One morning in Dugong Creek, the Onge men were engaged in chores ordered by the welfare staff. Be it fetching water or clearing undergrowth or anything else, the Onge referred to all work done for outsiders as *totale,* or cleaning up. Suddenly, Sita Venkateswar observed a group of Onge women arrive with brooms and angrily start to sweep the area. Each woman complained loudly that she was famished for pork but that the men were engaged in *totale* — her vigorous sweeping, continued throughout, invoking the demeaning connotations of the word. Each man went up to his wife and tried to appease her, to no avail. Finally all the men put down their tools and disconsolately returned to their huts to wait for their wives, but the furious sweeping went on for another hour.

The next morning all the men had left for the hunt, and *totale* ground to a halt for a week.

Venkateswar related another occasion when Onge women subverted the plans of outsiders. One of the children, Rocky, had been sick for a long time. The medical officer, who'd neglected him, suddenly realized that the child might die and that the consequences would be serious — to himself. The Onge being considered an endangered people, each fatality had to be explained to the seniormost authorities. In panic, he summoned a helicopter to transport Rocky to Port Blair for treatment.

The evening before it arrived, all the welfare staff pleaded with Simi, the boy's mother, to take him to Port Blair. Simi was reluctant, for her elderly husband, Kanjo, had similarly been transported away but not returned alive. Tambolai, Kanjo's son by an earlier marriage, was also torn, because as raja he was expected to speak for the welfare staff. Offered new clothes for the whole family, money, a suitcase to carry it all in, and other persuasions, Simi finally ran out of excuses and seemed to agree. The staff retired for the night, but tight knots of women continued to confer, suggesting that something was afoot.

At six A.M. the helicopter landed with considerable difficulty, because of the wind conditions. Each trip cost the administration dearly and had to be justified. The staff traipsed to the Onge huts to fetch Simi, but she'd locked herself in and remained silent to all the banging, pleading, and threatening. Ultimately the helicopter left, the pilot chastising the medical officer to the great amusement of the Onge.

The women had decided, and that was that. Over the next weeks, the medical officer, needing to ingratiate himself with the authorities, attended to Rocky diligently, and the boy recovered. But the Onge men's glee at the debacle came to be replaced by disquiet as the staff's taunts about their subservience to women hit home.

So far, it looked like Onge women had yet to submit to the men posted at the settlements, though the pressure was relentless. During Venkateswar's stay, the medical officer assaulted an attractive young woman, who defended herself with a knife.

The night before I left for Port Blair, I learned that a family of Onge was on the jetty. I made my way to a dark waiting area enclosed by lacy concrete walls which was loud with resonating voices. Along one wall were several humps: Onge children and a dozing woman. Lying in front of them, protectively, was a man. "It's become night," he said to me.

It was Bada Raju and his family, who'd be traveling to Dugong Creek the next day. Since they were half asleep, I offered to leave.

"But you didn't do your work?" Bada Raju asked. "We didn't talk."

"You people don't talk to me," I replied.

"You come back." After a while, he mused, "Another madam came, she left. And another madam came, she too left. Now you have come, you too will go. Another will come."

It was no accusation, just a statement of fact. I was but one of a string of onlookers who visited, took what they needed, and left, making no difference to the Onge's lives. Remembering I had a question, I asked if he got paid for the honey he'd given the social workers in South Bay. He shook his head and replied that he didn't eat all day. "Give me a big note, I'll get enough for everyone."

I gave him three ten-rupee notes, spreading them out and saying, "Thirty." He'd buy food in the morning. The kids were waking up, smiling at me in the dark, and giggling in musical peals.

"Will you get me clothes?" Bada Raju suddenly asked.

"What will you do with clothes? It's so hot here. I'll get you books. Do you read Hindi?"

"The children don't know anything," he responded. "The teacher teaches for just half an hour. Then he tells the children, you play." He was agitated; this was something he cared about. "Tell the *bada sahib*s in Port Blair to send a good teacher. Tell them Bada Raju said so."

Bada Raju is Hindi for "Big King." For the first time, he sounded like one.


On my return to Hut Bay some weeks later, I hitched a ride on a truck to the creek by the giant tree stump but found no boatman willing to take me to Dugong Creek. They were afraid of the social worker, who was away but had left instructions that they not transport anyone.

As I argued with the boatmen, a small canoe slid into the shelter with heavy plastic sacks. Baby boar killed within the Onge reserve, said the truck driver, who asked to buy two kilos. "I have to first clean them and give some to the forest guards," replied the poacher, then loaded the bags onto a bicycle and rode away.

Eventually I managed to hire a boat. "The tide is coming in," warned its owner as he cranked up the outboard motor. The line where the creek met the sea was guarded by high, crashing waves; the boat shot over each crest and slammed down on the other side.

When we got to Dugong Creek, the caretaker was on the jetty. To my surprise he refused to recognize me or to let me land, saying I needed permission from Port Blair. Replying that I had it, I defiantly clambered out of the boat, lugged my bag to the guest house, and dumped it on the back porch. A young man who introduced himself as the new schoolteacher — I'd transmitted Bada Raju's complaint, but I didn't know if he was the response — asked to see my tribal pass. He told the caretaker, who couldn't read, that it was still valid.

Scowling, the caretaker unlocked the room. It had been swept, the tabletops wiped clean of dead insects and gecko droppings, and a clean white sheet folded under the pillow. Miraculous. The defense minister had been scheduled to visit, I remembered.

One of the welfare staff was a nurse-cum-midwife. We walked through the Onge settlement late one evening, she armed with a stick against the dogs and shouting orders on either side in the same tone used by the male staff.

Bada Raju was building a shack in front of his cottage. He balanced on a fragile-looking frame made of thin, whiplike trunks of young trees, each a different hue of cream, brown, or red, tying them into place. His wooden cottage leaked in the rain, and he was preparing for the monsoons. "It's beautiful," I said, admiring his work.

Mohan, a portly and amiable Onge man, stood on his porch in a nearby cottage. He'd been given a job with the police but got fired because he lost his uniform and other insignia. Along with his salary, these were in a suitcase he'd left with some Onge men at Hut Bay; they were drinking, and by the time Mohan caught up with them, the case was gone.

When we got to the end of the line, Prakash's cottage was all shuttered and dark. "No one lives there," said the nurse.

I went up the steps and knocked, and Prakash opened the door. A tube light burned brightly inside. "It's so hot, and you have all the doors and windows closed?" I asked. "You won't get any breeze."

"There is no breeze," he replied. In an undertone, the nurse told me that an old man, Nabekutti, had just died and Prakash was afraid of his ghost. A small piece of wood was leaning against a wall: he'd been assiduously rounding and smoothing it with a knife to make a rolling pin for roti, Indian flatbread. I watched him work skillfully for a while. An array of clean, colorful pants and shirts was hanging on a line across the room, and from a nail on the wall dangled a new pair of sneakers he'd bought at Hut Bay.

In that season Prakash had killed four piglets, but he needed an adult male boar for his initiation, the *tanageru*. (The man introduced to me as Tanageru was an initiate when the welfare staff encountered him; they mistakenly continued to use the word to address him.) To become an Onge adult, an adolescent boy had to undergo a grueling spiritual voyage, his return from which rejuvenated the entire tribe. But since there weren't enough boys around, nor enough boar, the Onge had taken to spacing the *tanageru* out so that one occurred every few years. Prakash was well past adolescence — twenty-five, by his own estimate — but was yet to be initiated.

*       *       *

One afternoon I wandered through the woods and chanced upon an Onge man seated on palm leaves in a breezy spot looking onto the ocean. He was fashioning a long section of a sapling into a bow. He scraped its sides, picked it up, and squinted along the length with an air of appraisal that reminded me of my father aligning a gunsight.

"What's your name?" I asked.

"I told you," he answered, gesturing toward the huts.

Oh, no, I should have remembered. He was Muroi, a *torale*, a silent one who communed with the spirits. To cover up my faux pas, I offered, "My name is Madhu."

"Madhu?" He looked up in amusement.

A fortunate name, given how much the Onge liked *madhu*, Bengali for honey. I watched as he worked and warned him when he sliced the blade down toward his foot, which was supporting the lower end of the bow. He removed the foot and instead placed the end on a coconut husk. A communication; I was grateful for each.

A distant thudding made us look up: a helicopter from the Nicobars, on its way to Port Blair. When the defence minister was supposed to visit, the Onge were first groomed to meet him. Then they were told he would only be coming to Hut Bay, and some of the Onge would be taken there by helicopter. The doctor, making one of his rare visits, picked out the healthiest. One man, who got left behind, vented his rage by chopping down some coconut trees, symbols of outsiders.

Whether Muroi was impressed by the flying machine, I don't know. They said he did some soaring of his own.

When the hunters came back empty-handed time after time and the living was tough, the Onge would go to the *torale*'s home to request him to visit the spirits. They would bring carefully tended bones of ancestors to attract the latter's souls; old iron arrowheads and betel nuts the *torale* could offer as gifts; lumps of red clay to mask his body odor, so that malevolent spirits, who hunted the

Onge by smell, wouldn't follow him back home; and seeds of a vine related to the morning glory, which, when thrown into a fire, would burst with a bang to scare away any spirits who intended harm. "Go go go along with the winds," the visitors would chant, "above the forest [to] see our parents and children." For the spirits were reborn as the Onge's infants, the Onge in death became spirits, and living on Gaubolambe required consulting with these wraiths.

Only the *torale* knew how to meet the spirits and come back alive. "I will go, I alone can go to the forest," said Muroi to Vishvajit Pandya around 1984. He would carry a fire and keep it in his ancestors' hut. Then, spreading around him the bones he'd been given, he would put his head between his knees and go to sleep. The spirits would come and, being blind, would feel all over his body; he would start to shiver with the coldness of their touch. They would truss him up like a pig, and, throwing him on their backs, take flight.

After a few days, Pandya noticed that Muroi went missing. The others would not speak of him, as though he were dead; but his relatives wore strips of pandanus leaves, as if expecting an important visitor. Four days later Muroi reappeared, bathed and rested after his ordeal, and described how it felt to soar.

"I can see all the forest, the pigs in it, all the sea with the turtles in it, all the trees with the cicadas and honey in them, all the creeks with the crabs and fish in them, and all the ground under which are the tubers and the [stones for sharpening tools]," he related. This eagle vision was one reason for the hazardous journey. Once up in the sky, the spirits would untie him and argue about what to do with him; finally the bad spirits would leave with gifts of iron. The good spirits would tell him when and where they would be in the coming seasons, and just what the Onge should leave for them at the shoreline; they would remind him to make sure enough honey and cicada grubs remained for the spirits to eat. The *torale* would listen carefully, for he had to retain everything. Then the spirits would throw him to the ground in a place where there were lots of stones, so his skin became covered with bloody wounds.

But these stones were essential for the Onge to sharpen their arrowheads and adze blades, so Muroi would collect them. "I then warm up my body near the fire I had left, cover my body with clay paints and start my walk back home," he told Pandya. After he was rested he would distribute the stones and tell everyone what the spirits had instructed.

Without the knowledge the *torale* brought, they could not survive on Gaubolambe, the Onge believed. They would not know how to avoid the malicious spirits and keep the friendly ones satisfied, and everyone would become ghosts.

# Falling Apart

I n March 1911, census officials took on board some eighty Onge who were fishing and turtling on Rutland Island near Port Blair and proceeded south to Little Andaman. The Onge were delighted at getting a ride. Most were dropped off along with their canoes at Bumila Creek to the north, but twelve youths who were from the east side landed with the party on the northeastern coast to serve as guides.

They clearly knew the local Onge, whom they greeted by "sitting on each other's laps, embracing each other in silence, holding cheek to cheek for some minutes on one side and just a moment on the other, both sexes indiscriminately," noted forester M.C.C. Bonig, who led the expedition. For a long time everyone was quiet. But then the visitors "eagerly snatched" the fishing nets which the native women had brought as gifts, and the latter similarly divested their Onge guests of all cloth and ornaments.

Bonig noted that some of the Onge guides had worked as boatmen at the Andaman Homes. That could explain one of his observations. Farther along the coast, at a place he'd visited six or seven years earlier, he found three to four times fewer people: "I was told many had died, from what I understood, of pneumonia and bronchitis." Many of those present were washed with clay, a mark of mourning, and some of the Onge brought over from

Rutland carried "pieces of the skulls of their deceased children in cigarette tins tied around their necks."

In 1954, Cipriani took twenty-eight Onge to Port Blair to "present them" to the president of India; all developed high fevers and were hastily returned to their homes — along with their germs — after the official meeting. Onge numbers fell steadily through the twentieth century, from an estimated 631 in the 1911 census to around 100 in the 1970s, where it has since hovered.

The declining population has led to much speculation about underlying causes. It wasn't just diseases and accidents, for many Onge couples are mysteriously childless. Cipriani exculpated colonists of responsibility for the population slide, arguing instead for an inbuilt weakness of the natives: "Civilization," he wrote, "has in fact only hastened the disappearance of groups already heading for demographic decadence as the result of physiological factors which lie within the group itself . . . The intrinsic damage done by civilization as such has, in my opinion, been considerably exaggerated in some quarters." His argument falters on the simple matter of timing. The Andamanese flourished for thousands of years, only coming to grief in the late nineteenth and the twentieth century, when outsiders came. What can explain this coincidence, if not causality?

A more relevant question is how, unlike most other peoples, the Andamanese did not overpopulate their islands and thereby become sickly and undernourished. It seems as if the Andamanese achieved an exquisite balance: they evolved, culturally or biologically or both, to limit their numbers so that they could live well within their islands' resources. That scale, set at zero population growth, necessarily tipped when colonists arrived.

The infertility lately observed among Onge adults could be a result of past syphilis — acquired from outsiders — or of inbreeding in a group that has now become too small. More intriguingly, it could point to some adaptation that allowed the islanders to limit births. Among the possibilities are late menstruation and early menopause, which Cipriani remarked on. Another is homosexual practice, noted by a couple of observers. Or it could be something as prosaic as eating tubers containing steroids, which have contraceptive properties.

Another factor may be the so-called Westermarck effect: persons (and other primates) who were familiar with each other as children tend to be sexually indifferent to each other as adults. This instinct, which must have evolved to prevent inbreeding, implies that within a small group, in which everyone grew up knowing everyone else, sexual attraction is inhibited. The effect would balloon as the group shrank. (As a corollary, outsiders would become more enticing — which could be influencing the choices made by Great Andamanese women.)

Moreover, the Onge observed strict rules that ended up keeping the population down. For instance, a widow or widower, of whatever age, had priority in picking a spouse. So Tanageru was married to a woman old enough to be his mother. Suitable mates — those who were not closely related and who also satisfied the plethora of rules — were exceedingly scarce. Most of the young Onge men, who outnumbered the women three to two, had no hope of finding a spouse. Prakash was engaged to one of Bada Raju's tiny tots.

A final possible explanation for the Onge's poor "reproductive index" (as some scientists call it) is that they don't find life worth giving. One report noted the women routinely aborting their fetuses.

Those who counted the Onge made their own contributions to the dropping tally. M.C.C. Bonington, who directed the 1931 census of the Andamans, took three Onge men on a visit to the Nicobars, intending to later carry them back to Port Blair to study their language. The Onge got along well with the Nicobarese, who fed them amply and walked about with arms around their necks.

But during lunch, one of the Onge men strolled toward the trees, with the other two following. Someone remarked they were running away, and the Nicobarese "set up a wild shout," according to J. H. Hutton, the census commissioner of India. Startled, the Onge ran into the jungle.

Two were caught, shaking with fear, and brought on board the *Shah Jehan*. The third could not be found and was left on Car Nicobar, not to be heard from again. But that night one of the remaining Onge jumped overboard and the other had to be physically restrained from following. "He perpetually made signs that he wanted a knife apparently to cut his wrists and neck," Hutton noted. It's the only record of a desire for suicide among the Andamanese.

Back on Little Andaman, the lone survivor did not want to go ashore, perhaps because he did not want to tell the missing men's relatives what had happened. Forced off, he ran into the jungle. The officials related the tale to his tribesmen, who, "trembling violently," hurried after him.

Hutton, though a critic of British policies on the Andamans, blamed the incident on the islanders' being "very highly temperamental." It did not occur to him to question the offhand experimentation that led to numerous such deaths, albeit usually of disease, among the Andamanese.

Suydam Cutting, an American visiting in 1932, requested the occupants of an Andaman Home to take him on a hunt for dugong. It was midnight when, by the glow of a full moon, he descried two outrigger canoes coming toward him, each with a figure standing on the elevated prow. "It was a beautiful spectacle, the silhouettes of the pygmies splintering the silver light on the sea," he wrote.

Cutting perched in one of the canoes, which also contained an oarsman. The "pygmies in the pulpits" — as he called the men in the high prows — carried spears fifteen feet long, with detachable barbed heads. A spear point was tied, by means of a long rope, to its owner's boat. The man ahead of Cutting held his spear poised, "standing so motionless that he seemed to be a statue projecting from the bow."

They roamed for about an hour, then a whisper was heard from one of the paddlers: a dugong had been spied, perhaps by the phosphorescence it excited as it moved under water. "Almost imperceptibly the tiny figure at the bow tightened his muscles. The spear shot forward, and after it went the spearsman, diving cleanly into the water." Before Cutting could count to ten the man had surfaced, clambering back on board with the spear shaft. Then the boat shot forward: the dugong, agonized by the barb in its back, was heading out to sea.

"Giddily the canoe moved right and then left." They were getting into deep water; if the animal seemed strong enough to pull them into the open ocean, the cord would be cut. But finally the pace slowed, and the hunters were able to steer toward the steamer that had brought Cutting to that coast. In a few minutes the carcass, up to nine feet long, was hauled up on deck.

The same men then began to hunt for turtle. A whisper, as before, and a native lunged and stabbed vigorously into the water with his spear. The boat rocked, nearly tipping Cutting into the shark-infested sea. "Quietly the little pygmy at the bow who was strong enough to crack the hard shell of a seventy- or eighty-pound turtle waited" till his quarry stopped struggling and the boat again stilled.

The next day there was a great feast and a wild dance: "The surfeit of their favorite food had gone to their heads completely," Cutting reported. He carried away the skin, skull, and flippers of the dugong, which were made into a display for the American Museum of Natural History in New York.

Dugongs once grazed in herds of thousands on the sea-grass beds of southeast Asia. But Himansu Sekhar Das, a biologist who was also visiting Dugong Creek in 1998, said that in all of the Andaman and Nicobar Islands he'd learned of only forty of these gentle giants. The others had died off with the sea grasses, which suffocate in muddy water flowing off the shorn land just as surely as do coral reefs. In Dugong Creek, where the animals must once have been plentiful, a family of four still survived, the Onge told him — down one from their hunt of just two weeks earlier.

A band of the Onge led by Tambolai the raja had left the main camp at Dugong Creek and set up another one a mile or so along the shore. Himansu Das wanted to visit them, for they could tell him where to find sea-grass beds far more accurately than did the satellite maps he had. The pharmacist and I tagged along when he left the next afternoon.

We finally came to the renegade Onge camp, which was pleasant and breezy, sheltering under trees near the beach. As usual, dogs heralded our approach. Children hid under shacks and giggled, each peal rising in tone like a musical scale practiced on little bells.

The hunters had harpooned two green sea turtles. One was being cooked, while the other was still in the sea, tied by a long rope to a pole stuck in the sand. A tall Onge man, Koira, pulled on the tether and the creature stuck its anxious head out of the water like a periscope, checking to see where it was being drawn.

A young woman bore a baby on her hip. It was Simi, whose husband, Kanjo, had died four years before at a ripe old age; he was Tambolai's father. The Onge suspected that a married man had sired the baby and several of her other children. The accusations had caused a rift, so that Tambolai and his family and friends had left the main group.

It was all falling apart, no matter how hard they tried to hold it together.

# Assimilation

> When all the rocks and stones go away from the sea, like the
> ones we see now between us and Aberdeen, then nobody will go
> or come . . . All the pain will go away. No longer will the spirits
> get angry — our fathers and mothers will all remain with us . . .
> No one will die and there will be no [new] spirits. There will be
> no marriage and the giving of young boys to the old and the
> spirits.
>
> — Tambolai, told to Vishvajit Pandya, *Above the Forest*

WHEN A CULTURE DIES, the individuals who remain merge with the larger society. Where they fit in has always been clear.

In late 1927 Egon von Eickstedt visited the Andamans to make a physiometric study of its aboriginals. On Rutland Island near Port Blair he came upon some Onge who were camping for fish and turtles. Among them was a man who spoke Hindi, Nokai; through him, wrote von Eickstedt, "the government from time to time distributes those presents that shall instill the want for things with the Onges and shall buy their readiness for peace." Accordingly, Nokai was a raja.

In the next few weeks, becoming inured to the Europeans (and no doubt persuaded by peace offerings), the Onge allowed their bodies to be measured, their blood to be tested, their habits to be observed and photographed, their genealogies to be catalogued, their teeth and children to be counted, their hair to be collected and, in general, "a complete ethnographic collection" to be put together. The team then took the whole group of Onge to Little Andaman.

When they landed by a creek, men, women, and children materialized to gaze at the visitors, evidently entertained by their white faces. "They were put straight away, without complaints, on the measuring instrument, one after the other." Among them von Eickstedt discerned two variants of skulls. One, which was "phylogenetically higher ranked," belonged to a chief: "The brutal chin with the strong lower lip, the crookedly bent and very thin nose as well as the forehead contour and whole expression are completely unnegritoid," he opined. The type, he felt, was even better defined in an old man who'd refused to put down his bow: "[He] showed a long, fine face, which was completed by a high, splendid curved forehead, with a fine, bold aquiline nose, thin, solid lips and forceful chin; it virtually appeared as typological absurdity that this fine and kind senatorial head had deeply black skin and belonged to a dwarf-like small body."

The second morphological variant had a face "lowly and round, the chin often pushed forward snout-like, the top face flat with a short nose that is small and raised." These unhappy features were complemented by a receding chin and "bulging" eyes. He designated the type "chimpanzee-oid."

As such, it must have seemed appropriate that the Andamanese occupied the lowest ranks of human society.

Prakash was one of the few who accepted that mingling with outsiders required meeting their terms. One morning, when he showed up at the guest house, the men sharing the second room asked him to get me some water. He returned with two buckets balanced on a plank across his shoulder, sweat streaming down his face. I felt guilty for the imposition, which I should not have allowed.

We sat and talked. He once went to Port Blair and stayed there for six months with Boke, a boy who'd fallen from a coconut tree and had to be in the hospital. Boke, who couldn't speak, needed the company. I asked Prakash how he liked Port Blair.

"*Maza hai.*" It was fun.

"More fun than the forest?"

He shrugged. "You go there one day, you go two days, what is there to see?" In Port Blair there was a marketplace, where he'd spent time wandering. "You get eggs there."

"You get those here too," I pointed out. Chickens were pecking in the dust all over the Indian part of the settlement.

"They don't give us any," he replied, referring to the welfare staff. Nor could the Onge keep their own chickens, he confessed, for the dogs ate them. (Just before he arrived, I was watching a thin black puppy play with a scrawny adolescent chicken, and suddenly realized that the puppy had its friend by the head and was gnawing.) Yet the Onge routinely supplied turtle meat to the Indians.

We ended up on the back porch playing carom — trying to shoot, with a flick of the fingers, flat discs into holes at the corners of a board. Prakash could hardly hit the striker, and though I could, it made no difference to my score. In the matter of carom, at least, we were equals. We shot the counters around for a long time, me wiping sweat with a towel and he giggling at my total misses.

At enormous cost, the authorities had had experts from Madras compose bilingual primers for the Andamanese. I idly leafed through the one for the Onge, written almost entirely in Hindi. "Sometimes it so happens that we get neither fish nor wild boar as food. Then we eat rice and roti that we get free from the Society. The government meets all our needs without taking money."

*Prakash*

My hackles rose. What about the Onge being owed compensa-
tion for all the land they'd forfeited?

"Nor do we have money. Nor do we know how money is earned
. . . To earn money I have to first understand the value of money.
To do this I have to understand how to keep accounts. The Onge
only count one and two."

Of course the Onge could count beyond two; even some birds
can count to six or seven. True, the Onge didn't have specific
words for numbers greater than two: they marked off higher
numbers with their fingers. But Edward Man had noted that the
Great Andamanese had single words for ordinals such as "fourth
out of six" — perhaps for designating the order of children in a
family.

"The sea is full of fish," the primer continued. "But with one arrow I can get only one fish. Sometimes in the whole day I can get only three or four fish. This many fish is not enough for my family. But if I use a net, then I can get many fish at one time."

The sea *was* full of fish, and arrows were more than adequate for harvesting them. Henry Corbyn, the first keeper of the Andaman Home, wrote of two ten-year-old boys shooting fish with bow and arrow, leaping from rock to rock as their prey darted about underneath. "I have seen them obtain in this way a large basket of fish at times, when, on account of stormy weather, none have been caught by the convict fishermen" — armed with hooks and nets.

But with the reefs and sea grasses dying, the waters were no longer so productive. I watched several boys trying to shoot fish from the jetty, getting not a single chance to discharge an arrow. Even so, the Onge didn't need to be taught the use of nets: they used to weave large ones for catching turtles and small ones for little fish. (One ingenious design, the sample all torn and dusty in a cupboard of a Calcutta museum, had the form of a windsock supported by hoops of ever smaller size; the structure stretched out in the current of a small stream to trap fish at the far end.) The primer falsely implied that nets were a gift from civilization.

Just about every Indian I met on the islands, from the poorest to the richest and from the least literate to the most, was convinced of his intellectual superiority to the Andamanese. Repeatedly I heard that "they never learned to catch fish with a hook," "they don't wear clothes," or "they don't understand how to grow things." Every man assumed credit for the technical advances of modern society, taking helicopters, for instance, as proof of his personal prowess. Never mind that he couldn't explain the principles behind a helicopter or craft so much as a screw.

In reality, it's likely that hunter-gatherers are at least as intelligent as most civilized humans. They simply have a different strategy for survival: rather than using technology to mold their surroundings, they use an extraordinarily subtle understanding of their environment to live in harmony with it.

In the evening the Indians and the Onge played cricket on the helipad. An empty crate was the wicket, but the Nicobarese power station operator's small son had supplied a real bat. The wireless officer's tall assistant, his lungi hitched high, was taking time off from fishing to field, along with the pharmacist and the wireless officer. Four Onge boys showed up: Prakash, Rakesh, Boke, and Jain. The biologist Himansu Das did a lot of bowling and generally ran the show. Prakash didn't chase the ball, just giggled when he couldn't catch it. I was an enthusiastic, if inept, fielder, and Boke the most powerful batter.

Dense flocks of parakeets winged by overhead, strangely silent but for the whooshing of wings. The last rays of the sun caught them, lighting up their reds and greens and yellows. Das counted them, tens at a time, as we all stopped to watch.

It was one of the few interactions with the Onge that was purely pleasurable, not based on need. Soon no one could see the ball, and we all strolled back to bathe.

Later Prakash took me to a cottage to show off the turtle meat he'd cooked. He beckoned me into a room and lifted an aluminium pot full of cooked meat. It slipped and landed upside down, releasing a smear of oil and meat chunks onto the sandy wooden floor. I stared aghast. "It was hot," he giggled.

Surprisingly, the men on the porch didn't seem upset at their dinner's being on the floor. I squatted and helped Prakash pick up the pieces. A couple he cleaned in the kitchen, then returned with a mug of water. I licked my fingers — the taste was very Indian, but oily — and washed off.

I sat on the jetty, watching ripples of moonlight falling through the water onto the sand. The wireless operator's assistant was fishing with a line and hook. The caretaker perched on a large coil of wire and complained about the Onge. "They're becoming so smart, in five years they'll sell us on the street."

The wireless operator's assistant turned to me. "You should hear that Bada Raju talk. He says, 'Why have you come here? To make fools of us?'"

He jerked up a fish, diamond-shaped, and extracted the hook. The creature, silvery in the moonlight, thrashed on the concrete, flipping from side to side until it lay still, gasping. I asked him to kill it.

"Don't worry," he assured me. "It will die."

Despite their heartfelt efforts, the Onge would enter mainstream society, slipping right into the lowest rungs. The rest of society would move up one notch to accommodate them — and the resources taken from them.

Himansu had photos of Onge men at a Republic Day ceremony, singing the national anthem. And Tambolai saluted the Indian flag. The pictures shamed me.

Back in Hut Bay, I went to the bazaar to make a phone call.

"You don't know?" the storekeeper said, smiling as he dialed my number. "India exploded five atom bombs."

It took me a while to believe it. I could think of nothing that had happened, at least until I went to Dugong Creek, to prompt something like this.

"Shows the world what we can do," he went on, still dialing. "Gives us pride."

On the shelf in front of me, amid hand fans and other bric-a-brac, were arranged boxes of firecrackers, showing pictures of pretty children playing with bursts of light. "Standard Atom Bombs," said one box, and "Hydrogen Bombs," said another.

On TV, I watched a man from the Hindu nationalist party bask in the glory of the bomb and found myself gripped by a vicious fury. The explosion proved the prowess of a Hindu male; so far as I could tell, that was the entire rationale for the adventure. It was a phallic thrust at a world that would not take him seriously.

As a former nuclear physicist, I'd had plenty of time to rumi-
nate about bombs. The glee on this man's face told me he hadn't
heard of apocalypse, hadn't seen the photos of Hiroshima.

Oddly, many of the Andamanese were entering civilization at
the same time that the dominant culture was reaching its own cri-
sis of identity.

That night Himansu Das and I took the *Philopanja* to Port Blair.
The crowd was frightening. Pushing past two deckloads of passengers crammed into every available inch of space, we climbed to
the third deck and came to a halt at the top of the stairway. It was
blocked off by ropes; I stuck my head through and saw beautiful,
empty, breezy space, with only a few forms visible at the far end.

"They'll let the ropes go later," said Himansu.

So we waited, balancing our bags on the steps. The ship left. On
the empty deck I saw a few families and friends of the crew set-
tling down for the night. Finally I squeezed through the ropes and
walked up to a portly man who looked like he was in charge.
"Please open the ropes," I asked. "There is no space down there."

"No!" he shouted. He beckoned me to the balcony and pointed
down. "Do you see?"

From his commanding height the men, women, and children
crammed onto the first deck looked like a seething mass of colorful rats. The lower classes.

"You can let in a few people!" I protested.

"No, you go back down."

You're going to have to throw me down, I resolved, and asked
Himansu to hand me my case. In the darkness we furtively got
our bags up, he squeezed through, and we sat down, trying to
be inconspicuous. Two Frenchmen came up and a man shouted
at them, pointing down the stairs. Tourists got treated poorly
because everyone assumed they didn't have connections and
couldn't retaliate; with me they couldn't be sure.

We ended up on the rooftop. I lay down, watching clouds un-
dulate in front of a glorious moon and floating, in my mind, up

into the sky to see the ship far below on a vast, glittering sea, taking me away from the shadowy speck that was Gaubolambe.

A year later I got a call from the Strait Island pharmacist, who
mentioned that two young Onge men had drowned. They were
out fishing.

"What were their names?" I screamed into the phone.

"I don't recall."

"Was there someone called Prakash?"

"Yes, I think that sounds like one of them."

"Are you sure?"

"I think it was him."

For some weeks I hoped he'd turn out not to be Prakash. Later,
I learned that he was indeed dead, but I would never be sure how
or why he died.

*Jarawa*

# Hunted

The mirror-like expanse of the surrounding bay . . . how soothing
a sight was it, in contrast with the restless, furious, implacable
passions of the people who called that land and bay their own,
who . . . transformed a scene in which there should have been
the abodes of peace and plenty into a field of contention, strife,
and bloodshed, when civilized men came among them to offer
them a share in the benefits they themselves enjoyed, and to
instruct them in the truths by which their own minds were enlightened.

— Frederic John Mouat, *Adventures and Researches
Among the Andaman Islanders,* 1863

SETTLERS IN THE LATE 1700s, at what is now Port Blair, took
a captive in a skirmish. "He had the mark of a pistol ball
which had gone through his nose, and put out one of his eyes,"
wrote Robert Colebrooke of the Bengal Engineers. Nonetheless,
the man "appeared to be very cheerful, and quite reconciled to his
captivity." He evidently became the source for an Andaman vocabulary that Colebrooke published. It made no sense to later researchers until Portman recognized it as Jarawa spoken with a
Scottish accent: that is, the prisoner was a Jarawa.

Commodore Cornwallis, who was also at hand, desired that the
captive be given the chance to "desert." Accordingly, the man was

sent ashore in a boat to where a few other natives were visible. Overjoyed, he jumped out, threw off his hat, and ran toward them. "They did not immediately recognise him for one of their countrymen, as he had been clothed on board the *Ranger* with a jacket and trousers," Colebrooke observed. But soon he'd shed these accoutrements, whereupon they all raced into the woods.

Exploring up the coast with Cornwallis, Colebrooke spied a lone man fishing, whose hair "was rubbed with a kind of red earth, and the rest of his body smeared with mud. He wore round his neck and left arm a kind of ornament which looked like a fringe of dried grass." Although fearful of being captured, the native readily exchanged his bow and arrow for a knife and avidly ate the biscuits his interlocutors gave him. A couple of days later Cornwallis returned to talk to the same man. This time he was roasting shellfish on a fire, along with a woman and girl, "both perfectly naked and their skins daubed with mud." These people, who were not hostile, were Jarawa.

When the colony was resurrected in 1858, the area was occupied by the Bea. The Jarawa, who'd become friendly with the first settlers, might have been emasculated by some imported disease and thereby lost the territory to their enemies. Never again were the Jarawa seen on that coast, nor were those found elsewhere peaceable.

In the early 1870s, workers cutting roads through the forests of South Andaman would often encounter Jarawa, who'd take their tools but otherwise leave them alone. "[T]hey are milder in disposition," concluded the settlement's chief General Donald Stewart, "than any other section of the Andamanese whom we know." As gifts and germs rapidly diminished the threat from the Great Andamanese, the latter were pressed into the project of catching Jarawa.

Topsy, the Great Andamanese guide, was the first to warn the nineteenth-century colonists of an unfamiliar tribe in the interior jungles. At one time, when Corbyn proposed to explore up a creek, Topsy and Jacko "pathetically enacted" a death scene, showing an arrow piercing the heart and entreating him not to proceed farther. The word Jarawa meant "dark stranger" in the Bea language.

As for the captive Jarawa, Maurice Portman plotted to keep them "with the Officer in Charge of the Andamanese until they are to a certain extent tamed, and learn a little Hindustani; they might also be taught to smoke, thus establishing a craving which intercourse with us can alone satisfy." But the Jarawa proved less tractable than the Onge.

Some convict laborers in pursuit of Jarawa happened upon a group of them dancing. One of the Indians stepped into the clearing, holding up a pair of spectacles; the Jarawa ran, but a young man, who stopped for a moment to look at the glasses, was caught, as was a woman who was too heavy with child to run. After being held for two weeks, they were released. "They visited some of the nearest Homes and ought to have been convinced that we treat the islanders who do not molest us with much consideration and kindness," Stewart reported.

Meanwhile, the Jarawa had taken to killing outsiders they encountered in the jungle. Many tracks had been opened through their territory, explained an officer in 1883, "which they probably took to be a move on our part to hem them in and so capture them on their first appearance." A year later, an expedition sent to avenge the death of a policeman came upon some of the natives collecting honey; in the ensuing fight, one Jarawa died, while another was wounded in the leg and caught, along with a boy.

The injured man, Talai, recovered after about a month. "He was a young and well-made man, with a merry face, and was always full of fun," Portman wrote. Talai stayed in his captor's house and became very friendly with everyone, including the Great Andamanese. But when taken to Rutland Island, south of South Andaman, on another Jarawa search, Talai slipped away. He was tracked to the northern tip of the island, where he'd evidently made a raft and crossed over a strait to his own terrain. Because he'd been treated well since his capture, Portman hoped — in vain, as it turned out — that Talai would induce his compatriots to become more cooperative.

The Jarawa boy, Api, was too young to understand what had happened to him, and played about with the Great Andamanese children. Portman tried to return the lad to his people, but all the huts the party came to were deserted and Api refused to stay alone. Another time he was sent back with two captured Jarawa women who did not know him, but he reappeared, saying he got nothing to eat. "He was very young, accustomed to our ways and food, and had almost forgotten his own language," Portman explained.

Api later proved his worth in being able to converse with the Onge captives. He became very close to Kogio Kai, an Onge who became a guide for the colonists, and was allowed to go live with him on Little Andaman. Api died there, a few months later, of bronchitis. "He was quiet, gentle, and a rather stupid child," was Portman's epitaph.

Another time a girl of three or so was caught, and although adopted by a Great Andamanese woman, she soon succumbed to illness. The main impediment to carrying out his policy, noted Portman, was that "in captivity, the Jarawas sicken and die." That did not deter him from his course — though he was well aware that disease had brought the Great Andamanese to the brink of extinction. "There are very few Andamanese now alive who are acquainted with the Jarawa country," he complained about the lack of skilled trackers, "and those few are old."

At the same time, he commented, the situation had its advantages, for the Jarawa would likely kill any escaped convicts they chanced upon.

Clashes between Jarawa and colonizers worsened over the decades. In 1902, some Jarawa attacked and killed convicts who were felling trees for the forest department. Accordingly, a punitive expedition was dispatched to drive the aboriginals northward and put a stop to their raids. Beginning on the west coast, the British party searched the jungle and soon began to trail a band of Jarawa on their wanderings up a creek. "So close were we to them," officer Percy Vaux wrote in his diary, "that at one place where they had sat down to take their food, we found a live fish that they had caught in the creek." The Jarawa would camp for the night, which was the time to attack.

About four P.M. the Jarawa, oblivious of their pursuers, began to cut saplings to make huts; Vaux could "distinctly hear the voices of men, women and children." He waited until all sounds quieted at about seven-thirty P.M. and dispatched three Great Andamanese trackers to check on the situation. They returned after an hour to report that all the Jarawa were asleep. The attackers then approached, "in nearly absolute silence, at about the pace of a yard a minute," and ultimately could see the huts in the moonlight. All was quiet but for a baby who cried and was hushed to sleep.

As they crept forward, twigs broke underfoot, ultimately waking the sleepers: "[T]here were voices, exclamations, then figures could be seen emerging from the huts. A shot was fired from a rifle, then others, and all was confusion." Vaux caught hold of one woman, but she escaped in the melee; the Great Andamanese shot two arrows into a Jarawa man; and at Vaux's orders a girl of about seven years and a baby boy of ten months were seized. The party then spent the night at the vacated camp, eating the boar, fish, and tubers they found there and shooting off a rifle every fifteen minutes lest the Jarawa come back for their children. At daybreak they followed the blood trail and came upon two arrows, which the injured man had pulled out; but the tracks vanished.

Jarawa expeditions sound astonishingly like tiger hunts of a later period: the lying in wait, the shots in the dark, the following of blood tracks in the morning, even the taking of cubs. Indeed, they may have been even more exciting because, as one forester noted, the Jarawa had "all the skill and cunning of tigers and pan-thers and intelligence of human beings." But this hunt had an un-usual outcome, perhaps because Vaux was insufficiently ferocious for the job.

A contingency was developing: the baby was hungry. It must have been crying piteously, for Vaux changed his plans and the next day proceeded to Lakra Lungta, a point on the west coast where a Great Andamanese woman was known to be with milk. But she'd gone to the jungle and did not return for the night. He then sent the children to Port Blair in the official launch and pro-ceeded to seek more Jarawa.

Again the expedition tracked a band and waited for nightfall. The plan, reported forester C. G. Rogers, was to "rush the camp when the moon rose, and try and capture a woman to suckle the Jarawa baby Mr. Vaux had taken." After dark they spied the glow of smoldering logs and stole forward, holding hands so as to sur-round the camp.

"We crept down into a depression," wrote Rogers, "and then seeing dimly huts in front of us, Mr. Vaux sprang up and rushed forwards to the nearest hut." The Great Andamanese shot arrows into the melee — others had orders not to fire until Vaux signaled. But as he grappled with two people in a hut, he disturbed the em-bers at his feet, which flared into a fire. Seeing him, a Jarawa man in another hut shot two arrows, one of which, a barbed, iron-headed affair, entered Vaux's left side. "I am done!" he cried. "For God's sake take this arrow out." He asked for water and a light but died soon after.

Two women and six children were taken in this attack. Later the women and a few children were released, but two boys were kept along with the infant.

In February 1918, officer D. L. Morgan led an expedition into Jarawa territory. His strength consisted of twelve Great Andaman-ese trackers, sixteen armed policemen, and thirty-five laborers to help with the food and tents. Upon landing on the west coast of South Andaman, he sent an Indian policeman to scout along the beach. The latter returned to report the fresh footprints of nine Jarawa and two convicts.

The next morning Morgan viewed the tracks. "At one point it was clear that a Jarawa father had been fishing from a tree over-hanging the high tide, while his children had been playing on the sand nearby," he concluded. There were ashes from a fire, foot-prints of several more Jarawa — characterized by extremely small size — as well as those of "at least one man whose feet were larger than my own." Astonishingly (and alarmingly, to a British officer), the Jarawa were sheltering an escaped prisoner instead of slaugh-tering him.

Following the tracks along a creek, the party came to a pool of water and camped for the night. "As it happened," Morgan wrote, "had our trackers gone on another [half] of a mile, the exact posi-tion of the Jarawa village would have been discovered, and we could have killed them all early next morning."

At seven A.M. the expedition moved on and soon heard the aboriginals a little ahead. But before they could get "within killing distance," the Jarawa raised an alarm. One of the shouting voices sounded much like an Indian's. The pursuers rushed in, where-upon the Jarawa dropped everything and fled. Morgan saw a woman, a child, a youth, and a grown man, and "put 2 barrels of buck shot into the last at about 15 yards distance." The man dropped his bow and arrows but slipped away.

There was a "great deal of blood" in the creek, and the trackers followed this for some miles until they lost the trail in the jungle. The wounded man must have died an agonized death, for the per-forations caused by buckshot, if not immediately fatal, would get infected. In the next days Morgan found no more Jarawa, though he did come across twenty old encampments, burned two com-munal huts, and carried away an assortment of artifacts such as toy bows used by children.

The jungle was too thick, he concluded, for a group of flat-footed policemen to surprise the Jarawa. But "30 Burmans armed with guns and daos, with some Andamanese to track for them," wrote Morgan, "would wipe out every Jarawa in the place in 2 or 3 years."

The clearing of the forests forced the Jarawa northward into jungles vacated by the dying Great Andamanese. But as logging cut ever more deeply into the jungles, Jarawa resistance increased: on one occasion they even attacked a steam-powered train that was transporting logs, killing the driver and a couple of others. In 1905 the bush police was formed, with twenty Great Andamanese men, to hunt runaway convicts and punish errant Jarawa. "Like the Bushman of South Africa, the Jarawa is implacable and will continue to fight to extermination," predicted the census of 1931.

On a Saturday morning in 1997, a jeep arrived to take me through the Jarawa forest. Along with a driver I had an escort, an engineer from the public works department by the name of Pradip Kumar Dey; the three of us would share the front seat. My host, the lawyer Sen, drew him aside just before we left. Later I asked, in Bengali, what he'd said.

"I should be outside when we pass through Jarawa-infested area."

"So you get the arrow through the head?"

Dey smiled weakly.

The Andaman Trunk Road ran north from Port Blair along the mountain range that formed the Great Andaman's watershed. Opened in 1989, it effectively sliced off the eastern parts of Jarawa territory. The aboriginals had tried to stop its construction by setting up ambushes and roadblocks and would still attack travelers on it.

We navigated past schoolchildren, scooters, and dogs to the outskirts of town, where the traffic thinned out. The road was then bordered with rice fields or an occasional vegetable patch crowned by a hut, perhaps with a TV antenna sticking out of its thatched roof. After two bumpy, dusty hours we took a break at a public works department bungalow, built by the British in an airy style. Dey informed me that the cook, who served us tea and biscuits, had been hit by a Jarawa arrow.

The cook lifted his boxer shorts to show off the scars, black on brown skin. Two years earlier he'd been caretaker of a forest bungalow. One afternoon, while shooing cows out of the garden and beyond the gate, he glanced up to a nearby ridge and spied Jarawa perched there. He turned and ran but was pierced through the thigh by a heavy arrow. "Here's where it entered," he pointed, "and here it came out."

Back in the jeep, Dey offered to take the outer seat: we'd now be entering the reserve. I refused, for I should take the arrow if it came — moreover, since he didn't insist, I figured there was no real danger. Another jeep, with armed police, started up and followed us; at least the arrow wouldn't be through the back of my head.

Soon the forest started to show up, interrupted by agricultural farms and other government projects carved out of it. The fattest, roundest elephant I'd ever seen ambled by with its mahout. To the left, which was the western side, the reserve was thick and green, but whatever forest remained to the right was brown and barren, the evergreens replaced by commercial deciduous trees with leafless branches. We passed a group of road workers guarded by an armed man.

"Did the road have to go through the reserve?" I asked.

"It's so expensive to maintain," Dey pondered. "Have to truck the workers in and truck them out, provide guards. It could have been deviated, by the coast." Then he changed his mind. "It would be too winding if it followed the coast. Would have been a much longer journey."

Abruptly the jungle opened into a clearing with a few huts: a forest department outpost. Cows and chickens were grazing, and on the shoulder was a broken-down bus with passengers sitting around, waiting for rescue. "What do the forest staff do here?" I asked.

"Regenerate the forest." He pointed to a roadside stand of spindly leafless trees with no undergrowth.

"Now that the trees are grown, will they leave?"

"They'll cut them down and regenerate them again."

I glanced at him and decided he wasn't joking. Some more forest and another outpost, complete with tea stall, starving dogs, and huts. A village, really. Dey offered a fable: "The king's horses are given a caretaker. They get ten kilos of food. He keeps five. The horses are getting thin, so another supervisor is appointed. He keeps six kilos, and the caretaker keeps three. So it is with the forests: the more protectors it has, the less forest there is."

Just before we reached Jhirkatang, the last outpost for a while, I saw in the shadows a stack of enormous logs. "The forest department cuts them," Dey explained. The laborers would enter the jungle with elephants and armed guards, and so wouldn't get attacked by the Jarawa. "Our workers don't disturb the jungle," he added. "They just maintain the road."

Silently I thought of the pattern, all over the world. The roads seem innocuous at first, a thin strip cutting through. But they take people into the forest, who chop down the trees and settle in. Many of the outsiders living in the Jarawa reserve were first brought by the public works department to help build the road; after it was finished, they just didn't move.

Beyond Jhirkatang the jungle reared up on either side, coming into its own. Trees more than one hundred feet high dripped with masses of green lianas, lining the roadside in thick drapes. Delicate palm fronds stuck out in places; blue and green birds flitted by overhead, vanishing the instant they entered the foliage. We fell silent, as if under a spell. The primordial power of the curling ferns and the swaying aerial roots, the sheer abundance of life force, harked back to a time when nature ruled and we ran scared.

The jungle was shaved off the shoulders, letting in a strip of sun that glared off the greenery, rendering its depths perfectly opaque. Still, I strained to look in past the leaves and trunks. Sheltering in the unfathomed folds of this forest were humans with whom my people were at war. Someone could be standing behind that giant tree trunk, pulling back the string of his bow. There was a fear in my bones that reminded me of driving through a tiger reserve some weeks earlier.

In places the trees reached in, enveloping the road: it felt cool, peaceful, and green inside the embrace.

A sharp retort rent the air. Startled, I turned in time to catch a grin on Dey's face: the jeep had misfired. "They killed three of our laborers last year," he related. "Really horrible. One had his throat slit, and three arrows stuck in the cut. Another man must have run, hidden, and crouched. The arrow went through the top of his head, out through the chin and into his chest. I'll get you some photos."

"Thanks," I replied feebly.

Around a corner the road disintegrated into bumpy rubble. "It's hard to maintain the surface here because of the Jarawa," he apologized. The shoulder was taken up by gravel piles and a road roller, signifying future hopes of repair. Sometimes the Jarawa came at night, tipped over the tar drums, and shat on the roller, displaying their skill in expressing contempt. A dog limped by, going goodness knows where.

Then the forest was over. We reached the end of South Andaman and waited for the ferry. Inside the turquoise water a shoal of baby fish flowed past like a thick stream of silver. The police jeep left, for the Jarawa farther north posed no danger.

Beyond the creek was Baratang Island, which bridges the strait between South and Middle Andaman. Much of it was Jarawa reserve; but the tallest trees were gone, so the forest looked short and scant. The roadside greenery was plantation, trees set in neat rows so one could see from end to end, and no creature would venture in because it couldn't hide.

Past another strait we reached Middle Andaman and the sizable Bengali town of Kadamtala. The Jarawa in the depleted forests nearby were the friendlier ones who'd been accepting gifts from contact missions. But they came to the villages at night to take bananas and coconuts. The villagers called them Chor, or Thief, Jarawa.

Finally, we came to Mayabunder, a small town at the northern tip of Middle Andaman. The jeep swept into a blue-painted rest house atop a cliff. Indira Gandhi had sat in the garden and said it would be nice if there were steps to the sea; they had since appeared. I walked on the rocks down below, watching crabs scuttle into crevices, and when darkness fell, I headed back up. The breeze was strong, salty, and heady, and the power had been cut. For the first time in years I could see the Milky Way.

In the garden shelter were shadows of several men. Dey's voice introduced me to a superior; I couldn't see the man at all. He had a story about the bush police, who were then assigned to keep the Jarawa and the settlers apart.

"One day they told me, Jarawa will attack. I took no notice, how could they know? Two days later, my cook was attacked, got an arrow in his thigh. I went back to the police and asked, how did you know?

"They said, 'We went to the forest the day before. Saw two Jarawa, killed them.'" He paused. "During my posting there were many Jarawa attacks. All came after we had attacked them."

He stopped to watch as someone carried in a kerosene lantern.

"As long as there are bush police, there will be no peace with the Jarawa. A policeman said to me, 'If there is peace, I will be out of a job.' So . . ." he jerked his arms up and down in a pantomine of letting off a machine gun.

"In Middle Andaman, the Jarawa are more friendly. The contact team goes there with a doctor. The Jarawa called him into a hut to show him a man lying there. He had a bullet wound. The doctor did what he could, can't report it officially."

The next morning we left early, back by the same road to Port Blair. This time I let Dey take the outer seat while I talked to the driver, Haldar, a portly and opinionated Bengali. Through a mouthful of betel leaf he announced that the place was getting spoiled: the Bengalis were getting crowded out by Tamils. "They have all the shops, stick together, get rich."

"What do Bengalis do, farm?" I asked. The roadside was patchworked into rice plots, then dry and shorn. Kingfishers perched on roadside wires and egrets stalked the cows. The picture of rural Bengal — certainly poor.

Haldar had caught the Chor Jarawa in his headlights, running across the road, and seen them by moonlight cutting bananas from the village groves, one man standing on another's shoulder.

"Don't the local people object?"

"What can they do? They shut the windows and sit quietly in their huts."

Haldar hadn't seen the Tirur Jarawa, in the thick forests of South Andaman. "They don't take things, they shoot."

On South Andaman we had the police escort again. Dey took the outer seat. He didn't ask, and only later did I realize this was the dangerous part of the trip. The driver, Francis, a thin and white-haired old man, kept peering into the forest, twisting his head all the way round even as he somehow held the vehicle on the road. In my halting Hindi, I asked if he was afraid.

He grinned thinly. "At four they come out. It's four now. They sit above ground, in trees, on hillocks."

We passed a ridge on which a Jarawa man had perched just the week before to shoot down at a bus. The arrow had glanced off the side.

"Have you seen the Jarawa?"

*"Dekhna to marna."* To see is to die.

I joined Francis in scanning the jungle. He wanted to get through it as fast as he could. But the police jeep kept falling behind, making him even more nervous. The giant trees and their dripping folds of lianas were lit up in orange by the setting sun. An occasional leaf, high up, stirred in a breeze, and the eye flew to it instantly, probing, checking for danger.

## Visions of Control

A s BEFITS THEIR ROLE in the lives of the proletariat, the offices of government lounged on top of the tallest hill in Port Blair, their superior glance passing over the milling multitudes below to rest on the distant bay. The meticulously manicured VIP Road (where but in India would a road have that name?) linking the offices was perpetually abuzz with white Ambassador cars transporting their precious cargo: bureaucrats. The higher the rank, the fewer the digits on the license plate, and, incidentally, the greater the elevation of the official's home.

The arrangement suited me fine, for my abode was conveniently close to the offices I'd have to frequent for permission to visit Jarawa beaches and other tribal areas. Soon after arriving in Port Blair in 1998, I found myself a guest of Superintendent of Police Ujjwal Mishra, a friend of my father's college classmate. He'd left for the Nicobars, and I had a room, a bath, meals, and a houseful of servants to myself.

It wasn't too far up VIP Road to the glittering glass-and-concrete office of the director of tourism and publicity. With a forbiddingly stern expression he read through my resume and mission statement and finally turned to the phone. The director of tribal welfare was not available, but the secretary of tribal welfare was. "Go see him," said the director of tourism.

The secretary of tribal welfare glanced at me with a thoroughly bored expression. "There is a minorities commission here. I can't see you till next week." Trekking back, I told myself that I'd expected this, a runaround.

My pass would need authorization by the lieutenant governor, a Gandhian who'd recently arrived on the islands, but I had to traverse the proper channels to get to his door. After some days I found myself facing the chief secretary, the number two man on the islands. A tall thin man with a clipped accent and stern manner, he got to the point.

"In the past, people who have come to write about the tribes have shown India in a bad light. The tribes used to number thousands when the British came, now they are hundreds. They attribute that all to us."

I searched my conscience. True, I would not have flattering things to say about my countrymen. Was it my patriotic duty to praise them? I explained that the book was a personal project, not shaped by my American connections; I emphasized my scientific interests, downplaying the journalism. But I departed knowing I'd gotten nowhere.

A week later I had an appointment with the LG. He was reputed to be an honest man but addicted to red tape. I dressed carefully in a white cotton *salwaar-kameez* to look Indian, academic, and modest. I was as nervous as a schoolgirl preparing for an exam.

The man was frail and old behind a gigantic desk. He asked in Hindi what my mission was, and I quickly sketched my project: every second of this man's time was valuable. When I was done, he told me in a monotone that it wasn't possible for me to see the Sentinelese, the Jarawa, perhaps even the Great Andamanese. He explained why, but I understood nothing. He would refer the matter to others.

One evening I found my host, Mishra, sitting on the back porch, drenched in sweat from a badminton game with the home secretary. "Would you mind moving?" he asked. He'd been told it was improper to have an unrelated woman in the house. I lugged my bags to a municipal hostel farther up the hill.

Day after day, for the next three weeks, I walked up and down VIP Road, pleading my case fruitlessly to one dour-faced official after another. One evening I returned to my lodging to find that the lights were out: there wasn't enough diesel fuel to illuminate the marina as well as the desks of schoolchildren, studying for their final exams by candle flame.

I sat on one of the concrete pillars lining the road, and the hostel's dog came up to greet me. I reached out a hand to fondle her scruffy ear, thinking all at once of Jack Andaman lying down on deck with the ship's dog. I needed to touch a warm being, for the hostility and suspicion surrounding me had been bruising. She stretched out on the tarmac beside me and together we watched the scooters put-put by and a few men strolling in the darkness. Eventually I began to sing songs by the poet-philosopher Rabindranath Tagore that spoke of striving and humanity and justice, and it soothed my soul.

We, the administrators were telling me, hold moral authority and the right to judge you. The poetry shredded such posturings, reminded me of the caring among creatures that is at the root of all morals or should be. After an hour, when the lights came on, I'd recovered my strength, and the dog and I walked through the hostel gates.

Samir Acharya talked fast, in a mixture of English and Bengali. Thick black-framed glasses distorting his eyes, hair slicked back from his forehead, and a cloud of cigarette smoke shrouding his face, he looked unprepossessing. In the time I'd spent on the islands, though, I'd learned to respect him as a Bengal tiger who fiercely protected the things he loved. He was a true descendant of the freedom fighters who languished in Cellular Jail, a defender of the country.

Acharya ran a small business selling scientific equipment; the rest of the time he battled for the islands, their forests, beaches, and corals.

During the reign of an earlier lieutenant governor, he related, businessmen from the mainland would fly in with suitcases full of cash in the hope of buying timber. Wood could be exported only with a permit, which the LG would grant to certain politicians, to be instantly sold for large sums. The logs were extracted from legally protected forests in such numbers that bare patches began showing up in satellite scans.

Almost all the felling on the Andamans was done by the forest department and its contractors. (The exception was the government corporation devoted to denuding Little Andaman.) I queried an officer, N. Kala, about logging in reserve forests. "After some years trees die and are wasted," she explained. "We have to remove them."

I stared at her in stupefaction. Kala was with the forest department's wildlife wing, and dead trees are vital to wildlife. Insects breed in the decaying wood, which provides food and shelter to birds, small mammals, and reptiles, which in turn fuel the chain of life all the way up. "Timber is the only source of revenue on the islands," she added.

I asked for numbers.

"That I don't have." Somehow, no official could provide specifics — figures, charts, maps. Maps showing the boundaries of the Jarawa reserve were especially secret.

Acharya had a comment on the earnings of the forest department. "Frequently they do juggleries in arithmetic. A lot of the expenditure they take out, saying this is service rendered to the nation." Such costs included those of buildings, jeeps, and boats. If these were accounted for, it seemed timber was being exported from the Andamans at a net loss.

I pressed a friendly forest officer on the piles of logs I'd seen the year before along the Andaman Trunk Road.

The divisional forest officers were assigned quotas for timber extraction, he finally explained. During the fag end of the financial year, they tried desperately to meet their targets, taking trees from the edges of the Jarawa reserve. "It's quicker to extract along the road," he added. "The department doesn't own up to this happening."

The elephants used to extract timber were let loose to graze in the Jarawa reserve at night. A mahout entered the forest with an armed escort to find his steed when needed; the guards would shoot the Jarawa at sight.

"No one enters the Jarawa reserve," Kala stated blandly.

When Veer Bahadur, a logging elephant, went into musth, he would sometimes stand on the Andaman Trunk Road, swaying from foot to foot and blocking traffic. After a while his mahout would show up and patiently persuade Veer Bahadur to step aside.

One fateful day Veer Bahadur stopped the chief secretary's car. The CS stormed into the office of the chief conservator of forests to rail about the insult.

Being a government employee, Veer Bahadur could not be fired. Instead he was transferred to Havelock Island. But his mahout remained on South Andaman; consequently, Veer Bahadur defied control and escaped into the jungle. He took along with him three female elephants belonging to a timber contractor.

Veer Bahadur was a valuable elephant, but any loss to the government is readily written off. The contractor, though, wanted his animals back, and timber contractors had a direct line to the former lieutenant governor. The order went out to catch Veer Bahadur. Foresters protested, to no avail, that capturing a testosterone-flooded pachyderm is a dangerous and difficult task.

So a large party ventured into the jungle with a tranquilizer gun. Unfortunately, Veer Bahadur had watched a gun being used many a time. He trampled the man who pointed one at him.

Now he was a rogue and had to be shot. The contractor got his elephants back, and, according to Samir Acharya, Veer Bahadur's two front feet were transformed into wastepaper baskets.

In 1985 Romulus Whitaker, an independent researcher from Madras, estimated that only 77 percent of the islands' area was still forested; in 1998, Acharya gauged the forest cover to be less than 70 percent. (The official figure was 86 percent.) Most of the surviving jungle was devoid of the largest, oldest trees.

When the canopy provided by the tall trees was gone, the summer sun reached to the forest floor, drying it out. The rain forest never recovered. This year five forest fires had raged on the Andamans, where they'd been virtually unknown. "The only pristine forest left," concluded Acharya, "is on some very remote islands and in the Jarawa territory. The Jarawa are protecting the jungle."

Since timber was hardly available for use on the islands — it was all sold to mainland businessmen — construction required cement and steel shipped from Calcutta or Madras at great expense, and sand lifted from increasingly scarce beaches. The buildings thus made were unsafe, for the sand was lightweight and the concrete quickly developed cracks. What's more, the Andamans sat atop a tectonic fault and could have a major earthquake at any time.

An even more critical problem was that of water. In the 1950s the archipelago had nine months of rain, but in the 1990s it had five. To what extent the paucity of rain was due to the lack of forest cover is unclear. Tropical forests increase humidity and invite clouds; certainly the monsoons had receded in coincidence with the felling of jungles.

Everyone agreed that the lack of forest cover caused rain to run off. It didn't get caught in the undergrowth and had no time to sink into the water table. By mid-May 1998, the dam that supplied Port Blair had only a foot of water left. In the average home the taps ran every other day for ten minutes — and at five A.M., a bone-tired housewife told me.

TREE MEANS WATER. WATER MEANS BREAD. So said a forest department sign, appropriately placed by a pile of logs at a jetty. White banners exhorted the public to save water: EVERY DROP IS PRECIOUS. But near the Marina stood a fountain, spraying water up in fine droplets that I estimated to vaporize at least fifty gallons a day, and by it was a huge open-air swimming pool that was usually bereft of swimmers but complete with a cascading waterfall. The guest houses had ample water, as did the VIP homes. Conservation, it seemed, was for everyone but the administration.

The Indian mainland subsidized the Andaman and Nicobar Islands to the tune of at least $125 million a year, Acharya estimated. That came to Rs. 17,000 or so per person, more than the income of an average Indian. The numbers eviscerate the logic of settling refugees, or anyone else, on the Andamans. Every necessity of life — rice, lentils, wheat, potatoes, clothes, medicine, umbrellas, utensils, you name it — had to be shipped over, with the price of passage largely borne by taxpayers.

Government functionaries supplemented their incomes by peddling their multifarious powers. As a result, the black market had undergone inflation. To be appointed a schoolteacher on even a remote island like Car Nicobar could cost a year's salary in bribes. A family with no one in government service was correspondingly impoverished.

The most senior bureaucrats came from the mainland and were assigned terms of only two to three years for fear that they would develop corrupt ties with local officials. But they also got little time to develop a commitment to the islands. The rare administrator who tried to do his job was sure to step on someone's toes. "If you happen to do something, you will be punished for it," Mishra said in a rare burst of bitterness. "If you manage to do nothing you will become an important man" — rising through the ranks.

No one was responsible for the resulting mess. One could always blame the previous administration, a long line of pointing fingers fading into history.

From the 1950s to the late 1990s, the population of the Andamans grew twelve times because of immigration. The member of parliament from the islands was a Bengali and encouraged the inflow of people from West Bengal and Bangladesh; his Tamil rival pushed migration from Tamil Nadu and other southern states. These populations, which served as vote banks, were growing in frantic competition with one another.

The migrants cleared the forest and settled in. "Three hundred and fifty [settler] families live within the margins of the Jarawa reserve," said a forest official who declined to give his name. "If we try to evict them, politicians object." The member of parliament had been known to suggest that the Jarawa be rounded up and placed on another island, so that their forests would become available to his people.

The bottom line: the aboriginals didn't vote. Even if they did, their votes would have come to naught against those of a few hundred thousand outsiders who coveted their forests. So the senior administrators, even the well-intentioned ones, didn't take the essential step: preventing encroachment of Onge or Jarawa territory. That would invite the wrath of other bureaucrats and the politicians.

The authorities did have other tasks at hand. I wouldn't be permitted to visit the Jarawa, the chief secretary told me. "It's for your safety," he added.

The home secretary — small, thin, severe — had a further explanation: "We don't allow ladies." But women had been on the contact trip, I pointed out (wives of several officials, I didn't point out).

"Only in disguise."

"I'm willing to be disguised," I replied, astounded.

He ignored me. "You will get the permit. But we will restrict some areas."

The LG, I finally learned, was distressed at the thought of an unmarried — and presumably virginal — Indian woman interacting with the unclothed Jarawa. So with the chief secretary and the home secretary he'd instituted a new policy, of which I was the only victim so far: the Jarawa contact trip was for men.

Sita Venkateswar, the anthropologist, was the lone female on three contact missions. Most team members, she observed, were far from shy of naked bodies; rather, some of the men assumed a familiarity with the Jarawa women that "veers towards the prurient."

Flipping through a book of speeches given by the former lieutenant governor, I found he often referred to the Andamans as the "lush green" islands. In one place, a typing error had replaced the *n* with a *d*. If a *t* had also taken the place of the *h*, I mused, the phrase would have aptly described the modern Land of Naked People: lust greed.

# With the Enemy

While she was in the prison hospital at Port Blair she made several attempts to pull the clothes off her wardress and tear out
her hair, and she had to be kept in an empty cell and treated like
a wild animal . . . [B]ut as it was obvious that she could never be
tamed, it was decided to release her.

— *Blackwood's Magazine,* on a Jarawa captive, 1938

AROUND 1905, as forester Durgaprasad told a younger officer,
a convict laborer named Chacko was captured by the Jarawa.
Five or six of them closed in quietly and forced him to walk to
their camp. For days he was bound hand and foot and closely
guarded. But eventually, when his captors believed he was reconciled to his new life, he was married to a Jarawa woman with
whom he had two children. After seven years of jungle life, one
day he found himself in forests near his old village and deserted
his jungle family.

The next kidnapping by Jarawas doesn't show up, in the records
I perused, until 1975. The Jarawa attacked some settlers who were
searching for decorative shells, injuring three men and retaining
one; the police report didn't say if he ultimately returned. Four
men taken over the next ten years seem to have similarly vanished. Acharya described hearing of desperate messages for help
scrawled on the sand.

In 1986, an outsider cutting wood near the forest's edge was terrified to find arrows dropping nearby. Four or five Jarawa men suddenly surrounded him, held his mouth shut, and carried him into the jungle. There they removed his clothes, tied his hands, and took him to their shacks. The women laughed at his plight, while the kids amused themselves by pricking him with arrows or pretending to shoot him. But his captors did not intend further harm, the young man later told anthropologist Jayanta K. Sarkar. They untied his hands and offered him some pork they'd been cooking; and later, when he ran, came after him but ultimately let him get away.

As logging trails and villages pushed deeper into Jarawa territory, outsiders and aboriginals were forced into a tragic intimacy, exemplified by the kidnappings — on both sides.

Of the numerous Jarawa children seized by punitive expeditions, few survived. The 1931 census noted a seven-year-old Jarawa boy studying at a Catholic mission school in Ranchi, eastern India; he'd been taken in infancy during a campaign that claimed to have shot dead thirty-seven of his compatriots. Although described as "happy" living with a family of the Oraon tribe, he sometimes displayed a "violent temperament," eating earth in fits of rage. "It is hoped that some day he will return to the Andamans as a forester," wrote the census officer, M.C.C. Bonington.

That would have been ironic indeed, given that his job would be to decimate the very jungles his relatives died defending. But he fell to dysentery at the age of twelve.

A few Jarawa children, captured in 1938, fared slightly better. The Jarawa had killed a bush policeman and two others who were hunting near a forest outpost in Middle Andaman. In retaliation, police commandant A. Denis M. McCarthy organized a posse to chase the Jarawa from Middle to South Andaman while he stationed an ambush on diminutive Bluff Island, which the Jarawa would approach when crossing the strait. About fifty Jarawa were on a raft when police boats surrounded them and opened fire. Many died, others dropped into the water and got away, and an eight-year-old girl was shot and captured. Also taken were three boys, aged two, three, and four, and their young mother, who could have swum but preferred to share their fate.

Given biscuits, she was suspicious and at first wouldn't let her children have any, recalled forest officer B. S. Chengapa. The captives were placed in the charge of an Indian major and his wife. The girl's wound healed with treatment, and she came to be called Topsy. But the captured mother, whose name was Bathana, neglected Topsy while she lavished care on her three sons. She refused to learn Hindi, insisted on speaking Jarawa with the children, and instructed them to provide no information about their past lives. At the time of capture she was pregnant, and in six months gave birth to a boy.

Kept on Ross Island, Bathana would sometimes throw off her clothes and climb up the tallest tree, perhaps to gaze at distant jungles, or swim off a mile as if to escape. But the umbilical cord always pulled her back. After two years McCarthy built a shed on the edge of the Jarawa forest and left the family there with rice, utensils, and other provisions. Bathana would have rejoined her people, but the children didn't want to leave. Instead they would wander naked in the jungle all day and return to the hut at night.

Then the Japanese invaded, and everyone forgot about the Jarawa family. Over the next few years one of the older boys died and so did Bathana, after having a child by a local villager. At the end of the war Topsy and the three remaining Jarawa children were delivered to the care of John Richardson, a missionary on Car Nicobar.

The native-born Richardson had heroically defended his brethren from their Japanese tormentors; as a result, almost the entire population of the Nicobars converted to his Anglican faith after the war. A visitor described "some wonderful singing" of hymns at a school he ran. "Among the brown pupils I noticed three little boys as black as coal, with glittering pop-eyes," wrote Compton Mackenzie. The Jarawa boys wore blue shorts and shirts, with one sporting a small light bulb around his neck: "They were reported to be very naughty, but details of their naughtiness were withheld."

Anthropologist Asutosh Bhattacharya, traveling with two colleagues, met the children and their mentor at the jetty of Car Nicobar in 1949. Dede, the oldest boy, was given to running away to wander for hours by the seashore, where he'd pick up shellfish and eat them raw, then finally return home drained. Poppy was fearful and easily startled — from the trauma of his capture, Richardson guessed. Appa, who was born in captivity, was solitary and would sit apart while the other kids played.

Topsy was eighteen at the time, but with her slight, undeveloped frame, looked like a girl of at most nine. The scar from her bullet wound was clearly visible on her upper arm; her clothes were oversized hand-me-downs, and her toilette devoid of vanity. She was a headache, Richardson complained to Bhattacharya, for she'd flirt with his servants, and he couldn't imagine how to marry her off, for the Nicobarese were contemptuous of her.

As the men discussed her character, Topsy looked up with a glance that was serene and deep, but when asked about her capture she just looked down. Bhattacharya's companions now began to take photographs. She stood "still as a black stone goddess" while the anthropologists, prancing around her, subjected her to close-ups of her face, her hair, her pelvis, her elbow, her knees, even her immature bust, so that they could use the pictures for research.

The census of 1951 described Topsy reading with ease Nehru's famous letters to his daughter, written in English. "She and her three little brothers are doing arithmetic sums, and reading Hindi and their receptivity is amazingly good," the document noted. The youngest would, however, vanish into the jungle for days, and Richardson, by then a bishop, had to "use the birch to domesticate him." Evidently only two of the boys grew into adulthood, for a footnote in Cipriani's book tells us that "two Jarawas held in the Nicobars" showed no facial hair. (This feature, Cipriani noted, was unlike a Jarawa head collected in 1951.) Topsy eventually married a Nicobarese man and lived to an old age.

During the Japanese occupation, British commandos landed by submarine on the Great Andamans in spying ventures known as Operation Baldhead. The soldiers spent months in Jarawa territory, hiding in the jungle and traveling at night by boat while they gathered military information. One group, led by officer T. V. Croley, repeatedly stumbled on the Jarawa. Although heavily armed, the intruders did not shoot. Ultimately they came to be somewhat trusted: if they chanced upon a native camp, the women and children would run and hide while the men watched from behind trees.

Croley would examine the foodstuffs to identify everything edible, leave a small gift, and retreat. "The nearest I have got to anyone was perhaps 20 feet," he wrote. Curiously, among his offerings were iron arrowheads from a tribe in eastern India; these the Jarawa would immediately work into their own design.

Several Indian tribals and Karen Burmese — descendants of laborers brought over for logging — were living in the jungle at this time to escape Japanese roundups. According to the forester Chengapa, the Jarawa ignored them and allowed them to roam in their vicinity. But on two occasions the British soldiers, who did not reveal their presence, watched villagers from settlements near Port Blair stalk empty Jarawa camps with "every intention of causing trouble." Jarawa raids on forest camps, Croley opined, were always in retaliation for harm done to them.

For his part, McCarthy, the police superintendent who'd ambushed Topsy's band, roamed the forests at around the same time as did his former captives — and not surprisingly, his group had violent encounters with the Jarawa. When McCarthy withdrew from the islands, he left supplies for future operations on South Andaman, surrounded by a brick wall and primed with grenades in order to keep off the Jarawa.

Accountant M. L. Gupta decided in 1948 to see Jarawa in the jungle. After all, he'd spent eighteen years on the Andamans and was due to return to the mainland, where he'd have nothing to talk about. One could hardly tell stories about accountancy, he confided to anthropologist Bhattacharya.

Accordingly, in October 1948 Gupta and three other civil servants took a launch to Spike Island, in the strait between South and Middle Andaman (and just north of Bluff Island, where Topsy had been captured). After an elaborate lunch, the adventurers, each carrying a gun, disembarked with several bush police and trekked through the jungle. Soon one of them spied four or five Jarawa walking along the shore and shouted an alarm. Seeing the startled aboriginals reaching for their bows, the man fired. A youth and a boy came running toward the intruders, but, being shot at, raced back to the sea and jumped in; another Jarawa was wounded in the leg and leaped into the water as well. The sightseers kept firing over their heads so that they wouldn't return to shore.

The barrage of shots forced the swimmers into a deep channel, bordered by steep cliffs, between two islands. At length, two exhausted Jarawa were pulled onto a boat; the wounded man drowned, as probably did the boy. The civil servants trusted that their presence of mind in capturing two wild men alive would be duly appreciated by their superiors. Their one regret, Bhattacharya learned, was that the "war paint" had been washed off while they swam, and so could not be exhibited as proof of Jarawa savagery.

The two captives were kept in the home of forest officer Chengapa, whose wife wanted to study their language. She did not get far. One night three weeks later, when their guard fell asleep, they unbolted the locks and fled. They must have made it back to the jungles, for they were not seen again.

After forty-nine years in the Andaman police, Bakhtawar Singh had retired. I found him an imposing figure in khurta-pyjamas, a long flowing white beard, pale blue turban, and eyes obscured by thick glasses. Singh had joined the force in 1935, as an eighteen-year-old driven by poverty or restlessness from a home in Punjab to serve the British on this distant shore.

In those years, the Jarawa were on South and Middle Andaman, all the way up to Mayabunder, and punitive expeditions were frequent. "There were great casualties," Singh remembered. When the Japanese came, they installed a cannon on a beach belonging to the Tirur Jarawa. The tribe objected, killing two soldiers (one officer, in another version) with their arrows. So the Japanese had bombed their huts, with casualties unknown.

In 1952, Indian authorities settled Bengali refugees onto clearings deep within Jarawa territory, using punitive expeditions and police posts to drive aboriginals from the area. At the same time, the bureaucrats resumed Portman's policy of dropping gifts, so as to eventually "come to some understanding" with the Jarawa. Over the years, contact missions entirely replaced the punitive ones. "If you maltreat them and fight them, they never get friendly," Singh elaborated. The government boat would approach by sea, leave offerings on the beach, and retreat: "They see us, we see them."

One night in 1968, the villagers of Kadamtala were woken by a commotion: thieves! It had been raining; when the intruders ran single file toward the jungle, one slipped and fell, and he and two behind him were caught. They slashed at their captors with a knife, a schoolteacher losing his finger.

A Jarawa man in his twenties and two teenagers were taken to Port Blair. On the ship, anthropologist Triloki Pandit observed that they looked fearful. One would talk in a long monologue while the others kept silent, then another would start talking. They were housed at Cellular Jail, being given fish, rice, and other foods that they cooked themselves. Out on an evening stroll, they were offered a green coconut. ("One took two sips, passed it to the other, he took two sips and passed it on, and so on," Pandit recalled. "The spirit of sharing, how imbued it is in them.")

The captors also took them on jeep rides and technology tours. One time they saw the inside of a passenger plane and met a stewardess; later they watched the aircraft take off. "They had tremendous curiosity about new technology, and puzzlement," Pandit said, and would finger a jeep's steering wheel and engine, trying to figure them out.

After a month the authorities returned the Jarawa to the forest. Pandit believes it was this experience that eventually induced the Jarawa to accept gifts from the contact mission. The first friendly contact occurred early in 1974. When the boat landed, two Jarawa men who were thatching the roofs of their huts hid in the jungle. "We put the gifts there, went back to sea, and waited," said Bakhtawar Singh. "Next day two Jarawa swam to the boat, and we pulled them on board."

With repetition, the trips led to some familiarity. A photograph in a 1975 *National Geographic* revealed Singh stripped to the waist, with a grinning kid trying to get his hands to meet around the visitor's ample paunch. Another picture depicted a luscious Jarawa woman dancing with joy; evidently this image, torn from the issue, relieved Nelson Mandela's days in a prison cell.

When Heinrich Harrer and the King of Belgium visited the Andamans in 1974, they were invited on a contact tour with the Jarawa. They remained on board while Bakhtawar Singh went to the beach in a boat and brought over some Jarawa men and women. A deafening shout announced their arrival, as the aboriginals swung onto the ship "singing, shouting, gesticulating, dancing, jumping" and breaking on deck like a wave. An intimate ball of arms, legs, and bodies formed while the aboriginals perused the first whites they'd gotten their hands on.

"The Jarawa examined us like some strange objects that a storm tide had thrown onto their beach," Harrer wrote. They tugged on buttons, reached into pockets, and pulled hair. Spying the gleam of gold in a Belgian's mouth, they forced apart his jaws and scrutinized his tooth filling. Discovering a ballpoint pen, they watched with interest as someone drew with it on his palm. One man, evidently not sure if Harrer was male — he had longish hair at the time — reached into his pants and triumphantly displayed the proof to his friends. Yet another was attracted by the king's eyes and tugged at the skin on his face in the hope of exposing more blue.

Right away the Jarawa had claimed the colorful strips of cloth fluttering from a pole. Now Singh unpacked other presents: colorful glass beads, a big aluminum pot filled with meat, a steel hatchet, and a spade. The chief commissioner had insisted that he would not interfere with the Jarawa's lives, and Harrer noted the dissonance between the statement and the gifts. He had once presented a hatchet to a chieftain in New Guinea, explaining that it could cut trees faster. "Why do it faster?" the man had asked, and Harrer had to agree. Such things could only break the rhythm of the others' finely tuned lives.

The disruption Harrer feared came to the fore in 1977 when a Jarawa man of sixty and another of about thirty refused to get off the contact boat and were brought to Port Blair. "They were very delighted when they saw electric lights of Port Blair from mid sea," noted Bakhtawar Singh in a government report. The two stayed in a guest house for seven days, sleeping under a mosquito net and feasting on pork, fish, sweet potatoes, and other delicacies. After eating meat, they would paint their faces with red clay that they dug up in the garden. Driven around in a jeep, they were "thrilled" by the shops arrayed with fruit and awed by the dam (especially, one suspects, the older man, who may have remembered the site differently). They were intrigued by Loka and other Great Andamanese they were introduced to. As a member of the bush police, Loka was involved in Jarawa shootings of the 1940s: he once showed an anthropologist a site where several bodies had been buried. But the Jarawa did not seem to have recognized him.

Even this interaction was less significant than that with the Jarawa teenager En Mei, who was caught in 1996. He stayed in Port Blair for five and a half months, being treated for a broken leg. In the first days, sightseers filing past his hospital bed, four abreast, caught only a flash of frightened eyes as En Mei tried to hide under the bedclothes. The welfare staff treated the boy to a video of a contact mission, hoping to evoke comforting memories; but the moving images reduced him to gurgling terror.

In time En Mei became enamored of TV and other gadgets, as well as the elaborate cuisine of his hosts. "We said he shouldn't be fed masala," Bakhtawar Singh complained. "They said, 'Who is going to cook separately for him at a hospital?'" After his leg healed, the welfare staff returned him to Lakra Lungta, a beachside Jarawa camp at the southwestern tip of Middle Andaman. But En Mei took to demanding roti from the contact personnel, who would take him aside to give him some.

Far more startling, the next year En Mei started bringing some of his Jarawa friends to the jetty near Kadamtala. They swam and trekked for hours to get there, tarried awhile, took the coconuts and bananas they were given, and left.

"Why don't you just go there?" Singh suggested. "You might get to meet them."

# State of War

TOGETHER WITH a youngish man, Nasim — another acquaintance discovered by my father — I took trips to villages near the Jarawa reserve. In Tirur, just two hours' drive northwest of Port Blair, a farmer walked us across a bare field under the burning sun and pointed to a rivulet at the forest's edge. A month ago, in February 1998, Phoolmala Haldar was trying to catch fish there when the Jarawa shot her through the back of the head. She was sixty-three. I looked into the ditch; it had only eight inches of water. You'd have to be desperate to fish in there.

The Jarawa then leaped across into the fields, beckoning to another woman who was nearby. "They were calling me to come and get killed," she related. When she screamed, Phoolmala's son came running, and so did other men. The Jarawa vanished into the jungle.

"You could smell where they had stood," the farmer told me. "They smell so bad, don't clean themselves. We have to go into the forest for cane and leaves. We take dogs, they go ahead and if they smell Jarawa they come running back."

Many settlers believed that the Jarawa would not slay at random but targeted those who used their forests and streams. The police had warned Phoolmala not to go to that ditch, which was too close to the jungle. "When my time comes, it will come," she'd replied dismissively. Her family and others were settled here in a patch of cleared forest in the middle of Jarawa territory in the 1950s. On the barren soil the lush jungle yielded, the villagers tried to grow rice and a few vegetables. "They should put the Jarawa on another island," the farmer declared, handing me a slice of watermelon. "How can we live with them?"

Police officer Z. D. Khan had investigated a killing the year before. An uncle and nephew had gone fishing in the Jarawa streams. The nephew was shot through the heart; the uncle pulled out an arrow through his hip and managed to run to a bush police post. Later Khan took an armed party into the jungle on two boats to look for the nephew's body. They were stopped by arrows dropping into the water ahead: the Jarawa were on the banks, shouting and threatening.

Fearing an encounter, the police boats retreated toward the sea, upon which the Jarawa vanished into the jungle. "I thought maybe they would set up an ambush near the mouth of the channel, so I gave instructions to stay near the other bank," Khan related. Indeed, the Jarawa were waiting; some seventy arrows came at them, all falling short. Khan showed me a small arrow, two and a half feet long; the iron arrowhead was exquisitely crafted.

"From the bank they were calling us, 'Ao, ao'" — which in Hindi would mean "Come, come." A few days later Khan tried again, this time with dogs, and found the body. "They'd cut off the right foot, stabbed him on both knees and arms, many times. There were no eyes, maybe fish ate these."

At Kadamtala in Middle Andaman I met a shrunken man with a large cut across his scalp, crisscrossed by fresh stitches. He was fishing with four other men in a stream in the Jarawa forest when they attacked. One of the party was killed instantly by an arrow through his temple.

On the wounded man's arm was another scar. The arrow went through the arm, and when he jumped into the water and tried to swim, the arrow got in his way. So he pulled it out and kept swimming.

"Will you go fishing there again?" I queried.

He folded his hands, invoking the protectress Kali. "Never."

Two months before, in early 1998, three men from Burma had staggered out of the forest into the Bengali settlements. They'd landed on the western beaches for timber. The Jarawa had attacked them, killing some; the rest had reportedly fled in their launch. But the settler Kartik, who went to the Jarawa streams to fish — though his brother was killed there seven months ago — said he'd seen thirteen bodies lying in the forest, along with an abandoned boat.

Late one night at a forest outpost, bush policeman Mahanand Tapoo switched on the light to call his station. An arrow slid into his stomach. He turned off the light, pulled out the arrow, bandaged himself, and started shooting.

"Could you see them?" I asked.

"I shot into the air," he replied. Or so were the instructions. First several rounds of blank fire, then live rounds above their heads. "They know the sound of blank fire. For live rounds they run. They can hear the bullets go past." Another arrow passed through the bamboo walls of the hut and into Tapoo's kidney, which had to be removed.

And in a recent attack, the night before Phoolmala died, the Jarawa had gathered around an elevated police post and shaken its pillars violently in an attempt to bring it down. It held. But one policeman was stunned by an arrow, and two others became nervous wrecks. The posts had since been provided with flares. The nightly fireworks, plus blaring Hindi music, had been keeping the Jarawa away.

"We have no security," complained a policeman. "The public shouts at us because we can't protect them, and the officers shout at us if we use live fire." One officer had recommended that the police posts, which were deep in the jungle, be brought in close to the villages, so as to better protect them. But the village headmen and the politicians wouldn't allow it. "The people who go to the forest to hunt, they spend the night in the police posts," the policeman explained. "They don't want the posts brought in, they feel safer going into the forest because of them."

The stated purpose of the bush police posts was to protect the Jarawa from the settlers, and vice versa. But in reality they served as bases for poachers — and prevented Jarawa groups from moving freely. Some of the posts were four miles deep, in a jungle that was often only eight miles wide. In effect, they cut the area of the Jarawa reserve down to two-thirds or less of the demarcated three-hundred–odd square miles.

An engineer's wife who lived in Kadamtala for many years told me a singular tale from the 1990s. Six men went to a Jarawa locale to hunt pigs with a gun they'd paid a forest guard for. Two stayed in the boat and kept watch while the other four went ashore. "They took things from the Jarawa huts," she related, "and killed two children." (The Jarawa adults had gone to find food, leaving behind kids who were too big to carry but too small to traipse along.)

The Jarawa were not far away; they must have seen or heard the intruders, for they were watching from behind the trees. When they attacked, the gun failed to go off. Seeing the turn of events, the men in the boat started to move away. The Jarawa shot arrows at them: one died, while the other had his nose cut off. He jumped into the water and returned home after two days of swimming. "He hid there without a word to anyone," said the woman; but there was a commotion because the others didn't come back. So the police went to his house, where he told them what had transpired.

The police took a big party and searched the area, bringing

back three bodies hacked to pieces. They showed the remains around, saying, "This is what will happen if you go there."

One evening Nasim and I strolled into Kadamtala, asking to hear Jarawa stories. An old man pulled his rope-webbed cot under the streetlight, and soon a small crowd gathered to listen.

"We came here on August 11, 1954," he began in Bengali. "There was nothing here but jungle. The forest department had cut some trees, but we had to clear out the stumps and branches. For three months we had no food at times, except for the pumpkins we grew. One man died from just living on pumpkins.

"Then, the Jarawa wouldn't shoot. They would hit the mangrove roots, make a thump you can hear from very far away. To warn, 'We are here, don't come.'" (The Jarawa drum signals to one another on the flaring buttress roots, anthropologist Pandit believes.)

"One day I said to this young boy, 'I'll show you a Jarawa home.' We rowed for three hours north to a hut on shore. We looked in, and when we came out, I threw a fishing net in the water. Suddenly the boy saw a Jarawa aiming his arrow at us. We started screaming and running, and he missed. We jumped into the water and swam to our boat, got slashed from head to foot on the corals." He pulled up his vest to show me the scars on his stomach.

"It used to rain here nine months a year," he continued. "Now that the forests are gone it rains for five months only. They don't have enough water or food. We Bengalis are greedy. We go into the forest for bamboo, cane, we kill their boar. We made them hostile."

On South and Middle Andaman, the streams flow mostly eastward, out of the Jarawa forest into settled areas. The police post they recently attacked overlooked one of the rivulets in the reserve that both settlers and Jarawa used. This summer Jarawa attacks had intensified: from what I could see, an outsider was getting killed every week, far more often than the year before. Villagers said the aboriginals were coming out of the forest in search of food and water.

Early one morning, back in Port Blair, I awoke to a phone call informing me that some Jarawa had shown up at Kadamtala jetty. In a frenzy of excitement I bathed, dressed, and was on my way with Nasim in half an hour. The driver raced over the potholed road, wiping sweat from his forehead every few minutes. When we stopped in a small town, I bought a cascade of ripe bananas from a roadside stall. At the jetty a small boat was waiting for us.

I could scarcely see them, so perfectly did their forms blend with the light and shade of the mangroves. The policemen had hidden them in a dinghy under the trees, far from the crowds on the jetty. As our boat drew near, a Jarawa man leaned forward and put out his hand. I touched his fingers with mine, and couldn't help turning over my palm to look at the tips in wonder.

Their faces were curious, excited, searching my face as intently as I searched theirs. Should I have been surprised that after thousands of years of our being separated, their expressions were so readable to me?

They were all boys and men, clad in waistbands, armbands, headbands, and necklaces, made of leaves and shells and red threads. They had no facial, body, or pubic hair that I could see. They were not self-conscious about nakedness, and in that heat, it was my neck-to-ankle clothing that felt out of place. Wearing only ornaments seemed natural and logical.

I broke off a banana and offered it to a small boy who bore a bold look and regal posture that belied his size. He smiled, accepted it as though it was a tribute, and peeled it, the yellow and white brilliant against his dark brown skin. The Bengali fishermen called him Raja and had taught him a Hindi movie song.

Then the others pointed to the bananas as well, keeping me busy. The boat was full of bananas and coconuts given by the Department of Tribal Welfare. One young man tugged at my T-shirt;

I'd made the mistake of wearing red, a coveted color. I shook my head regretfully. I couldn't give him my shirt and still hope to keep this visit secret from the powers in Port Blair. I couldn't tell if he understood the gesture.

Sitting down next to Raja, I gingerly touched his hair, tiny tight curls laid flat on the scalp. Between the curls, bare skin showed through, as if the head had been meticulously shaved. It was peppercorn hair, as on Kalahari Bushmen and Congo Pygmies. I tried out some words that Bakhtawar Singh had taught me: *ino* for "water" (splashing a little for emphasis) and *ani pika wor* for "ornament" (touching the threads around his neck). But he looked puzzled and chatted instead in long sentences while I stared at him blankly. Eventually he realized that I understood nothing and slowed down to single words: "Lele, lele."

En Mei, whose sojourn in Port Blair had led to this outing, sat at one end of the boat, bantering with the local fishermen. He was a young man, and he looked self-possessed, confident, sure of his status as the one who communed with the enemy. In his hand he held a flashlight someone had given him.

One Jarawa man squatted apart, watching the proceedings. This was the first time, they said, that he'd visited the jetty. He looked awed and apprehensive, but before long a disbelieving smile spread over his face. Like me, he was astonished at this meeting between peoples normally at war.

A young man to my right put an arm around me and with the other cupped my left breast, looking intently at my face for a reaction. The touch was gentle, so I didn't protest. Then he pulled forward the neck of my T-shirt and peeked in, getting a confusing glimpse of flesh in bra. (Why wear not only one, but two overlaying pieces of clothing?) After satisfying himself that I did possess breasts, he forced apart my legs. But my jeans concealed everything, and his curiosity was not satisfied.

My interrogator then tried to slip off my watch with its black band. I put it in my pocket, and he didn't insist. Around his neck, along with the red threads, he was wearing a metal zipper, with the rectangular piece one pulls on serving as pendant.

Another young man with jagged teeth signaled to me, offering me his armband in exchange for my shirt, to be shredded and made into more jewelry. When I took out my camera and pointed it at him, he bobbed his head out of the way. I refocused and he did it again and again, laughing at my frustration until suddenly he stopped and gravely posed. This time my hand shook, so that in the shot the outlines of his noble face are fuzzy, like my memories.

Now they had to leave, and the engine started up. The fishermen would give them a ride to an island an hour away, else it would take them many hours of trekking and swimming to get home. They gathered their possessions: net bags, some made of plant fiber and some of plastic, Styrofoam floats picked up on some beach, and every last banana and coconut, and they checked under the floorboards for any that might've fallen through.

As the boat pulled away a chanting welled up, musical and hauntingly happy over the roar of the motor. I tentatively held up a hand. One man, seeing it, held up his as well.

What can I say? It was like a dream.

The Jarawa had an ease, a power, a sense of rightness in their being. They'd met me, touched me, and talked to me as rulers of their land for millennia. What a contrast to the Great Andamanese, in whose eyes I'd read the awareness that I was a memsahib, to whom they could only be servants.

# Where Worlds Touch

A man of the *Aka-Cari* tribe who was with me in Rutland Island had a cold on his chest. He asked me for permission to return to his own country, explaining that the spirits of Rutland Island were, so to speak, at enmity with him, and that if he stayed longer he would be seriously ill, and perhaps die, while on the other hand, the spirits of his own country were friendly towards him, and once he was amongst them he would quickly recover.

— Alfred R. Radcliffe-Brown, *The Andaman Islanders*, 1922

OVER THE BAY raced masses of clouds, shades of gray jostling and losing to ever darker shades. I watched entranced as they covered the hilltops in wind-tossed shrouds. The first drops touched me, and then a torrent raged.

At times the rain quieted, leaving swaying green leaves stunningly lit by a glow that filled the space between the earth and the clouds. Then the rustling started up and rain rushed in again. Finally, the Andamans were saved.

With the monsoons having set in for 1998, the chances of the Jarawa emerging from the forest were scant: trekking and swimming were easier during the dry months. But the best way I could think of spending my last few days was at the jetty where I'd met them. Waiting for the bus to Kadamtala early one morning, I spotted a policeman from up north, in civilian clothes. "Have the Jarawa been out lately?" I asked him.

He nodded. "En Mei was sneezing and coughing, really badly."

That scared me. Decades of visiting doctors have observed only injuries among the Jarawa, no illnesses — not even the common cold.

I stood most of the way on the bus. Children perched on the laps of strangers, while men and women fell asleep on their feet or on me. The stuffiness became unbearable when rain started up and those near the windows pulled them shut. The man next to me had lived in Kadamtala for years, so I asked him about the Jarawa. "They haven't reached the human stage yet," he complained. "If the administration wished to, they could have made them human long ago."

To be fair, "making human" is how Bengalis speak of bringing up a child — of creating an adult, with a set of desired sensibilities. But to this tradesman, I believed, the Jarawa were not like children; they were subhuman.

Adventurer Kanak Tilak Banerjea described in a 1998 Calcutta newspaper his encounter with the Jarawa, a people who "hopped out of the cave, cleared the copper and bronze ages, borrowed from the iron age . . . and are making a jump into the modern age." He'd paid a boatman to take him toward Lakra Lungta; but when the natives saw the boat, piled with green coconuts and bananas, they plunged into the sea and swam toward it. Alarmed, the visitors threw their gifts overboard and got away behind an island.

After an hour, they returned to the jetty near Kadamtala to find the Jarawa waiting for them. One young man, who "appeared to be quite mad," insisted on Banerjea's cutting open one of the green coconuts he'd thrown to them. But the bows and arrows were stashed away in the jetty's rest room, and much hugging and other pleasantries dispensed his fears. "These innocent children

of the wilderness displayed their ignorance of proprietory rights,"
opined Banerjea, for they ran their hands over everything, rum-
maged in his pockets, and even fingered the sacred thread he wore
as a Brahmin. They stowed the sweets and biscuits they were given
in net bags; the latter were a major advance, he declared, "for they
are supposed to still be in the parasite stage" — as he regarded
their hunter-gatherer lifestyle.

Being among a "bevy of black beauties in their innocent nudity" was a particularly intriguing experience: "That women are a
curious species is well-known, but these Jarawa women were almost childish and, at times, downright embarrassing." He wasn't
too bashful, however, to break into "a snatch of Onge song" he'd
heard at Dugong Creek, which "drew enthusiastic chorus!"

Jayanta Sarkar, of the Anthropological Survey of India, visited a
Jarawa beach in 1986. Standing in front of a baby in its mother's
lap, he put his palm over his mouth and made a trumpeting
sound. The infant laughed and kicked; he repeated the sound and
it giggled again. Seeing the baby's joy, its mother's eyes began to
sparkle.

Several other children and adults came up, requesting that he
repeat the funny sound, and the kids put their hands over their
mouths to imitate him. Another woman placed her infant on his
lap and indicated that he should trumpet. He had to entertain the
two remaining babies as well. "Along with the others I too became
filled with pleasure," Sarkar wrote. "The love I have seen Jarawa
mothers and fathers exhibit I have seen nowhere else in my life as
an anthropologist."

It wasn't just their own children that the Jarawa liked. That year
fifteen Jawara, including one woman, spent the night on board
with the contact team. The ship was at anchor near Kadamtala
jetty, and by dawn several hundred settlers were jostling for a
glimpse of the aboriginals. Boatloads of men, women, and children began to circumnavigate the ship. The Jarawa entertained

the sightseers by posturing, pretending to threaten, and jumping about. Then some of the aboriginals pointed to the women in the boats, asking that their children be brought to them.

Two brave mothers were finally persuaded to part with their offspring. The Jarawa elbowed one another aside to get at them. "Each one took the babies in turn in his lap and said so many things. Some of them gently patted their bodies. One or two of them looked in the clothes to check if it was a boy or a girl. One or two rocked them in their arms. In their eyes and faces was unalloyed pleasure."

At Kadamtala I got a room at the public works department guest house. The day was dark, heavy, and still. The air had expectancy, a promise of rain at any instant, but nothing happened; not a leaf stirred. The stillness was irritating. How could it be so utterly breezeless, how could the skies be perpetually poised on the brink of rain?

At the small marketplace I rented a bicycle, a ramshackle affair that rattled enough to scare the most insouciant cow. On the jetty some teenage boys were playing cricket, occasioning frequent dips to retrieve the ball. Nilu, a boatman I'd met before, had a smile for me on his plump face.

"Is it true," I asked, "that En Mei was sneezing and coughing?"

"Yes, the last time he came" — a couple of weeks earlier, in mid-May. "In late April — maybe the twenty-third? — we even had Tirur Jarawa." This tribe, which was from South Andaman, had never accepted gifts from the contact team and was believed to be implacably hostile.

That time, En Mei had visited the jetty with ten others, and, as customary, all were given a boat ride back to their beach. But many unknown Jarawa were gathered on the south side of the channel, and about thirty of them swam onto the boat. Not quite knowing what to do, the police had brought them to the jetty and treated them to bananas and coconuts. "But we couldn't control them. They went here, went there, snatched things. Eventually we got them all onto the boat and decided to drop them off. We concealed a gun, in case something happened."

When they returned to the southern beach, some sixty to one hundred Jarawa were still waiting. The boatmen were afraid to land, but their guests gave them no choice. When they beached, most of the Jarawa jumped off but a few remained on board. "This *meyechhele*" — a disdainful term for a woman — "she came and put her arm around me, wanted me to get off the boat," Nilu related. "I patted her on the back, tried to explain I didn't want to." Then came another man, and another, all trying to lift him off the boat. When these men in turn left to get several others, Nilu asked a boatman to start the engine. The propellor plowed through the sand and got the boat into the water; the Jarawa on board jumped off.

"When En Mei came back to the jetty, I said, 'Why did they do this?' He said, *'Badmash.'*" Hindi for bad men.

The hunting was poor for the house geckos that night. No electricity, and therefore no insects by the light bulb. One gecko sat hopefully by my candle, placed on the rim of the verandah's rails. The flame barely stirred.

Anup Mondal, a small, shy man in his early twenties, had recently been posted as a social worker for the Jarawa. I asked him why they were coming: "For food?"

"They were here for an outing," he replied. "The last time, they were all children, with two young men." The jetty had become a tourist attraction, a place where the Jarawa could touch the outer world and taste its enticements.

I also asked him about En Mei's cold. "He had a bad cough," Mondal agreed. "I took him to medical. The nurse gave him a cough syrup and white tablets."

I, who'd suffered a hundred-odd colds, still got knocked out for a couple of weeks sometimes. Things could get very rough for someone who'd never had one. Certainly he would spread it to his companions. And if, as it looked, they had contact with the Tirur Jarawa, the latter would be infected as well. Could it prove fatal? What other diseases had been transmitted?

Could En Mei not be coming because he was too sick?

I woke the next morning to a cacophony: the grinding and roaring of buses leaving for Port Blair, the crowing of a hundred cocks, the gurgling and tapping of pigeons on the roof, the screaming of children, and the fighting of street dogs. It was five-thirty A.M. I made it to the jetty on foot — the bike had vanished — waited for the Jarawa till noon, and walked back. Over the next days I made several more trips to the jetty, but no Jarawa.

On the return trip to Port Blair, I got a bus seat all to myself. But soon the shaking on the potholed road started to get to me, and after two hours I became convinced my innards were popping out of place. Finally, in my room, I lay prone on the floor with a fever. It was time for me to return to the souls of my own land.

## The Taming of Tigers

T WO YEARS LATER, in April 2000, I returned to the Andamans for a brief visit. Much had changed: I had a baby, Prakash had apparently drowned, and the Jarawa had suffered epidemics of pneumonia and measles.

My first task was to visit the information clearing house, in the form of Samir Acharya. He and his shop looked exactly the same, but his status had levitated. From unpopular watchdog he'd become informal adviser to the islands' new member of parliament.

"I still don't quite believe it," Acharya confessed. Incredibly, this politician wanted to do things right. Acharya had helped devise a new five-year plan, which envisaged, for one thing, stopping the export of timber and using the logs, instead of imported concrete, for local construction.

At the same time, other problems had worsened. The depredations of foreign poachers had escalated. Some of them, brandishing power saws and machine guns, were taking timber from remote islands and ornamental fish from the reefs, and on Little Andaman were plucking a rare fruit by felling the trees that bore it.

As for the Jarawa — "Just go to Kadamtala," he suggested.

\*       \*       \*

"One boy was singing Hindi songs," Souren, my sister's friend, said with a laugh. *"Hum kaale hai to kya hua, hum dilwale hai."* What does it matter that I am black, I'm spirited.

"Some missionaries were teaching a group of Jarawa to sing Hallelujah," reported Nasim.

Acharya had some stories as well. "We were returning from Kadamtala, were held up by thirteen or fourteen little boys, all between six and eight. They were intimidating us with their tiny bows and arrows." What did the highway robbers want? Cookies. "They took biscuits, folded their hands, thanked us."

He also noted some Jarawa teenagers who'd just returned from the hospital in Port Blair. They went into the forest, took off the government-issued clothes, put on their bark chest guards, got knives, and started threatening bystanders. They were deliberately using their "savage" outfit to intimidate, Acharya observed. From a peddler, "They ordered some green coconut, stood there and drank it, called their friends over for some, and when the man asked for money, lifted a *dao* and threatened him." Locals would be compensated by the administration for their losses and so didn't make much of a fuss.

Another time, Jarawa teenagers stood in the middle of the road to stop Acharya's car, knowing they wouldn't be run over. They opened the boot and ran off with some telephones he was transporting: "We ran after them and recovered some."

Acharya believed the youngsters were followers of En Mei, who brought them the outside world. When at the hospital recently, En Mei had demanded his own air-conditioned room with a color TV. "We've made him into a VIP, before he was nobody. I think it's led to a rift in their society. The older people never come out of the forest."

"It was a *mela*," Mishra told me, a street fair. Tour operators were taking busloads of visitors sightseeing along the Andaman Trunk Road: "It was one day Jolly Buoy, one day Havelock, one day

Jarawa." As superintendent of police, he'd stopped the bus tours and removed stalls from the jetty, where tourists were buying goodies to give to the Jarawa. He'd also prohibited photography of the Jarawa, which was being used as pornography.

The aboriginals didn't take kindly to the "fun, frolic, and adventure," as Mishra put it, being over. In April 1999, a few weeks after the tours stopped, over 150 angry Jarawa, from Middle as well as South Andaman, gathered on the road in a show of force. Some built shelters on the shoulder, the better to hold up buses. The next day they'd vanished into the jungle to find food — a reminder that only agricultural people can sustain campaigns.

Two days later some sixty Jarawa forcibly boarded two buses; they were taken out by the police and returned to their jungle. The aboriginals were furious and a showdown seemed inevitable. Fortunately, some of their women emerged to request the police to leave for the time being, and bloodshed was averted.

In Tirur, where the Jarawa had started raiding in broad daylight, the villagers had demonstrated against police inaction. "People are saying I'm weak because I won't register cases against the Jarawa," Mishra complained. Bengali youngsters had vowed to give their own "treatment" to the *junglees*. Some clash must have taken place, he guessed, for the Jarawa were no longer coming to the village.

For the first time, policemen had trekked to the Tirur Jarawa's homes. One woman "started shaking and screaming" when she saw them, but others had offered food. By now all the major Jarawa camps were marked on maps.

Instead of killing intruders, the Jarawa of Middle Andaman had begun reporting them to the authorities. Some were dismantling animal traps set by poachers, having learned the technique from a forest ranger. Social workers delivered to Lakra Lungta the doses of bananas, coconuts, and iron implements they'd grown habituated to.

"A lady here has gone to court claiming that under the Constitution of India the Jarawa have a right to receive the fruits of civilization," Mishra commented. "She says this administration has taken a decision not to allow fruits of civilization to reach them." A letter-writing campaign by Survival International, an aboriginal rights group based in London, had bolstered the newly discovered official stance that assimilation was equivalent to annihilation. "This administration deserves credit," Mishra concluded. "We have made the Jarawa go back to the forest."

But that was not entirely true. I had a window seat on the Rangat Rani, a deluxe bus going northward. It drizzled for a while and then stopped. Near the end of the Jhirkatang jungle the bus slowed, and I stared in astonishment at a naked Jarawa boy on the road. He couldn't have been more than four years old, but his little hand was held out to stop the bus. He gazed in disappointment as we passed. Every boy I knew loved a ride, including my six-month-old.

When we caught up with the bus ahead of us, it had four Jarawa kids on the roof rack. They faced forward, shirts blowing back in the wind. When the buses came to a stop at the jetty, the children climbed down.

Several Jarawa boys were already there. A couple had bunches of bananas hanging onto their backs from string held by their foreheads, and one also boasted a plastic bag of puffed rice. One was eating a banana. An image from another place, far away, elbowed itself into my mind: macaques begging from buses, peeling bananas by the roadside. From fearsome tigers to amusing monkeys, quite a transition.

Some of the Jarawa wore shirts and shorts, while others were naked. One young man even had on a khaki uniform and was hanging out with the policemen posted at the jetty. Why would someone wear a uniform that forever marked the enemy?

The ferry arrived with a bus going the other way, and I watched some of the boys climb onto the roof for the return trip to Jhirkatang.

*          *          *

At Kadamtala, I deposited my things at the guest house and walked down the road to the hospital. I saw more astonishing things.

Four black imps perched on the green boundary wall overlooking the street and another one, even smaller, was trying to climb up to them. A Jarawa boy was playing cricket with the hospital staff. En Mei took the ball and expertly bowled. He was impeccably dressed in a short-sleeved shirt and long pants, a cowrie necklace the sole remnant of his past. He was serious, unsmiling.

Several other boys were lolling around. Sitting on the steps of the hospital, looking shy, were a few Jarawa women, all in maxis or other concealing clothes in bright patterns. I tried not to stare, for the change was stunning.

Raja was also fully clothed. He remembered me; astonishing, for we'd met briefly two years before. Since then he'd encountered hundreds of strangers. "I'll stay here in medical," he said in Hindi and English. "Go to school, learn A, B, C, D." The social worker, Anup Mondal, cuffed him playfully.

Mondal, of the AAJVS, the Society for Upliftment of Andaman Aboriginals, had been shy and frail. Now he boasted a paunch, rode a motorcycle, and seemed very sure of himself. He spoke to the Jarawa boys familiarly, sometimes in their language. Toward me he was guarded and wary, the standard social worker stance; he'd been much friendlier before. A boy of about three, in a long yellow T-shirt, was hanging around him, and I asked what he was there for.

"He got burned," Mondal replied. "But he stays here. Has no parents."

"But," I protested, "they love children. Why would the Jarawa give him up?"

"His mother wasn't married."

Stranger and stranger. The kids seemed to be having fun, and no one looked very distressed. I couldn't help staring at a beautiful Jarawa girl. She had a perfectly heart-shaped face set with huge almond eyes and small lips, an exquisite little doll. All the Jarawa children — except for those with cheeks swelled by mumps, the current epidemic — had heart-shaped faces and large eyes. They looked very much like one another, unlike the Onge kids, who had a spectrum of features.

"Are the children living here?" I asked.

"They go back when they are cured," said Mondal.

But several of the boys didn't look sick at all. Raja plumped down on some thatching and squawked loudly like a hen. Other kids joined him in a chorus.

I looked at En Mei, still playing cricket as darkness fell. I wanted to talk to him, but I didn't have the language skills. What would I ask? I wondered. Why did you leave the forest? What is it you want to do now? Even if I could ask him, would I get any real answers?

At the guest house I met M. Sreenathan, a linguist with the Anthropological Survey of India. He'd been on many contact trips. "The Jarawa adapt very fast to any changes in circumstances," he observed. "They opposed the road building and saw they couldn't win, so just stopped. Now they are fixing [Styrofoam] on the chest and swimming. Use plastic bottles, I don't see nautilus cups." The Lakra Lungta camp was strewn with Coke and mineral water bottles: the global economy had reached there.

Visiting a Jarawa beach in 1999, Jayanta Sarkar of the Anthropological Survey was surprised to find large blue flies swarming over coconut husks, banana peels, and other foreign garbage. Worse, the exuberance so inescapable on past visits had been replaced by gloom. A woman he remembered as an irrepressible chatterbox was quiet and somber; another turned out to be ill with pneumonia. A puppy moved among the children, harbinger of another big change — the Jawara had always killed dogs, which poachers liked to use. "I kept asking myself," Sarkar wrote in a Bengali essay, "did we start contacting [the Jarawa] to see them become this silent and subdued society?"

*     *     *

Next morning I found the doctor, Ratan Chandra Kar, at the hospital, discharging some Jarawa children for return to the forest. He was a friendly, loquacious Bengali, very proud of having — thus far — saved the Jarawa. He deserved much of the credit for having ensured that the measles epidemic had claimed remarkably few lives.

Starting in July 1998 — a month after my previous visit had ended — many of the Jarawa visiting the jetty had been diagnosed with pneumonia, bronchitis, and other serious ailments and were transported to Port Blair. But because Port Blair was becoming a tourist attraction for the Jarawa, so that even healthy men and women were claiming to be sick, Kar was posted in Kadamtala in November of that year to take care of their ailments.

"When I first went to the forest," he related, "I saw just some sores on the feet. No high blood pressure, no dental caries, no thyroid disorders, no congenital disease, they delivered babies without our help. Never saw umbilical sepsis. No parasites."

A young woman with puffed cheeks and hangdog eyes, wearing a maxi and a necklace of wilted leaves, wandered in. She wanted to return to the forest but couldn't until her mumps was cured. Kar put the stethoscope on her chest and back, and she breathed in and out, a practiced patient. Then she watched herself wistfully in the mirror in his chamber, turning her cheeks from side to side.

In January 1999, a police patrol discovered nine Jarawa men sprawled unconscious in the jungle by the roadside. "They all had stomach pain," Kar said. "Many were lying in the forest, we found them and brought them in." Luckily all survived. They'd eaten an introduced tuber that probably contained natural narcotics, and, on getting sick, had run toward the hospital until they collapsed. "They showed us the tuber, it was in an area close to our villages."

A young Jarawa man came in and sat on the chair by Kar. He wore a rippled pink-and-white woman's blouse and a metalwork necklace of a kind made in Calcutta, but he looked somber. "This is Naru," Kar said in introduction. "He was about to die" of a respiratory infection. "One lung was fully collapsed and the other one, half was collapsed. He used to have a powerful build, has killed many outsiders. Now he is skin and bone." Naru looked pensively at me while Kar related his story. I felt he'd like to touch me, but he knew the rules.

The measles epidemic broke out in September 1999. Sensing trouble, the director of health services for the islands had toured Jarawa camps; she'd brought in many patients, pulling some out of creeks where they were fishing with high fevers. (The sick Jarawa were wearing headbands braided from a creeper and were easy to spot.) One woman, who'd refused to go to the hospital, had died; since then, most of the Middle Andaman Jarawa would come to the hospital when sick. "I don't let them go home without the course of medicines being finished," said Kar. "They sit and make necklaces out of whatever they get. If they insist on leaving, I go to the forest and give them the medicines there."

One old lady, Kar suspected, had died of yet another pathogen, tuberculosis. Drug-resistant strains of the disease were common in India, and who knew where this infection might lead.

I even suspected that no one knew the true death count so far. "I see very few old people," Sreenathan had remarked, going on to explain that hunter-gatherers had short life spans. But I found that explanation rather too pat. Portman had estimated the Great Andamanese life span to be sixty, and British efforts to capture Jarawa had roped in many old men and women. True, they were easier to catch than the youngsters, but at least they were there.

They were also the first to get sick in captivity. It was entirely possible that the early phases of the epidemics had wiped out the elderly.

"This whole tribe is now like a newborn baby, getting all the infections," said Kar. "After five years it will stabilize, they will have gotten everything."

In return for his services, Kar was revered by his wards. At one time, noting terrible sandfly bites on his hands, an old lady had brought a paste of leaves and plastered it on. "In five minutes the itching died down."

On another trip to the forest he'd come upon a group of Jarawa returning with knives, spades, and other implements stolen from villagers. At Kar's suggestion, the policemen escorting him had taken the things, annoying the raiders: "They were pointing arrows. I said to them, *pitipiti*, bad." He'd eventually returned the loot but refused to treat them. "Some days later they showed up at the hospital, shamefaced."

Raja entered with a piece of paper on which someone had written for him 1, 2, 3, 4 . . . Kar examined his scribbles. "He's very sharp," the doctor remarked. "I said to administration, send him to Ananda Marg school here, I want to make him a teacher. Then he will teach the others. I will give him books."

The Ananda Margis were Hindu radicals, and I wasn't surprised the administration had declined. But the situation was fraught with dilemmas. If Raja wanted to go to school, why should he be denied?

Since a long line of Indian outpatients was by then waiting for Kar, I let him work while I sat on the hospital doorstep and looked around. Raja wandered by with his papers and, in Hindi, asked me the time.

"Ten minutes to ten," I told him. Did he understand that? I wondered; and why did he care? A Jarawa boy with swollen cheeks hid behind a pillar with a plastic ball. His target turned out to be a dog, which yelped at the hit and ran away. Raja and another boy tried out someone's bicycle and fell.

I'd been told En Mei could ride not only a bicycle but also a motorbike. His wife, a teenager from the Tirur area, was playing with a pretty little girl in a yellow dress; they were racing around the hospital compound. En Mei came up and they hid; he discovered the two girls in the recess of a wall. Soon he lost interest and climbed up to a hillock where Indian men were working on building a Jarawa ward. It was to be a thatched, open structure made of wood with sleeping platforms, electricity, and running water. Kar also envisioned a banana plantation that the patients' families, who often came along, would be taught to take care of.

At lunchtime, I checked out a Jarawa plate: huge amounts of rice, yellow with turmeric, plus a little of something else. It was all starch, like the usual Onge meal. Kar had stated that the Jarawa got food without salt or oil, which were alien to their cuisine; he hadn't said anything about turmeric. Again, should I care? They were getting our strongest medications, so why not our spices, our traditional preventives as well?

Later I cornered Kar. "All the Jarawa here are from Middle Andaman. What is going on with the Tirur people?"

He didn't want to say but eventually relented. "They will die in the forest. Some Tirur Jarawa came here, swam across with bronchitis and pneumonia, recovered in five days at the hospital. We know they visit the Lakra Lungta people, so cross infection must be going on." But most of the Tirur Jarawa never left the jungle, nor did they seek medical help.

In 1988 the contact team took fifty-five Jarawa from Middle Andaman onto their ship and traveled to the Tirur coast. There two Jarawa men, one woman, and a ten-year-old boy swam to the boat.

One of them gave a young man on board some news: Jayanta Sarkar of the Anthropological Survey heard the Jarawa word *bechame*, meaning dead. The man screamed out and collapsed, sobbing loudly. Two women from his home, Lakra Lungta, quietly sat down and placed their hands on him. After a while the man who'd brought the news, his woman, the bereaved, and another woman sat together in a circle, their hands on one another's backs and their heads together, crying. The others sat in silence, communing with their grief.

After half an hour the group broke up, but the first man — whose brother had died — continued to sob until he fell silent from exhaustion. Later, when the messenger departed, the bereaved man took off his bark chest shield and gave it to him to put on, probably for protection from the jungle he'd have to cross.

In the evening I found that a new group of patients had come in: Tirur Jarawa, brought by dinghy from the jetty where they'd showed up.

They were slumped, naked and dusty, on the clean white sheets of a hospital bed, men, women, and children. I glanced at them and away, for in the foreground was a man feeling his genitals. They looked — I have to use the word — wild. A woman crowned by wilted leaves, her breasts flattened by nursing, strode by scratching her behind and calling loudly. It was a shock to see her, and to realize that for all my reading and reasoning, total nudity, such *casual* nudity, unnerved me.

I'd seen many artsy photos of nude models, but this was different. Even the naked men I'd met before, En Mei and his friends, had seemed more decorous — their manner more like ours — than these people from Tirur. The sterile hospital environment, the starched bed sheets all stained with mud, heightened the effect.

Though it was evening, Kar had come to check on them and seemed annoyed. "They aren't sick. They've come to visit their friends here at the hospital. We'll feed them tonight and tell them they have to return tomorrow."

I didn't have permission to go to Lakra Lungta. But welfare personnel, I was told, had built shacks in the jungle, and Kar had given health clearances to ten laborers who were charged with developing orchards of banana, mango, guava, and cashew. I needed to know how intrusive outsiders had become.

Earlier, I'd asked Mondal, the social worker, if I could go to the jungle with him, and he said he'd think about it. But when he showed up, it was clear from his evasive eyes what the answer was.

Next morning I caught a bus back to Port Blair. A ferry took us across the channel to South Andaman, where I saw a Jarawa kid, carefully dressed in a long-sleeved shirt and pants, sitting on a post by the water. A tall, thin young Jarawa man guided the bus off the ferry by blowing on a whistle and hitting its side with a stick in the manner of a bus conductor. As the bus took off, two Jarawa boys came up for a ride.

"Go onto the roof," said the conductor in Hindi.

"*Gir jaiga,*" retorted one, in the same language. Will fall.

So they got to come in. One sat on a low stool while the other stood near the open door, right next to me. When I asked his name, he pursed his lips and looked away: they must have been told not to talk to strangers.

He had on long pants but no shirt, and wore a whistle on a chain as well as several safety pins strung in a decorative line down his chest. The boy on the stool wore a pinkish full-sleeved cotton shirt and olive pants, both well fitting. A worn leather belt with a metal buckle held up the trousers. His fingers sparkled with several silvery rings, one bearing a large red stone, and around his neck was a chain from which hung a whistle. He had the heart-shaped face and enormous eyes common to these uncommonly attractive youngsters. Neither of the teenagers wore a shred of Jarawa jewelry.

After about half a mile, the other boy wanted to get off.

"*Ruko!*" shouted the one on the stool, whistling in the manner of a conductor. Stop!

He continued to sit after the bus slowed down to let off his companion. A video came on, with an awful Bombay movie jittering all over the screen and speakers turned way too loud. It was a deluxe bus. He stared at the picture with amazement in his huge eyes, the only surprise any of them had shown so far.

\*  \*  \*

*Jarawa men and Raja*

"All the boys want to be police," said Mishra.

He showed me some photos taken at a Jarawa beach, featuring the grown men I'd never met because they refused to come out of the forest. They looked powerful and self-assured and had on their faces the most amazingly open, trusting, warm smiles. They think we're their friends, I realized with sadness.

Next to them was Raja, naked as I'd first met him, pointing a plastic gun.

# On Full Modernization

On more than one occasion the Jarawa ran away when a match was struck before them. On some occasions, they became furious and even took out knives and threatened the person who lit the match. On other occasions they snatched lighted cigarettes from the mouth of crew members and threw them away . . . But in the course of the last three years a change has been observed in this respect. Now when they see matchboxes they ask for them.

    — Jayanta K. Sarkar, *The Jarawa*, 1990

W HEN I FIRST learned of the Andamanese, one question in my head was: What do they make of our technology? our matches and ships and airplanes? I never got around to asking.

But I found something of an answer in an account from the 1930s by logger and writer James Howard Williams. He was on North Andaman, gauging timber resources, when from his boat he spied a naked figure run along the shore and vanish into the jungle. It was one of a group of four, perhaps the last Great Andamanese still to survive in the jungle.

The explorers filled up a Johnny Walker whiskey crate with some canned food, a fishing line, and hooks, and floated it ashore. Although fearful at first, over the next few days the aboriginals became trusting enough to accompany Williams back to his logging camp, with their canoe in tow and their possessions on board, "a pathetic collection of tropical junk" that included an eternal fire: "What they treasured more than anything else was an earthenware bowl, the shape of a large fruit dish, in which burned, or rather smouldered, a few pieces of touchwood similar to charcoal, which they fed continually as if it were a God of Fire . . . They seemed to regard themselves as keepers of the flame. When we showed them how to make fire by striking a match, they were not in the least interested, which I thought evidence of their good sense; for what was the use of their learning to strike matches, if after we left there were no more matches to strike?"

Getting close to camp, though, Williams and his companions realized the problem of bringing naked women into the presence of convict laborers. So the four natives were dropped off on a beach near the camp with ample provisions. They visited the loggers over the next days, especially the younger woman and the personable patriarch. "They would both spend whole days with us at camp or at work, watching what we were doing with an interest that was intelligent a lot of the time. The old man we named Friday." They became mascots of sorts for the outpost.

Some days later two aircraft, which were scouting the surrounding waters for Japanese ships, flew in. The Andamanese men were in the camp; they "looked up at these strange roaring birds 3,000 feet up in the sky," ran screaming down the beach, jumped into their canoe, and "started paddling as if they were in a canoe race, the prize for which was life itself." The onlookers roared with laughter.

The next morning the planes left. Not having seen the natives for several days, Williams and a friend paid a visit to their beach. They found only three of them, daubed with gray ashes and mud. "The old woman and the young man seemed to be stricken with a dumb grief," while "ungovernable sorrow shook the girl." The old man had been up on a cliff when one of the aircraft had flown very low past him. In terror he'd fallen off and smashed onto the rocks below.

The girl's emotion was extreme, Williams guessed, because while the resourceful patriarch was alive there was still a chance they might all find a way to survive: "What she bewailed was not the death of the old man, but the end of her race and the fire in the bowl." All encounters between the Andamanese and outsiders must end in tragedy, he speculated, because the cultures were too different to come to terms.

Isolation was the only way to save the Jarawa. But with isolation having become an illusion, the new question was: How could one help the Jarawa cope?

Advocate Shyamali Ganguly's small office in Port Blair overflowed with papers and legal volumes. She sat solidly in the middle like a Buddha, unkempt hair falling all over a plump face shadowed by stress. When I asked about her case against the administration, she became even glummer. "I went to Mayabunder, I saw things on the road I didn't like, I thought someone should do something."

She'd seen the Jarawa running after cars, calling for water, and feared there might be an accident. One child on a joyride subsequently had his hand cut off by an oncoming vehicle. She'd noted "malnutrition, awful colds, and coughs," and demanded medical help for the Jarawa. But what bothered her most was the nudity she'd spotted. "At least give them some clothes!" She shuddered in disgust. "I couldn't even lift up my eyes to look at them."

The sight of genitals was so disturbing that in 1999 some locals had chased seven Jarawa men off a bus; the men had in turn vented their anger by entering a settler home and tearing the clothes off two women. (As mentioned earlier, the Andamanese have not been known to rape.)

The administration had tried to deal with the Jarawa's wanderings, ailments, and apparel. The problem with Ganguly's case stemmed from a further demand: "to provide immediately all sorts of facilities of modern life and protection to aboriginal Jarawas, rehabilitating them in their own habitat as it had been done for the Onges and Andamanese." Thanks to Samir Acharya, several foreign anthropologists had written to the administration, pointing out the problems inherent in making the Jarawa sedentary, and within fifteen days of filing her case an astonished Ganguly had received a flyer from Survival International criticizing her.

"What did I say wrong?" she asked indignantly. "The prime minister came, they were put into clothes, taken to meet him, shook hands, sat on chairs under a fan, ate cashews. He left, and they take off their clothes and put them back in the jungle. What did I say wrong that they be civilized?"

Ganguly's assistant, Nurul Ikram Khan, was polished and articulate. In the 1970s, he recalled, the Jarawa were coming all the way up to the school field in Port Blair, but their jungles had since receded to Jhirkatang. The encroachment, he charged, had so robbed them of resources that they were now "knocking on the door of modern civilization" for help. Moreover, the Jarawa had for years been tempted by offers of friendship from the contact mission. The administration, he held, had a duty to oblige them.

"Do you think modernization has worked with the Onge?" I asked.

"The process of rehabilitation has harmed them," Khan retorted, "not the principle." He pointed to the Onge's rations of tobacco; likewise, he argued, immense resources had been wasted in providing coconuts and bananas to the Jarawa. What he envisaged instead was their jungles being protected, while simultaneously they were trained in the crafts of civilization, most prominently cultivation.

"People will say," I put in, "that we were not able to teach the Onge to grow things. How do you teach the Jarawa?"

"The Onge haven't been taught properly," he insisted. Instead of coconut trees, which bear fruit after ten years, they should be given banana trees or tubers. "Humans have instinct to learn some things," he added. "First is agriculture."

His smooth hands had never held a hoe. But Khan's was the prevailing view. The aboriginals had to enter civilization at the lowest rung: they must submit to the back-breaking, soul-withering toil of the field, which would keep their eyes and aspirations firmly fixed to the ground. "What is the alternative?" he asked rhetorically.

"Education," I suggested. Another kind of modernization, it could tear children from their roots, alienate them from parents and traditions, and intensify the pain of assimilation. But without it, the Jarawa would grope their way into our world like the Onge and the Great Andamanese, vanishing into the underside of society.

"The level of IQ they have you cannot ignore," he replied. "You can find archers, maybe. There is [an Indian] tribal now going to the Olympics."

"Why the contact?" I asked Triloki Pandit.

A tall, graying man, he was a former head of the Anthropological Survey of India. Along with Bakhtawar Singh, he was a prime mover behind the Jarawa contact trips.

"There were violent incidents," he replied. "We thought, it's better to have a more conciliatory interaction. People were getting killed, the majority cannot be totally ignored. The MP would get friends in parliament to ask questions."

It can't be denied that several anthropologists had built careers on the contact program. Science — and "friendly relations" — provided the rationale behind contact even if, in later stages, VIP tourism provided much of the impetus. The amount of knowledge that emerged from three decades of contact was, however, astoundingly small: as the anthropologists admitted, the arrival of the boat created a synthetic situation in which the Jarawa couldn't be observed living their day-to-day lives.

Moreover, their society was undoubtedly disrupted by the provision of hundreds of coconuts and a thousand-odd bananas each month. The gift-giving created a demand for novelties; it also led the Jarawa to believe that manna was theirs for the asking. In the 1980s their raids intensified, with the aboriginals emerging during full moon nights to take cloth, utensils, tools, cooked rice, bananas, and other things that the contact team had taught them to use. They might not have thought of themselves as raiders, points out anthropologist Vishvajit Pandya, but simply as "gift takers."

In short, the contact missions forced the Jarawa out of the jungle and into the arms of the administration — as was the intent. In 1969 a committee had recommended that "such gifts be distributed as may gradually make the Jarawa economically dependent on the Administration." One expert, Rann Singh Mann, later suggested that just as Portman had pacified the Onge by capturing them and keeping them awhile, so should the Jarawa "be properly trained and convinced of the friendly attitude of outsiders to them" — by catching some while they crossed from South to Middle Andaman and holding them prisoner. The aboriginals were even shown where to go if they should venture into civilization, being routinely brought to the jetty near Kadamtala to meet settlers. "Once the fear psychosis that exists on both sides is eradicated, mutual trust and faith is bound to grow," wrote Jayanta Sarkar, who now claimed that recent developments had upset the Anthropological Survey's carefully laid plans.

Neither as ruthless nor as clear-sighted as Portman — even with the benefit of hindsight — the government's advisers followed his precedent partly because it was the only one around. "Anthropology is an imperial science whose purpose is to conquer and control," the linguist Sreenathan told me. "Indian anthropologists are practitioners of British anthropology . . . People were trained in anthropology or administration, both in British tradition. The attitude is to govern and conquer."

Of course, no Western government, past or present, would stand for its citizens being routinely killed, as the Indian government did for decades. That tolerance stemmed, I cynically believe, from the Jarawa's endangering just the poor: in a century of strife, Percy Vaux appeared to be the only upper-class individual to have died at their hands. In recent years, those venturing into the Jarawa forests were held responsible for their own fate.

That fate, of course, was prompted by a series of administrative decisions, the first being the settlement of refugees in the midst of Jarawa jungles in the 1950s. Although the law ostensibly protected tribals' rights to their land, it also allowed key people — in this case the chief commissioner or lieutenant governor — to take away such land if he deemed it to be "in the public interest." In later decades, the government abetted further encroachment. Suddenly an entire Bengali village, Phooltala, had been "discovered" deep within the reserve. "We only got to know about it because the Jarawa attacked it," said Police Superintendent Mishra; yet, inexplicably, the administration legalized the settlement in the 1970s. With the completion of the Andaman Trunk Road, something had to give.

In 2000, no settlers were getting killed. But that raised another question: If the Jarawa were no longer feared, what would happen to the forests and beaches they were defending? Would these now be trucked away, making the demise of their way of life — and ecological death of the islands — inevitable? So it seemed.

In 2001, following a petition by Samir Acharya's organization, Society for Andaman and Nicobar Ecology (SANE), the High Court issued its verdict in the Shyamali Ganguly case on modernization of the Jarawa. The court directed that the Jarawa reserve be strictly guarded against intrusion and further encroachment, with civil servants being subjected to penal measures if they failed in this duty; that the boundaries of the Jarawa reserve be clearly demarcated; that aboriginals be discouraged from venturing onto the Andaman Trunk Road; and that settlers be taught that the Jarawa were "not inferior but . . . different."

The judges also asked for research to determine whether the Jarawa had enough food and why they had been emerging. In the summer of 2002, I learned that a massive team — of anthropologists, zoologists, botanists, nutritionists, medical researchers, foresters, social workers, and their assorted helpers, a total of sixty to ninety heads — was camped on Jarawa territory. "It's a picnic," reported one policeman. Cooks provided meals at three campsites, while other assistants fetched water, washed up, and ran errands. (The Jarawa, if no one else, were surely learning about social structures.) Trash disposal was into the forest or sea, and although toilet tents had been set up, most of the men preferred the beach, trusting the high tide to cleanse it of their droppings.

So far, the Jarawa hadn't had epidemics of dysentery, jaundice, or other maladies caused by contaminated drinking water; they now might. The judges could scarcely have expected their thoughtful verdict to be put in place on such a thoughtless scale. The bureaucracy was being led by yet another LG; I'd been furious with the Gandhian one, but I now wished he was back, for he'd cared about the Jarawa. (In any case, I'd again been denied permission to visit them.)

Sadly, even the more enlightened administrators failed to grasp that posting outsiders in aboriginal areas was a prescription for harm; moreover, those assigned were government employees who couldn't easily be disciplined for their misdeeds. Such constraints ensured that the best of intentions would be warped in the implementation.

Acharya's SANE and other nongovernmental organizations in India had filed a second public-interest case to stop the illegal harvesting of trees in the Onge reserve. In the documents submitted, the litigants had included information on the environment of the entire archipelago. The Supreme Court verdict, issued in May 2002, was stunning in its scope. It banned all felling in protected forests on the Andamans and demanded that encroachers — including those in the Jarawa reserve — be evicted. To halt immigration to the islands, it required that all inhabitants be issued identity cards. Most startling, the court ordered two stretches of the Andaman Trunk Road that traversed the Jarawa reserve in South and Middle Andaman to be closed within three months.

A lunatic, a fraud, a publicity hound — such were the verdicts on Acharya. He was the most hated man in Port Blair, held responsible for the decimation of thousands of livelihoods. I found him at home one midday, unshaven and in a faded khurta full of holes, his eyes bloodshot and the inevitable cigarette dangling from his fingers. We sat on a bed to talk, for much of the furniture had been confiscated over a bank matter that in normal times would've been negotiable. Sensing the surge of popular anger, the member of parliament had withdrawn support for Acharya's ventures.

He might have saved the Andamans, but I wasn't too sure Acharya could save himself. "It's a great democracy," he insisted. "I am alive still, my family is unmolested. I'm permitted to fight."

# End of the Road

TOPSY WAS ALIVE! Captured as a child in 1938, she was living in Mus village in Car Nicobar and must have been seventy-two. Thrilled, I wrote her a letter: "I feel as if I know you." But she showed no interest in my missive, they told me.

Her Jarawa "brothers" had died in their twenties. With Bishop Richardson, Topsy had toured India, visiting major cities and viewing the Taj Mahal. When she was twenty-eight, her mentor had arranged her marriage to his subordinate, Reverend Ezekiel. All the villages of Car Nicobar had been invited to the feast, on a day she recalled as the happiest in her life. The first son, Sylvanus, was athletic, the backbone of the Mus soccer team; he'd drowned while diving to disentangle a ship's anchor. The remaining children, a boy and a girl, had fallen in their teens to a viral fever, and her husband had passed away a decade ago. In 2002, Topsy the eternal survivor lived alone and in poverty, sewing clothes and gathering fibers in the forest to weave baskets and mats, saved from starvation by the Nicobarese sense of community.

She was withdrawn, said my emissary, and didn't talk to outsiders. She recalled no life in the jungle, spoke not a word of Jarawa, and insisted she was born in Port Blair. Just to be sure, I confirmed that she indeed bore a scar. Perhaps the trauma of her capture was so unbearable that she'd permanently blocked it from memory.

At the tribal welfare department I informed the new assistant director, Kritish Ghosal, about Topsy, and he picked up the phone to issue instructions to the tribal council in Mus. At least her last years wouldn't be spent in want, but loneliness seemed to be in her stars.

At the jetty near Kadamtala late one afternoon, I encountered Toamba, an attractive Jarawa woman of perhaps thirty. She wore a girdle of golden rushes, a headband of red wool, and a long golden tassel hanging down her back. Beside her rested a jet-black wooden bucket, bound with exquisite basketwork in a yellow twine. She had made the bucket herself, Toamba confirmed. It was lined with leaves and contained green shoots, possibly bamboo.

Toamba pointed to an eight-year-old in muddy blue shorts hopping on and off a concrete stump: her son. I gestured to suggest my own boy, now two and a half, and in response she held out her right hand, at her knee and then at her waist, and trailed it up to the sky. The setting sun lit up her look of stark grief. Her daughters, aged two and six, had gone to the spirits.

A bus stopped in front of us, waiting for the ferry, and a line of unblinking eyes at the windows stared down at Toamba's nakedness. She gazed back without defiance and without shying away. I didn't know how long I could take such stares. Several of the Jarawa women were in the government-issue maxis, while all the men were clothed. They were taking the ferry across to Baratang, where they'd collect honey.

When the ferry was ready to leave, Toamba got up and with a folded green leaf wiped off a patch of menstrual blood she'd left on the concrete. It showed a futile fertility, for her husband too, she said in faltering Hindi, was lost to the sky.

A year earlier, a young Jarawa man named Ohame had fallen from a tree and broken his spine in several places. Brought to the Kadamtala hospital in a sack, he was flown to Chennai (formerly Madras), where he died after an emergency operation. To Ratan

Kar, the doctor, fell the unhappy task of informing the family. He got off the boat on Spike Island, an hour westward from the jetty, and told a couple of Jarawa youths the news. They walked over to Ohame's mother, some fifty feet away: she thrashed so violently that four men had to hold her down. Finally, when Kar went up, he said, "She turned and gave me a look that I will never forget" — of a woman devastated, betrayed.

"She sent him to me, and I couldn't save him," the doctor lamented. In three years, not a single Jarawa had died in his care: "They didn't know someone can die at a hospital." The family had "buried" the body in a deep alcove between the buttresses of a giant tree. For days afterward the Jarawa had stayed in the forest, mourning.

Kar pointed to a photograph of Ohame on the wall. It was the young man who'd been curious about my body the first time I met the Jarawa, four years ago.

The Jarawa incumbents at the hospital were three small boys, there with a gangrenous snakebite, a sting from a foot-long centipede, and an abscess, respectively. (An orphaned Jarawa had been living at the Kadamtala hospital two years ago; Kar had since persuaded his mother's brother to adopt him.) The smallest child was En Mei's brother, Oto; their father had died in 1999 of a respiratory tract infection, perhaps the first of the family to fall victim to contact. En Mei himself did not come out of the jungle anymore but tended to his fourteen-month-old daughter.

Of the two other boys at the hospital, Kelaotu had lost a hand in an auto accident but had since learned to use the stump to shoot arrows; worse, he'd lost his father. And Taote was missing a brother. With great concentration they pored over the photos from my first encounter with the Jarawa, in 1998, pointing to faces and whispering names. Several of those I'd met were from Tirur, evidently touring the jetty with En Mei as guide. Three times the little boys stopped and said, "*bechame*" — dead. They said it of

Ohame, and of Aluala, who'd borne the look of delighted disbelief, and of a little boy named Ohagame. The latter two fell to *ulade*, illness, in their forest home of Tirur.

Of at most ten individuals identifiable in the photographs, two had died of disease. In 2000, the administration's experts had estimated the Jarawa population to be 350; in 2002, they counted less than 250 and claimed that the lifespan was only forty-five years. The oldest Jarawa alive (apart from Topsy) was a man of no more than fifty-two. I could well believe that the Jarawa lifespan was down to forty-five or less, but I couldn't accept that was what it always had been.

The epidemics of the past two years included malaria, which Kar was convinced the Jarawa had never had before. It was evidently another introduced pathogen — and, judging by the fevers of early settlers, one of the first to reach the islands. The doctor had isolated the first victims of conjunctivitis. More curious was another report, from medical researchers in the Jarawa forests, that almost half of the aboriginals had hepatitis B. Astoundingly, none showed the symptoms.

By now, most of the Tirur Jarawa were seeking medical care. But there still was no answer to a crucial question Kar had been asking for years: Which vaccines should he administer to the Jarawa? They remained vulnerable to easily preventable but readily fatal maladies such as tetanus. Just as worrisome, Kar had requested a transfer. (He wouldn't say why, but everyone in Kadamtala described his difficulties with superiors.) Watching him with the three Jarawa kids, I realized that for a new doctor to build up such a bond of love and trust would take years, if it could be done at all. Should Kar's departure coincide with the onset of a new disease, disaster would ensue.

The Andaman Trunk Road was to be closed in a few months, but I could still catch a bus southward. The wayside jungle was lined with Jarawa shacks, most of them abandoned, but in the dense jungle of South Andaman we slowed to a stop. On the road several Jarawa children were gathered, while in the shelters nearby lounged two women, along with a dog. The boys handed up to the bus driver bunches of a yellow-green fruit and a can of what I suspected was honey. The fruit had sweet-and-sour white flesh with four red seeds. I asked the driver what he gave in return: food, he replied.

But I was told the Jarawa were getting just about every substance. Some of the women would vanish into the jungle with truckers who stopped on the road, for rewards unknown (and taking a generic route for the spread of AIDS), while young Jarawa men routinely begged for *sukka,* the then popular form of chewing tobacco. Two years earlier, the police were confiscating the valuables that Jarawa youths took from outsiders and returning them to their owners; but now I heard the aboriginals were getting alcohol and tobacco in exchange for their takings, which were discreetly sold back to the public. (Police Superintendent Mishra was gone — he'd made a difference, I believed.)

Using official transport, the Jarawa were quickly traversing the length of the Andaman Trunk Road and beyond, in pursuit of previously unimaginable ends. At Tirur, the remote village in South Andaman, a farmer had gathered gold jewelry and expensive saris for his daughter's wedding. "I've lived here for thirty-five years," he declared, "and I've never seen a Jarawa nearby." But weeks before the wedding, eight Jarawa men had invaded, threatened him with knives, rammed open the door to the bedroom, broken the lock on a metal trunk, and carried away a box inside that held all the gold. They'd also taken the saris, a wallet they fished out of a pair of pants slung over a line, and cash hidden under a bamboo mat. While running into the jungle, they'd discarded some little boxes that held rings and earrings, but not the tiniest stud of gold.

No Jarawa had, however, been spotted with the metal, which in India is 22 carat and very valuable. I did not doubt that an outsider had fingered this house to the raiders and taken over their loot. Further, these were the worldly Jarawa from Kadamtala. None of the robbers had been spotted in Tirur since the raid — though aboriginal groups had been camped for months at the jungle edge where they once killed the old lady Phoolmala. Lately, the Tirur Jarawa stripped vegetable gardens of flowers that they wove into headbands ("We can't grow okra or pumpkins anymore," mourned a villager) and stole water that locals collected in jerry cans and pails. If they got hold of gold jewelry, they were still innocent enough to wear it.

"We know the faces of our Jarawa," said Nilu the boatman at Kadamtala. "So they don't do bad things here. But they can go elsewhere and do what they want." I could think of one kind of inducement for such a daring robbery: an addictive.

At the jetty I also met Raja, taller, heavier, and looking no more like a child. His picture had been in the papers, for he'd testified in court about a hit-and-run accident that had maimed one of his friends. But when he came up to me, the cheerful spark in his eye was replaced by a sad, dulled knowing, and his clothes were dirty.

An autorickshaw stopped by us, and the driver asked Raja to sing a Hindi song. He obliged, throwing out a few lines and vigorously miming sex with the vehicle, to the suppressed giggles of his audience.

*Sentinelese*

# Small Earth

The tide has gone down over the reef. I walk round the world.
There is great wind and rain.

— Great Andamanese song, in *The Andaman Islanders*, 1922

T HE CHAIRMAN of the National Commission for Scheduled
Castes and Scheduled Tribes felt "anguished," noted the *Andaman Herald* in April 2000, that little attempt had been made to
civilize the Sentinelese. "No citizen of India can be allowed to live
in the wilderness or as savages after more than fifty years of country's independence," he was reported as saying.

"That was just for the public," Mishra assured me when I asked
about the statement. The administration had a new, hands-off
policy on North Sentinel: no one, not even the contact mission,
was allowed near it. Predictably, people did go. "There was a navy
exercise last month," he said. "They took the ship very close to
shore. The Sentinelese were on the beach, with taut bows and arrows, waiting. Signaled to them to go away."

Two years earlier, three rather unusual men had visited
Kadamtala along with some Jarawa. "They were pointing arrows,
were very violent, and unused to interaction with outsiders. I have

a suspicion they might have been from Sentinel. It's only a four-hour swim."

"The Onge are great swimmers," asserted Harry Andrews, a researcher with the Andaman and Nicobar Environmental Team. "They couldn't have drowned." I was asking everyone who might have a clue about the deaths of Prakash and his companion Entogegi. Andrews was convinced that the youths were murdered: "We were there that day, near South Bay. The sea was calm." Evidently one of the young men had complained about the depredations of poachers.

"They went to catch fish and didn't return," related a pharmacist who was posted at Dugong Creek shortly after the deaths. "No one made much of it, seems that sometimes they'd be away for days." Ramu, one of the Onge men, had found the bodies on a northern beach; he'd also said that the young men were drinking.

"Prakash and Entogegi went turtle-hunting at night, three other dugouts went too," explained Kanchan Mukhopadhyay, an anthropologist. "The weather was cyclonic. The other boats returned, they did not. I heard one report that they were both drunk."

I didn't know what to make of the alcohol rumor. I'd been in Prakash's hut on three evenings and seen no sign of liquor. Neither could I find real evidence of foul play, nor think of any motives: Onge complaints, however vocal or specific, hardly posed a threat to anyone's interests. I had to believe it was an accident, if only because the alternative was too horrible.

One evening I visited some divers at their haunt; they'd had a good day and now looked very merry and tipsy. "This shark was so close, swimming so slow," said one, his face aglow with the ecstasy that divers on the Andamans floated about in. "We were at a wreck. New corals were growing in it, it was so beautiful."

"We saw a large trawler very close to North Sentinel, four to five kilometers from land," another interjected. He feared that fishermen were being tempted by the shoals in the island's pristine waters.

"How are the corals there?" I asked. "Have you seen them?"

The two exchanged glances. "They're dying, like everywhere else," the first one finally volunteered. In 1998, the extraordinarily hot summer — caused by an El Niño on top of global warming — had killed off half the world's corals, including many on the Andamans. "But we also see new growth."

The divers clearly had been at North Sentinel, not South — the latter is known more for its surfing. They were checking out a wreck, I was told, and fled when four dugouts, each with three men, approached them very fast.

The first glimpse of the Sentinelese was evidently in 1867, when Jeremiah Homfray, a keeper of the Andaman Homes, went to their island in pursuit of escaped convicts: "We saw some ten men on the beach, naked, long haired, and with bows and arrows, shooting fish." They hid on seeing the boat approach. The Great Andamanese on board were frightened of the men and told Homfray that they hailed from Little Andaman and were very fierce. He did not land.

Portman, as Officer in Charge of the Andamanese, went ashore on North Sentinel in 1880 to search for natives. He found the island was composed mostly of limestone and coral, the jagged edges of which made walking difficult. "The soil is light and admirably suited for the growth of coconut palms," he observed, "the surface drainage being excellent. The jungle is in many places open and park like and there are very beautiful groves of bullet-wood trees." His party came across magnificent specimens of *Bombax malabaricum* and measured the buttressed root of one to be "27 feet long and 15 feet high where it left the trunk."

Portman also found some villages and managed to capture a woman with four small children. After a few days he released the woman and one child with the usual gifts. Some days later — and after one snake-infested night on shore — his group encountered in the jungle an old man with his wife and child. The man drew his bow but was thwarted by Portman's convict orderly, who jumped on him. The three captives, along with the children taken earlier, were transferred to Port Blair. But they became ill and the two adults died. "[S]o the four children were sent back to their home with quantities of presents" — and, undoubtedly, germs.

Recommending that the government convert North Sentinel to a coconut plantation, Portman suggested a familiar course of action. "Search parties should go through the jungle and catch some of the male [Sentinelese] unhurt, and should keep them in the camp." As always, the danger of disease did not cause him anxiety. "In features the North Sentinelese most closely resemble the Jarawas on Rutland Island, and there is a peculiarly idiotic expression of countenance, and manner of behaving, common to both." That was his last word on them.

In 1896 the corpse of an Indian was found on the shore of North Sentinel "pierced in several places by arrows, and with its throat cut." Remnants of a bamboo raft and clothing bearing numbers of three convicts were also floating about. Evidently two of the escapees had drowned while the third had made it to land, only to be killed by the natives.

Lieutenant-Colonel M. J. Ferrar landed on the island in 1926, where he glimpsed three of its inhabitants. Taking bows, arrows, a paddle, and a skeleton for research, he left in their place the usual medley of files, mugs, plates, red cloth, and so on. The Sentinelese seemed to shoot birds, for their arrows were unusual in being barbed with birds' bones and decorated with feathers. Ferrar, who explored the island for six hours, estimated that it sheltered about sixty heads. Based on calculations of food supply, anthropologists estimate that the island can support no more than one hundred individuals.

"In 1967 we landed on Sentinel," related Triloki Pandit.

First went a large force of police, armed and in uniform. The

Sentinelese, who were on the beach, vanished. The intruders followed a path into the forest and came to a village of eighteen huts. Four or five fires burned in the corners of each hut, being fenced off from the center for safety. "We didn't take anything," Pandit continued. "But the police — you know how they are — they took some things. I told the chief commissioner we should confiscate."

"Are those the things in the museum?" I asked.

He nodded. "But we couldn't get everything. They had an arrow tipped with bone, we couldn't get them to give it up." The chessboard displayed at the museum must have floated onto North Sentinel from an upturned fishing boat or some other wreck and been picked up by the islanders.

A team from the Anthropological Survey of India visited North Sentinel in March 1970. After anchoring the ship off the island, some men went ashore on a small boat but were chased off by determined natives approaching from two directions.

In the morning many islanders were visible on the beach, displaying their weapons and shooting some arrows that fell into the water. But on being thrown some fish, they picked them up and gestured for more. Women came out of the forest's edge to watch the goings-on. "In their height and stature they were equal to the men except that the lines were softer and they carried no arms," noted an anonymous observer — who thought the natives to be about six feet tall and "akin to the African Zulus."

Intriguingly, local fishermen who'd glimpsed the islanders from afar also held them to be much taller than other Andamanese. Just as strangely, all of those seen in recent times had cropped hair, unlike the ones described by Homfray: a different tribe might now be inhabiting the island.

The survey team dropped a few fish farther along the beach and tried approaching the men again. But though they picked up the gifts and shouted "some incomprehensible words," they remained threatening. The visitors shouted back, equally incomprehensibly, that they wanted to be friends.

"At this moment a strange thing happened — a woman paired off with a warrior and sat on the sand in a passionate embrace. This act was being repeated by other women, each claiming a warrior for herself, a sort of community mating, as it were," wrote the observer. It's likely, however, that the scene represented not a mating ritual but the meeting ritual: men and women from all over the island had gathered to fend off the new threat and were greeting one another by sitting on laps.

Around 1974, Pandit took Tambolai, his father Kanjo, and another Onge man on a contact mission, with the idea that the Sentinel islanders might understand their language. Raised high on stools, Kanjo and the others shouted Onge words of friendship. But the Sentinelese replied with a barrage of curses. "We could see their faces through our binoculars, they looked very angry, were giving them hell," Pandit recalled. The Onge men seemed to understand their threats: terrified, they hid in corners of the boat.

Another time some Sentinelese men raced out of the forest toward the contact team, which was loitering on the beach, causing a VIP to fall flat on his face in the rush back to the boat. His bodyguard fired into the air, upon which the natives shot an arrow that missed him by inches. After that the contact mission tended to stay away from shore, only landing to drop gifts: "Aluminium and plastic pots and pans, a live pig and iron tools were left there each day," wrote Pandit in a newspaper article, "Close Encounters with the Stone Age." One time the islanders killed and buried the pig but took the other gifts. Sometimes they shot arrows at the boat and "acted out insulting gestures, such as, turning their backs towards us and sitting on their haunches as though defecating."

Two ships were wrecked on North Sentinel in the 1980s. The crew was rescued and the wrecks sold to salvage companies whose laborers spent months hammering and blasting in full view of the islanders. Just what interaction they had with the natives — who also wanted iron from the wrecks and who must in any case have resented the presence of outsiders — is obscure. Some said they gave coconuts to the Sentinelese; others claimed to have shot them indiscriminately.

Whatever the cause, during that decade the Sentinelese became noticeably less hostile. In 1988 they picked up gifts just ten yards from the contact boat. "The long and patient efforts carried over two-and-a-half decades jointly by the Andaman and Nicobar administration and the Anthropological Survey of India has slowly but steadily made its impact," Pandit stated. In January 1991 came a "historic moment" when a Sentinel islander came up to the boat and took the gift handed to him.

In February of that year the Sentinelese came on board and picked up bagfuls of coconuts. The contact trips never progressed further, perhaps because some observers pointed to the harm they might inflict. In recent years the islanders had tended toward hostility.

Nasim, who'd helped with my trips to see the Jarawa, was late by a full hour. I'd been pacing up and down the whole time, my bag hidden behind a doorway. I was surprised to see a woman with him; it turned out he'd persuaded her to come along with us. He'd learned over the years that being spotted alone with a female was more dangerous than going to North Sentinel.

At Wandoor jetty to the southwest of Port Blair, two boatmen greeted us at five A.M., then promptly got on a motorbike and vanished. "They had to get something," Nasim reported. "Maybe they hid the boat somewhere, have to fetch it." I walked to the water and looked in. It was pitch dark except for winking points of light, which turned out to be the reflections of stars. A bird started to call loudly on the other side of the creek, hoarse and staccato like a frog. *Chuck chuck chuck.*

We thought the men would be gone only minutes, but when they got back three-quarters of an hour later, it was light. I was awfully annoyed; it turned out they'd gone for headache pills, which both Nasim and I had packed.

The boat was large, with two motors, but we still took ages to get away from the shore. We passed an island I'd photographed years ago, the hands-down winner of the Cute Island Contest. It had a white beach and a green grove and looked exactly large enough for one shipwrecked mariner.

The sun peeped over the horizon. To my surprise, I spotted a long shadowy outline to the west: North Sentinel was only eleven miles from South Andaman. It sat low and flat, with dark green edges and a slightly elevated center that was redder or browner. Global warming would surely drown it.

For the next two hours I watched the island approach. White trunks of tall trees showed up as the first detail, silhouetted against unbroken green. Then brilliant spots of light flashed on and off behind the rolling waters, resolving into bits of beach. They finally merged into a peaceful, unbroken white corona surrounding the island. Off to the south was what looked like a ship; it turned into a tiny spit of land abutting the main island.

North Sentinel was larger than I'd imagined and more luxuriant, brushed with myriad hues of green. The mangroves looked like they'd been combed uphill, their canopies lining up into sloping bands. Under us the water was a brilliant aquamarine, in its depths visible the streaks of corals. It was the purest, lushest, most serene environment I'd ever seen. A turtle surfaced, ponderously gulping air before it dived again.

Please, please, please, let us not destroy this last haven.

I had decidedly mixed feelings about the trip. The Sentinel Islanders should be left alone, I completely believed. On the other hand, many fishermen approached the island because of its rich waters, and one heard of foreign poachers as well. I felt I needed to know if the islanders were interacting with outsiders, for that was the beginning of the end. But I recognized that most anyone could construct a rationale for why she and no one else should have access to an endangered people.

The boat was now circling the island clockwise, and I strained to look for figures on the beach. We might not see anyone, I finally decided. Past the islet to the south the sea was calm with odd bits of detritus floating on it; the depths were dark green. Three dolphins dived in unison and vanished under the surface. Beneath the boat was a whole universe I was blind to.

A wreck came into view, the red rusted skeleton of a small ship, cleanly broken into three pieces and beached. Past it the sea got rough, and we spotted the first waves I'd seen on the Andamans. They crashed on shore, their raised heads all froth and blue glass.

A cloud was hanging over the island, and suddenly the sea was gray and weather threatened. A funnel had dropped all the way down, wispy clouds twisting and rising within it. "The cloud is drinking water," said the boatman. It wasn't quite a waterspout, but spray from the waves did seem to be rising up, the Onge goddess Dare climbing to the sky to tell her angry children of the antics of humans. Monsoon was near.

Just as suddenly we passed into a realm where the sea was sunny and calm. Close to shore black posts stuck out of the water, the remnants of another wreck, mostly submerged. It was likely the one overgrown with coral.

There they were. Some figures perched in a boat by the beach, barely visible against the towering dark trees behind them. Another two men stood in a dugout, poling it over the breakers toward the sea. The men seemed tall and slender, and in the middle of the dugout was a small form that looked like a seated child. They were between one-quarter and one-half mile away.

Our boatman pulled off his shirt and waved it. The men in the dugout saw us and responded; they seemed to be coming toward us. "*Ao, ao!*" shouted the boatman, Come! The Sentinelese replied with a musical yell.

From under the boards the boatman pulled out a *dao*. And I spotted Nasim transferring a large revolver into his trousers. I stared at the men in alarm. The motors were too loud to shout over, so I made my way to Nasim.

"We can't let things get to that stage."

"It's just a precaution," he assured me.

But I was frightened. I was responsible for the situation and had little control over it. The boatmen wouldn't listen to me but to him alone. "Let's go away," I pleaded.

"Let them get a bit closer," Nasim said. "We should take out the cloth."

"No," I replied. "We shouldn't give them anything." Rather late, I'd remembered that I didn't want to teach the Sentinelese to take gifts, to let them think we were friends. In the excitement of planning the visit I'd forgotten my own strictures and we'd brought cloth and nails, I'm ashamed to record, at my suggestion.

"People are doing it anyway," said the woman.

The Sentinelese solved my problem. As our boat moved toward them, they turned around and poled back to shore. Thank heavens, their curiosity was tempered by fear.

We moved away and the dugout tried once more to traverse the reefs near shore. But the moment we turned around, they went back. Clearly they just wanted to fish, and we were an irritant. Two figures were on the beach, keeping an eye on the encounter. When we finally took off, they returned to the forest.

I was elated and relieved. They were there. It was a curiously prosaic moment, just a few men fishing. But for me it had magic, this glimpse of a people whose defiance — of airplanes, computers, answering machines, and everything else that made up my world — I'd come to worship.

The return trip took forever. The sun's glare, the diesel stench, and the rolling nauseated me.

I sat on the prow and watched the water. Frothy patches signaled shoals of jumping fish, churned from below by a darting predator. Small lavender-colored jellyfish floated about, their receding forms giving a sense of the depths underneath.

I wondered what the Sentinelese made of the coral die-off, and whether it made fish hard to find. I wondered if their streams had dried out in 1998, for on such a small island the freshwater supply must be exceedingly fragile. I wondered if the monsoon came with uncommon violence, throwing down trees that crushed them and throwing up storm surges that washed them away. Scarcity of seafood and water, coupled with ever more violent hurricanes as the earth heated up, would make the island unlivable long before the flood formally drowned it. In 2003, when El Niño again added its strength to global warming, temperatures would probably peak even higher. How would they cope?

What would kill off the Sentinel islanders, ultimately, would not be the impoverished populations nearby, which are now held at bay. It would be the flatulence of the wealthy society where I lived, at the other end of the globe.

After about an hour the hot sun suddenly vanished. A dark cloud had been hanging over Middle Andaman, and the boat was now under its fringes. Rain began, and I unfurled my red umbrella while the others sheltered under blue plastic sheets. The raindrops stirred up the sea, studding its surface with zillions of tiny crowns tipped by foam drops. I sat under the umbrella, water dripping down my back, and watched the downpour as the sky got darker and darker.

I wasn't afraid, for the dinghy was big and had two engines. But the frothy heaving surface and heavy gray skies made my thoughts drift to another time. In the pitch darkness of a cyclonic storm uncoiling at night, two young men fought lashing waves in a desperate attempt to stay afloat. And spent, they sank into the inky depths of the waters that after tens of millennia had finally failed to shelter them.

Prakash, rest in peace.

# Afterword: Origins

THE GREAT ANDAMANESE had a variety of legends about the origins of fire. In most of these, the kingfisher stole it at great risk from Biliku, the angry goddess of the northeast wind — but its throat was burned crimson. In another, a fish performed the feat, thereby becoming colorful.

Given the long association of humans with fire, it's odd how often we hear of its having been stolen from others. The most ancient hearth seen so far is 400,000 years old, made by a creature not quite human. But such a fireplace — around which one imagines young ones gathered, waiting for food brought home to be cooked — evokes a society that is recognizably like ours. The use of fire is as integral to human heritage as is walking on two legs.

So it's even odder that the Andamanese forgot how to start a fire. Instead they took great pains to safeguard it, keeping it burning in each hut and in key locations in the forest. One wonders how often our ancestors similarly lost the art of kindling a flame, and, having run out of embers, ended up stealing from their neighbors — perhaps even from other species of humans. The possessors of fire, aware of its advantages, would have defended it as vigorously as did the gods.

Among the Andamanese, legends about fire were complemented by tales of a deluge that endangered it. "During the flood, the monitor lizard and his wife, the civet cat, managed to save fire by carrying it up a tree. Those ancestors who could not climb the tree became fish and other forms of sea life. Once the water subsided, those ancestors who could not climb down the tree became birds. Only the monitor lizard and the civet cat . . . were able to keep the fire in a clay pot. They would scare all the other animals away or burn them to death with this fire." So goes an Onge legend quoted by Vishvajit Pandya.

Before the flood, humans and animals were one. But after the flood, the monitor lizard and the civet cat, possessing fire, walked on earth as the first humans. To the islanders, fire marked the difference between humans and animals.

During the Ice Ages, the glaciers had sucked up seawater, sinking the oceans by around four hundred feet. A land bridge might have opened up between mainland Asia and the Andamans, allowing early humans to walk to the islands.

In Calcutta, I located the cartography division of the Geological Survey of India. Jibitesh Bhattacharyya rolled out several charts on a long table. A few were reproductions of exquisitely detailed British admiralty maps, referring to surveys as old as Archibald Blair's, in the eighteenth century; others, post World War II, warned of mines laid for submarines. We peered over the more recent charts. Much of the sea between Myanmar and the Andamans is shallow, but the channel between Preparis Island, south of Myanmar, and the island of Great Coco farther south, is more than 1,500 feet deep. Someone traveling southward during the Ice Ages would have had to cross it.

Measuring the span between the contours on either side of the channel, we came up with less than eighteen miles. A swimmable distance, and one easily crossed by dugouts — as well as, to judge by species distributions, many plants and birds. Furthermore, the Andamans would have been combined with Great and Little Coco into one large island, with its shadowy tree-covered outlines beckoning to adventurers on the Asian shore.

To get to the Nicobars, however, would not have been easy. The Ten-Degree Channel (named after the latitude through it) is more than three thousand feet deep, and even in the Ice Ages would have meant a crossing, from the Andamans, of around fifty miles. That there never was a land connection between the two island groups is clear from the creatures. Unlike the Andamans, the Nicobars boast the megapode — a hen-like bird that flies poorly and is remarkable for incubating its eggs in heaps of sand and humus — and the crab-eating monkey.

The Andamans do share with the Nicobars a species of monitor lizard that is fairly large and harmless to humans. Revered by the Onge as an ancestor, it roams with ease under the sea, on the ground, and in the towering trees. The more southerly Andaman islands also have in common with the Nicobars the bizarre robber crab. It climbs up coconut trees, nips off the nuts, collects them on the ground, and cracks them; it can easily break a man's wrist. I assume the crab-eating monkeys eat some other kind of crab.

Pranab Kumar Banerjee, a marine geologist at Jadavpur University in Calcutta, has concluded that the Bay of Bengal dropped by four hundred feet around fifteen thousand years ago, and that five thousand years later the glaciers melted and the seas began to swell again. This deluge offers a compelling explanation for why the Andaman tribes have distinct but related habits. The Andamanese told Portman that "before this cataclysm they were all one tribe, and spoke the same language, but that after it the survivors became separated into tribes, their languages gradually differed until at last they became mutually unintelligible." They further said that the oldest remaining kitchen middens (heaps of garbage that over centuries have turned into partially fossilized mounds) were started at higher elevations after the original ones drowned.

The sea rose fast enough, Banerjee pointed out, for the shrinking of the shoreline to be visible over a person's life span. Moreover, the process was far from gradual. During the Ice Ages the monsoons had quieted. But when the earth warmed up they returned with a vengeance, in terrible storms and tidal surges that would have brought great walls of water crashing over the islands. The rise was spasmodic, unquestionably cataclysmic, the stuff of riveting tales told over thousands of evening meals by the warmth of a fire.

The flood was ultimately useful in one respect, however: it decisively cut the Andamans off from mainland Asia. The islands became too small to harbor large predators such as tigers: the Great Andamanese languages even had words, such as *uchu*, for frightening beasts that no longer existed. Better still, they became easy to defend from other humans.

Victorian scholars noted similarities in appearance and material culture — bows, arrowheads, and huts — between the Andamanese and two other vanishing groups, the Semang of Malaysia and the Aeta of the Philippines. These peoples, who were designated as Negritos (for "small negros"), lived in embattled enclaves surrounded by peoples who were more recognizably Asian. Their dispersal suggested they were the remnants of an ancient group that once roamed over much of Asia but was beaten back by later comers.

To the casual eye, the Andamanese looked somewhat like the highlanders of New Guinea and the aboriginals of Australia. The prevailing wisdom was that these populations superficially resembled Africans because they evolved in a similar climate. The tropics favored the survival of people who were short, slender, and dark: short and slender because such people had more skin area for their weight, so their bodies stayed cooler, and dark pigmentation protected them from ultraviolet rays.

The popular "out of Africa" theory holds that modern humans can be traced back to a few men, women, and children in Africa some 100,000 years ago, whose offspring traveled to reach the ends of the earth. If so, some may have settled on the Andamans during the Ice Ages, when falling seas had opened up an almost continuous land bridge with mainland Asia. They were cut off when the seas rose again and remained almost entirely isolated until modern times. The islanders might have continued to resemble their prehistoric ancestors because they ended up in a similar environment.

In historic times, most dark aboriginals in these regions remained hunter-gatherers, rather different in manners and appearance from their horticultural or agricultural neighbors, whose ancestors hailed from southern China. Around four thousand years ago the latter began the great ocean expeditions that populated places as far away as Polynesia and Madagascar. The voyagers reached the Nicobars and the lowlands of New Guinea and must have failed to colonize the Andamans, Australia, and the New Guinea highlands because these were already taken.

Evidence of past encounters can perhaps be discerned in the flora and fauna. For an archipelago in these oceans, the Andamans had a mysterious botanical feature: the virtual absence of coconut trees. That fact, displayed on the skyline, probably spared the inhabitants numerous visits from ships in need of provisions. British colonial officers, searching for an explanation for the oddity, pointed out that the aboriginals would pick up and eat any coconuts that washed ashore, and they surmised that the plants did not get to take root. But the ocean voyagers from China, who carried coconuts as sources of drinking water, developed on the Nicobars into horticulturists who offered their wares — coconuts — to passing ships. Presumably, neither these peoples nor their coconuts could land on the Andamans, or at least survive such a landing.

But some livestock that the ocean migrants carried struggled to shore, for the wild boar that the islanders love to eat is related to the southern Chinese pig. A Great Andamanese legend says that at first, pigs had no eyes, ears, or noses and were easily caught. Then Mita — wife of Tomo, the first man — drilled holes in their heads, "two for eyes, two for ears, and two for nostrils." The pigs ran off into the forest and became hard to corner. One anthropologist interprets such stories as meaning the boars were originally domestic and only later became feral.

Moreover, both the outrigger used by the Onge and the pottery they made until recently are similar in style to those of the Nicobarese. Taken together, these clues suggest that the Onge have had some peaceable interactions with their southern neighbors.

Another possible puzzle piece: in the forests of Great Nicobar hides a very shy and fast-declining band of hunter-gatherers, the Shompen. They have straight hair and other features not dissimilar to the Nicobarese, but their skin is darker. The Shompen could conceivably be a combination of Nicobarese and Negritos; no one has a clue.

The habits of some ancient peoples show curious connections. Reading *The Forest People* (1961) by Colin Turnbull, I realized that apart from the Andamanese having seashores, their lives were remarkably like those of Congo Pygmies. Both peoples roamed dense, moist tropical forests in small bands. They could not light fires and instead carried them around. They would sit on the ground with legs outstretched, trim their peppercorn hair very close, paint their naked bodies, find communal solutions to disputes, use bows, arrows, nets, and their extraordinary botanical knowledge to find abundant food, believed the dead lived around them as spirits, and so on and on.

Perhaps these similarities arose from the two peoples having found the same solutions to life in a similar environment. But some part of me wanted to believe in a closer link. If modern humans evolved solely in Africa, as the "out of Africa" theory posits, they must have migrated, over thousands of years, to populate southeast Asia. Some wanderers could have become isolated on the Andamans and not have changed substantially since leaving Africa.

William Howells, one of the grand old men of anthropology, found a few African links in the Andamanese skulls he examined. But the skulls also resembled those of islanders in Micronesia. All in all, he wrote to me, the Andamanese didn't look much like "leftovers" from a migration out of Africa.

The origins of Andaman languages are also mysterious. Joseph Greenberg of Stanford University noted that the Onge and Great Andamanese vocabularies were so different as to suggest a long period of mutual isolation. In 1971 he postulated that the "Andamanese language family" — if there was such a thing — belonged to a larger clan of Indo-Pacific languages that included oddities such as the extinct Tasmanian. But Norman Zide of the University of Chicago argues that Andamanese languages are too poorly documented to support such a conclusion.

The world's languages belong to two classes, the linguist Edward Sapir is quoted as having told his students: Andamanese and all the rest.

One day late in 1998 I found in the mail a cutting from a British newspaper: researchers at Cambridge University had studied DNA from Great Andamanese hair collected by Radcliffe-Brown and found a closer genetic link to African Pygmies than to other Asians.

Incredibly, the next year I ran into Erika Hagelberg, one of the experimenters, in Port Blair. She was working with Lalji Singh, director of a molecular biology lab in Hyderabad, India, correlating his genetic analysis of Onge blood with characteristics of other populations. The next phase of the research would involve a few Jarawa.

In the past, human tissue ostensibly intended for academic research had ended up in labs of multinationals, which screen for genes that might have medical uses. As a result many governments, including that of India, have become reluctant to let such material out of the country. The ethical dilemmas don't stop there, however: collecting human samples involves an imbalance of power. The newest protocols require that the subjects of research understand and acquiesce to the ultimate objectives. But as Hagelberg herself pointed out, "When you say 'full informed consent,' how can you say that of the Jarawa when you can't even speak their language?" Moreover, the studies would benefit not the Andamanese but the curiosity of outsiders.

In late 2002, the journal *Current Biology* accepted the DNA study for publication. From that study, this much seems true: the Andamanese are only distantly linked with Africans, being far closer to Asians. Moreover, the Andamanese's DNA has some characteristics not found in other humans, suggesting that the Jarawa, to a large extent the Onge, and to a lesser extent the Great Andamanese have been genetically isolated for tens of thousands of years. The Andamanese are probably among the last of the planet's first humans.

# Acknowledgments

O F THOSE WHO HELPED me on the Andamans, my most heartfelt thanks go to Nasim.

I am grateful to the Guggenheim Foundation, whose grant couldn't have come at a better moment. Michelle Press and John Rennie of *Scientific American* found me time to pursue this project, especially in 1998. Anthropologist Sita Venkateswar read the manuscript and suggested important modifications. Laura van Dam, my editor, helped with the structure and with precision trimming. Anna Ghosh, my agent, proved faithful after a couple of others had bailed out. Patricia Wynne drew a lovingly detailed and accurate map.

Among former colleagues, I want to thank Marguerite Holloway for teaching me to be a journalist, John Horgan for his encouragement and advice, and Kate Wong and Dave Schneider for insightful conversations. I also wish to thank journalist Jean Kumagai, archeologist Zarine Cooper, coconut specialist Hugh Harries, anthropologist Triloki Pandit, paleontologist Ian Tattersall, and Dr. Fernando Merino and Dr. Debal Sen for discussions.

I owe particular thanks to George Weber of the Andaman Association for unstintingly sharing information, especially his exhaustive bibliography. I am grateful to the Anthropological Survey of India for the use of its library in Calcutta, and especially for permission to view the Portman collection. In the initial stages of my research, the National Library in Calcutta yielded some rare volumes. The astonishing collection and facilities at the Regenstein Library of the University of Chicago allowed me to hunt down books and articles that had eluded me for years. Material from the book *Above the Forest* is reproduced by permission of Oxford University Press, India.

Stefan Schramm, my husband, uncovered many rare accounts of the Andamans, bought some over the Internet, and translated those in German. My mother-in-law, Wera, helped with the German books and the baby. Deepawati and Souren Sen provided support and encouragement, as they always have, and so did Yoichiro Nambu, my former thesis adviser. My friends Bob Carr and Lee Herman came to my aid when I desperately needed help — again, with the baby — and Chandana Sailo watched over him during my stints in Calcutta.

My mother, Sabita, bought me precious time by taking care of the baby and me for months at a stretch, and occasionally queried when I would stop researching and start writing. Finally, this book would have been missing key chapters without help from my father, Biren, whose phone calls got me rather unusual access to the Andamans.

# Bibliography

BOOKS

Alexander, James Edward. *Travels from India to England: Comprehending a Visit to the Burman Empire, and a Journey Through Persia, Asia Minor, European Turkey, Etc., in the Years 1825–26*. London: Parbury, Allen and Co., 1827.

Awaradi, S. A. *Computerized Master Plan, 1991–2021, for Welfare of Primitive Tribes of Andaman and Nicobar Islands*. Port Blair: Andaman and Nicobar Administration, 1990.

Balfour, Patrick. *Grand Tour: Diary of an Eastward Journey*. New York: Harcourt, Brace and Co., 1935.

Basu, Badal Kumar. *The Onge*. Calcutta: Seagull Books, 1990.

Bhattacharya, Asutosh. *Andhakarer Andamane* (In the Dark Andamans). Calcutta: A. Mukherjee and Co., 1983.

Boden Kloss, C. *In the Andamans and Nicobars: The Narrative of a Cruise in the Schooner "Terrapin," with Notices of the Islands, Their Fauna, Ethnology, Etc*. London: John Murray, 1903.

Bonington, M.C.C. *Census of India, 1931. The Andaman and Nicobar Islands*. Calcutta: Superintendent Government Printing, India, 1933.

Campbell, Colonel Walter. *My Indian Journal*. Edinburgh: Edmonston & Douglas, 1864.

Chakraborty, Dilip Kumar. *The Great Andamanese*. Calcutta: Seagull Books, 1990.

Cipriani, Lidio. *The Andaman Islanders*. New York: Frederick A. Praeger, 1966.

Clifton, Mrs. Talbot. *Pilgrims to the Isles of Penance: Orchid Gathering in the East.* London: John Long, 1911.

Coxon, Stanley W. *And That Reminds Me: Being Incidents of a Life Spent at Sea, and in the Andaman Islands, Burma, Australia, and India.* New York: John Lane Co., 1915.

Cutting, Suydam. *The Fire Ox and Other Years.* New York: Charles Scribner's Sons, 1940.

Ehlers, Otto E. *An Indichen Fürstenhöfen* (An Indian Court). Berlin: Allgemeiner Verein für Deutsche Litteratur, 1898.

Hagenbeck, John. *Kreuz und quer durch die indische Welt* (Crisscrossing the Indian World). Dresden: Verlag Deutsche Buchwerkstätten, 1922.

Hamilton, Capt. Alexander. *A New Account of the East-Indies.* 2 vols. 1739. Reprint, New Delhi: Asian Educational Services, 1995.

Harrer, Heinrich. *Die Letzten Fünfhundert* (The Last Five Hundred). Frankfurt: Ullstein, 1977.

Heindl, Robert. *Meine Reise nach den Strafkolonien* (My Travels to the Penal Colonies). Berlin: Ullstein, 1913.

Krishnatry, S. M., ed. *Retrieval from Precipice.* Port Blair: Andaman Adim Janjati Vikas Samiti, 1977.

Lowis, R. F. *Census of India, 1911. The Andaman and Nicobar Islands.* Calcutta: Superintendent Government Printing, India, 1912.

———. *Census of India, 1921. The Andaman and Nicobar Islands.* Calcutta: Superintendent Government Printing, India, 1923.

Majumdar, Niranjan, ed. *The Statesman: An Anthology.* Calcutta: The Statesman Ltd., 1975.

Majumdar, Ramesh C. *Penal Settlement in Andamans.* New Delhi: Ministry of Education and Social Welfare, Government of India, 1975.

Man, Edward Horace. *The Aboriginal Inhabitants of the Andaman Islands.* 1883. Reprint, New Delhi: Sanskaran Prakashak, 1975.

Mann, Rann S. *The Bay Islanders.* Calcutta: Bidisa, 1980.

Mouat, Frederic John. *Adventures and Researches Among the Andaman Islanders.* London: Hurst and Blackett, 1863.

Moyne, Lord. *Walkabout: A Journey in Lands between the Pacific and Indian Oceans.* London: William Heinemann Ltd., 1936.

Mukhopadhyay, K. et al., eds. *Jarawa Contact: Ours with Them, Theirs with Us.* Calcutta: Anthropological Survey of India, 2002.

Myka, Frank P. *Decline of Indigenous Populations: The Case of the Andaman Islanders.* New Delhi: Rawat Publications, 1993.

Nostitz, Pauline. *Travels of Doctor and Madame Helfer in Syria, Mesopotamia, Burmah and Other Lands.* 2 vols. London: R. Bentley & Son, 1878.

Page, Michael F. *A Sea with Many Islands.* London: Robert Hale Ltd., 1952.

Pandit, T. N. *The Sentinelese.* Calcutta: Seagull Books, 1990.

Pandya, Vishvajit. *Above the Forest: A Study of Andamanese Ethnoanemology, Cosmology, and the Power of Ritual.* New Delhi: Oxford University Press, 1993.

Portman, Maurice V. *A History of Our Relations with the Andamanese.* 2 vols. 1899. Reprint, New Delhi: Asian Educational Services, 1990.

Radcliffe-Brown, Alfred R. *The Andaman Islanders.* 1922. Reprint, Glencoe, Ill.: The Free Press, 1948.

Sarkar, Jayanta K. *The Jarawa.* Calcutta: Seagull Books, 1990.

———. *Nritattiker Chokhe Andaman* (Andaman in the Eyes of an Anthropologist). Calcutta: Shibrani Prakashani, 1999.

Suryanarayan, V., and V. Sudarsen, eds. *Andaman and Nicobar Islands: Challenges of Development.* New Delhi: Konark Publishers, 1994.

Symes, Michael. *An Account of an Embassy to the Kingdom of Ava, Sent by the Governor-General of India in the Year 1795.* London: J. Debrett, 1800.

Tomas, David. *Transcultural Space and Transcultural Beings.* Boulder, Colo.: Westview Press, 1996.

Trevelyan, Raleigh. *The Golden Oriole: Childhood, Family, and Friends in India.* London: Secker & Warburg, 1987.

Venkateswar, Sita. *Policing Power, Governing Gender, and Re-imagining Resistance: A Perspective on the Andaman Islanders.* Ph.D. diss., Rutgers University, 1997.

Williams, James H. *The Spotted Deer.* London: Rupert Hart-Davis, 1957.


ARTICLES

"Adopted in Andaman." *Chambers's Journal,* March 24, 1860: 177–179.

"The Andaman Boy: A True Story." *Asiatic Journal* 8 (1819): 465.

Bamshad, Michael J. et al. "Female Gene Flow Stratifies Hindu Castes." *Nature* 395 (October 15, 1998): 651–652.

———. "Genetic Evidence on the Origins of Indian Caste Populations." *Genome Research,* November 2001: 1–11.

Banerjea, Kanak Tilak. "Among the Jarawas." *Sunday Statesman,* February 8, 1998: 8.

Banerjee, P. K. "Imprints of Late Quarternary Climactic and Sea Level Changes on East and South Indian Coast." *Geo-Marine Letters* 13 (1993): 56–60.

Busk, George. "Description of Two Andamanese Skulls." *Transactions of the Ethnological Society* (London) 4 (1865): 205–211.

Chengapa, B. S. "In the Land of Hostile Jarawas and Other Wild Tribes of the Andaman Islands." *Indian Forester,* February 1958: 108–120.

Colebrooke, R. H. "On the Andaman Islands." *Asiatick Researches* 4 (1795): 385–394.

Connor, Steve. "DNA Links 'Stone Age' Tribe to First Humans." *Independent* 31 (August 1998).

Cooper, Zarine. "Analysis of the Nature of Contacts with the Andaman Islands During the Last Two Millennia." *South Asian Studies* 5 (1989): 133–147.

Croley, T. V. Letter to the Editor. *Indian Forester,* July 1958: 449–450.

Cutting, Suydam. "Natives of the Andaman Islands." *Natural History* 32, no. 5 (1932): 521–530.

Dobson, G. E. "On the Andamans and Andamanese." *Journal of the Royal Anthropological Institute* (London) 4 (1875): 457–467.

Eickstedt, E. von. "Die Negritos der Andamanen" (The Negritos of the Andamans). *Anthropologischer Anzeiger* 5 (1928): 259–268.

Fytche, Albert. "A Note on Certain Aborigines of the Andaman Islands." *Journal of the Asiatic Society of Bengal* 30 (1861): 263–267.

Gates, R. Ruggles. "Blood Groups from the Andamans." *Man,* nos. 62–63 (April 1940): 55–57.

Gibbons, Ann. "Indian Women's Movement." *Science* 280 (April 17, 1998).

Greenberg, Joseph. "The Indo-Pacific Hypothesis." *Current Trends in Linguistics* 8 (1971): 807–871.

Guha, B. S. "Report of a Survey of the Inhabitants of the Andaman and Nicobar Islands During 1948–49." *Bulletin of the Department of Anthropology, Calcutta,* January 1952: 1–7.

Harding, Luke. "DNA Secrets of Stone Age Travels." *Guardian* (London), May 12, 2001.

Haughton, J. C. "Papers Relating to the Aborigines of the Andaman Islands." *Journal of the Asiatic Society of Bengal* 30 (1861): 251–263.

Heine-Geldern, Robert. "Archaeology and Legend in the Andaman Islands." *Festschrift Paul Schebesta zum 75. Geburtstag.* Wien: St. Gabriel-Verlag (1963): 129–132.

Hutton, J. H. "Notes on the Andamanese and the Nicobarese." *Man in India* 11 (January–March 1931): 1–5.

Jagor, F. "Andamanesen oder Mincopies" (Andamanese or Mincopies). *Zeitschrift für Ethnologie* 9 (1877): 41–65.

Lehmann, Herman. "The Andaman Islands." *St. Bartholomew's Hospital Journal* (April 1955): 99–112.

"Maga's Log: A Visit from the Ongees at Port Blair. By Enterprise." *Blackwood's Magazine,* March 1938: 386–391.

Mukerjee, Madhusree. "Out of Africa, Into Asia," *Scientific American* (January 1999): 24.

Pandit, T. N. "Close Encounters with the Stone Age." *Sunday Times of India,* April 28, 1991: 1–2.

Pandya, Vishvajit. "From Photography to Ethnography: Andamanese Documents and Documentation." *Visual Anthropology* 4 (1991): 379–413.

———. "To Contact or Not? The Jarawas of the Andaman Islands." *Cultural Survival Quarterly* (Winter 1999): 59–65.

Pycraft, W. P. "Diagnoses of Four Species and One Sub-species of the Genus Homo." *Man* 25 (October 1925): 162–164.

Sarkar, Jayanta. "Sondhikkhone Jarawa Samaj" (Jarawa Society at a Cusp). *Ekti Samudra Pakhi, Bihan.* Silpasahitya Sanskriti Sankhya, 2001.

Scott-Clark, Cathy, and Adrian Levy. "Survivors of Our Hell." *The Guardian* (June 23, 2001).

Singh, Raghubir. "The Last Andaman Islanders." *National Geographic* 148 (July 1975): 66–91.

Taylor, Frederick. "Native Life in the Andaman Islands." *Century Magazine* 82 (October 1911): 891–904.

Temple, Richard C. "Extracts from the Bengal Consultations of the XVIIIth Century Relating to the Andaman Islands." *Indian Antiquary,* April 1900: 103–116.

———. "Remarks on the Andaman Islanders and Their Country." *Indian Antiquary,* July 1929.

———. "The Trade in Andamanese Slaves." *Indian Antiquary,* March 30, 1901: 120.

———. "An Unpublished XVIIIth-Century Document about the Andamans." *Indian Antiquary,* June 1901: 232–238.

Venkateswar, Sita. "The Andaman Islanders." *Scientific American,* May 1999: 82–88.

Whitaker, Romulus. "Endangered Andamans: Managing Tropical Moist Forests." *The Environmental Series Group.* World Wildlife Fund, India, April 1985.

Wolfers, Andreas. "Rükkehr auf Heickles Terrain" (Return to Tricky Terrain). *Geo* 10 (October 1996): 58–63.


WEB SITE

The Andaman Association. Lonely Islands: The Andamanese. An On-line Documentation by George Weber. www.andaman.org.

# Index